THE PRINCIPAL'S OFFICE

Frontispiece. "Administration," from *The Annual,* Hamilton High School 1929 yearbook, Hamilton, Ohio. Courtesy of Butler County Historical Society.

THE PRINCIPAL'S OFFICE

*A Social History of the
American School Principal*

KATE ROUSMANIERE

STATE UNIVERSITY OF NEW YORK PRESS

Published by
STATE UNIVERSITY OF NEW YORK PRESS, ALBANY

© 2013 State University of New York

For information, contact
State University of New York Press, Albany, NY
www.sunypress.edu

Production, Laurie Searl
Marketing, Fran Keneston

Library of Congress Cataloging-in-Publication Data

Rousmaniere, Kate, 1958–
   The principal's office : a social history of the American school principal /
Kate Rousmaniere.
      p. cm.
   Includes bibliographical references and index.
   ISBN 978-1-4384-4823-7 (hardcover : alk. paper)
   ISBN 978-1-4384-4824-4 (pbk. : alk. paper)
   1. School principals—United States—History.   2. Educational leadership—United States.
I. Title.

   LB2831.92.R68 2013
   371.2'012—dc23   2012045315

10 9 8 7 6 5 4 3 2 1

CONTENTS

ILLUSTRATIONS

ACKNOWLEDGMENTS

I wrote this book while serving as chair of my university's Department of Educational Leadership, which, as it turned out, was the perfect setting for thinking about school principals. My department offers an excellent master's and licensure program for aspiring school principals, and my observations of those brave and energetic students, and the former school administrators who serve as their faculty, taught me more about the great possibilities of school leadership than could any library. I am especially grateful to and admiring of professors Steve Thompson, Kathy Mecoli, Larry Boggess, Ray Terrell, Michael Dantley, and Jim Burchyett, all former school administrators, who extend their commitment to progressive education by preparing future generations of school leaders. Also helpful in my thinking was my role as department chair, which is the higher education version of the principalship: a middle managerial position with fast-moving, multifaceted tasks that range from addressing long-term university policy demands to responding to immediate student and faculty needs. The work is intense, complicated, and exhausting, and for good reason is the position grimly observed as the most difficult and thankless position on campus. Yet I found the work personally rewarding and exciting, and those nine years in the chair's office gave me a closer sense of, and admiration for, the work of K-12 school principals.

The historical records of school principals are not easily identifying or accessible, and I am grateful to the guidance of staff in a number of libraries, cited in the selected bibliography at the end of this volume. Many thanks to the Albert Shanker Educational Research Fellowship, offered in conjunction with the American Federation of Teachers, which allowed me to spend three lovely winter days of research at the Walter Reuther Library, Detroit, Michigan. The staff at King Library, Miami University were exceptionally helpful as always.

Although this is a national study of American school principals, my work has been enlightened by collaborative work with international scholars who have provided new perspectives to my analysis. I send special thanks to my colleagues at the International Standing Conference for the History of Education; the national history of education societies of Brazil, Canada, Mexico, the United Kingdom, and Australia-New Zealand; the Kolkata

Institute of Development Studies, Kolkata, India; and the editorial staff at the *Journal of Educational Administration and History*.

As always, many scholars and colleagues helped in the research and writing of this book. Many of those people are recognized in my notes. I also want to thank Jackie Blount, Dan Golodner, Elliott Gorn, Bob Hampel, Lauri Johnson, Judith Kafka, Craig Kridel, Catherine Lugg, and especially Wayne Urban, and my department colleagues Kathleen Knight Abowitz and Richard Quantz. The American History of Education Society has been an intellectual and professional home base for this and all of my scholarly work. Finally, none of this could have happened without John Bercaw.

This book is dedicated to the future generation, especially to my nieces and nephews. May we live and grow as our ancestors have taught us to, by choosing careers that make a difference in people's lives.

INTRODUCTION

GO TO THE PRINCIPAL'S OFFICE

This study of the history of the school principal began, literally, at the door of a principal's office. A few years ago when I walked the hallways of a high school with my five-year-old niece Evie, she remarked, without prompting: "There's the principal's office: you only go there if you are in trouble." As an educator and an aunt, I wondered how the office of an educational professional had come to be symbolized in such a decisive way in the mind of a child, particularly a child who had yet to enter formal schooling. As I scanned popular representations of the school principal, I found that Evie's impression was hardly unusual. Across popular and professional cultures, the figure of the school principal is commonly reduced to a small, often disagreeable functionary of bad news, the wet blanket of progressive teacher practice, the prison guard of students' freedom. As I asked friends and colleagues about their impressions of school principals, few actually knew what principals did, and many people confused the role of school building principal with school district superintendent. Most remarkably, those very people who did not understand what a principal did were often the first to argue for the abolition of the role.

As a historian, I was also struck by the absence of studies of the principalship. When I began this work in 2006, historians had only a sketchy understanding of the role and exhibited very little interest in understanding more. One reason for the great lacunae of historical research on the principal is that educational historians in the past fifty years tended to focus on either institutional and policy history at the central office level or on the social history of teachers, students, and communities. Principals fell through the middle, seemingly neither players in policy development nor in the day-to-day life of the classroom. Historical references to principals also tended to blur the distinction between building and central office management, collapsing the principal into a larger, indistinguishable category of bureaucratic administrator. In educational history, school principals appeared as one-dimensional functionaries, white men in dull-colored baggy suits who obediently completed administrative tasks and ordered others to be obedient to them.

The sole exception to this pattern was a pocket of historical studies on African American principals. Through the late twentieth century, black principals were completely excluded from predominantly white public schools in both the legally segregated southern United States and in the north, where virtually no African American held a principalship in any school with even a minority white population until the 1960s. In their racially segregated school systems, black principals played a critical role, serving as important role models and respected servant leaders in their communities. Historians had examined black school leaders in racially segregated schools with significantly more interest than any historians had expressed about white majority principals, and that research provided me with an insight into the possible historical significance of all school leaders.

I suspected that one reason why the history of all school principals had been largely ignored was that historians shared with others a personal predilection against school principals. In our own life history, many of us remember an inspiring teacher, but we may remember the principal only for an unfortunate, and assuredly unfair, disciplinary encounter. For women and people of color, the principal is often a position not of us, and not attainable. Personal experience is reinforced by a long cultural history of alienation between school administration and classroom teaching: Teachers who become administrators are often seen by their peers as crossing a boundary much like the river Styx—a one-way passage to a place not all that pleasant. The principal's office holds an unsavory tinge, and the people who sit in that office are viewed with some misgivings. Memory and methodology reinforce each other: when historians have written about movements for civil rights, student activism, and educational progressivism in schools, the principal has been folded into a battalion of upper-level administrators who stood on the other side of social justice.

My own interest in the history of the principalship was heightened by these observations of the persistent avoidance of the topic, particularly as I began to see the powerful impact and diverse identities of school principals in the history of American education.

In American public schools, the principal is the most complex and contradictory figure in the pantheon of educational leadership. The principal is both the administrative director of state educational policy and a building manager, both an advocate for school change and the protector of bureaucratic stability. Authorized to be employer, supervisor, professional figurehead, and inspirational leader, the principal's core training and identity is as a classroom teacher. A single person, in a single professional role, acts on a daily basis as the connecting link between a large bureaucratic system and the individual daily experiences of a large number of children and adults. Most contradictory of all, the principal has always been responsible for student learning, even as the position has become increasingly disconnected from the classroom.

The history of the principal offers even more contradictions. Contemporary principals work in the midst of unique modern challenges of ever-changing fiscal supports, school law and policy, community values and youth culture. At the same time, the job of the contemporary principal shares many of the characteristics of their predecessors two centuries ago. While social and economic contexts have changed, the main role of the principal has remained essentially the same over time: to implement state educational policy to the school and to maneuver, buffer, and maintain the stability of the school culture at the local level.

The reason for this paradoxical history of change and constancy is that even as the broader context of education has changed over the past two centuries, the core purpose of the school principal has remained embedded in the center of the school organizational structure. Located between the school and the district, and serving both, the principal has historically been a middle manager who translates educational policy from the central office to the classroom. Assigned both to promote large-scale initiatives and to solve immediate day-to-day problems, the principal has always carried multiple and often contradictory responsibilities, wearing many hats, and moving swiftly between multiple roles in the course of one day. This mobile, multitasking role has always described the work of the principal, even as the nature of those tasks has radically changed.

This book offers a way to understand this leadership paradox by exploring the historical development of the American public school principal. It is a study of how the school principal's position, which I refer to as the principal's office, developed over time amid the conflicting external and internal pressures on the people who sat in that office. Focusing on the broad shapes and outlines of the history of the principal's office, I trace both the changes in the position and the ways in which the principal's office has maintained its stable identity across periods of educational change.

The complex role of the principal is not an accidental by-product of history; rather, the principal's position at the nexus of educational policy and practice was an intentional component of the role when it was originally conceived. Indeed, of the many organizational changes that took place in public education in North America at the turn of the last century, few had greater impact on the school than the development of the principalship. The creation of the principal's office revolutionized the internal organization of the school from a group of students supervised by one teacher to a collection of teachers managed by one administrator. In its very conception, the appointment of a school-based administrator who was authorized to supervise other teachers significantly restructured power relations in schools, reorienting the source of authority from the classroom to the principal's office. Just as significant was the role that the principal played as a school-based representative of the central educational office. Created as a conduit between the district and the classroom, the principal became an educational middle manager in an increasingly complex school bureaucracy.

The introduction of the principal's office radically changed the overall machinery of how public education was delivered from central authorities to the classroom. Located as the connecting hinge between the school and the district, the principal was critical to the success of newly designed school systems in the early twentieth century, in much the same way that the creation of middle managerial structures in business in the same period helped to consolidate the control of independent enterprises under a corporate umbrella. Modern administrative practices, including scientific management, greased the wheels of this development in late nineteenth-century American business, providing managerial techniques, a hierarchical decision-making structure, and an occupational culture of rationality. In the business world, middle managers were the engine behind the expansion of corporate bureaucracy, providing the smooth transition of responsibilities from the central office to the shop floor.

Like the foreman in the factory and the mid-level executive in the office building, the position of school principal was designed to be an administrator who was responsible for day-to-day building operations rather than strategic policy decisions. Standing between the district and the classroom, principals were, as C. Wright Mills described such white-collar positions, "the assistants of authority" whose power was derived from others and who were responsible for implementing managerial decisions but had limited opportunities for influencing those decisions. Like other middle managers, the principal had a "dual personality," standing "on the middle ground between management and employee," as both a loyal sergeant to a distant supervisor and a local administrator who had to negotiate with workers in order to get the job done properly.[1] Larry Cuban aptly describes principals' historic and contemporary role as "positioned between their superiors who want orders followed and the teachers who do the actual work in the classrooms." Principals' loyalties, Cuban argues, "are dual: to their school and to headquarters."[2]

The historical development of the principal reflects the growing pains of an emerging state school bureaucratic system. Through the mid-twentieth century, the principalship was an inconsistently defined position, as often a teacher with administrative responsibilities as an administrator who supervised teachers. These early principals were flexible teacher leaders who maintained a close connection with classroom work and the school community in ways that might delight contemporary educators who feel burdened by bureaucracy. But for all the freedom offered by such positions, early principals suffered from the absence of an administrative scaffold to support their work.

At the turn of the nineteenth century, as educational reformers built up the bureaucratic framework of the state and local public school system, they realigned the primary attention of the principal from the classroom to the central administrative structure. This professionalization process involved proscribing lines of authority and accountability, establishing entry requirements and academic training, and improving compensation for the work. While professionalization improved the stature of the principal's office, it restricted the types of people who sat in that office, increasingly excluding women, people of color, and educators who prioritized community engagement over administrative tasks. Indeed, through the mid-twentieth century a majority of elementary principals were women, and the totality of principals of segregated African American schools were black. The professionalization process changed all that, as it also formalized the division between teachers and administrators, between doing education and supervising education, between classroom and office, body and mind, experience and intellect, and between women and men. The irony of professionalization is that it emphasized the identity of the principal as an administrator in the middle of an educational bureaucracy and not an educator in the middle of the school house.

As the principalship evolved away from the classroom to the administrative office, the principal became less connected with student learning, and yet more responsible for it. Isolated in the new principal's office, the role of school head changed from instructing students to supervising teachers of students. Further complicating the principal's role in the mid-twentieth century was that as public education became more responsive to and reflective of the public, principals were swept up in changes initiated by state and federal governments, legal requirements, and the increasing demands of local communities. Modern principals came to have less to do with student learning and more to do with upholding administrative structures and responding to public pressures.

Yet by the nature of their background and role as educators, principals have always been concerned with student learning, and principals across time have played a pivotal role in shaping the educational culture of schools. Middle management, after all, is a multifaceted role that can open up both possibilities and constraints, and some school principals in the past and present have been able to initiate progressive educational practices in their schools, often in spite of bureaucratic restraints. Indeed, across history, many principals' own vision of student learning has adapted to community needs and student interests. For all those efforts, however, the history of the principalship is marked by an increasing discrepancy between the popular image and the actual work of the position. Ironic too, is the dominant image of the principalship with an office, given the great variety, mobility, human interactions, and community relations of principals' work.

The experiences of principals in the past can teach contemporary educators about leadership strategies for improving schools. Throughout *The Principal's Office*, I offer evidence of principals who have led from the middle, who were able to adopt different leadership strategies to improve student learning, while attending to all sides of their increasingly complex educational context. In my effort to introduce positive portrayals of principals from the past, many of the school leaders chronicled here are examples of effective educational leaders who focus on enacting progressive educational visions of student achievement, teacher empowerment, and community engagement. Other principals who appear in this book are examples of the many school leaders who were simply survivors, trying to accomplish their jobs of great complexity and pressure, often with little support or guidance. Still others played out their administrative roles with cruelty and arrogance and stand as examples of the worst model of school leadership, which is, sadly, the model most prominent in popular culture representations of principals. My intent here is not to judge the work of individual principals; rather I have focused on understanding the working conditions of the principal's office. All principals, across time and circumstance, have faced a contradictory and perplexing job, straddling a range of expectations and ever-changing working conditions, even as they shared common struggles across time. By thinking of the middle managerial role of the principal as a trajectory from the past, contemporary educators can think differently about how to change schools in the future.

CHAPTER ONE

PRECEPTORS, HEAD TEACHERS, AND PRINCIPAL TEACHERS

School Leadership through the Late Nineteenth Century

Before the creation of the principal's office, school leaders worked under limited organizational structures, with minimal guidelines and expectations of their work. This thin administrative framework left them largely reliant on their own individual leadership skills and directly dependent on community approval. The simplicity of the system allowed for both flexibility and constraint: With virtually no local or state administrative standards to follow, school leaders were free to lead schools by their own vision and initiative. Yet, the absence of any administrative infrastructure kept school leaders occupied with the most basic of operational tasks and completely dependent on the opinions, wealth, interest, and support of their community. The irony of the early years of American educational leadership—from the colonial period through the Civil War—is that principals' freedom to develop and institute their own educational vision was compromised by the absence of a protective administrative structure. With the creation of a more centralized public education system in the late nineteenth century, school leaders experienced more professional security, but also less independence.

This chapter surveys the history of school leaders, alternatively called preceptors, head teachers, or principal teachers, from the colonial period through the Civil War. Here we see that even though school leaders in these days were not monitored by a guiding administrative bureaucracy, they still played a middle managerial–type role in their work with communities and governing authorities.

EARLY SCHOOL LEADERS

The first schools in America were unregulated and eclectic operations with no standard educational processes or administrative procedures. Colonial and Early Republic communities that funded local schools offered only elementary education in one- and two-room schools with no attendance requirements, no common curriculum, and no standard policies or practices. Without a set curriculum, students proceeded at their own pace and teachers taught multi-aged classrooms, basing their instruction on memorization for basic reading and mathematical literacy and relying on whatever texts were available, be it the Bible, *Webster's Dictionary*, or early reading primers such as the McGuffey Readers. Well through the American Revolution, barely half of all children in what became the United States even attended elementary school, and far fewer attended more advanced programs, variously called grammar schools or high schools. Girls enrolled in the early levels of education, but were dissuaded or excluded from more advanced education. For African American children in both the South and the North, and for the most destitute urban and most isolated rural children, education through the mid-nineteenth century was even less accessible.

In the years before the creation of state and local school systems, the administration of these early American schools followed a simple and direct hierarchy. Community school boards or trustees acted as a combined parent association, personnel office, and supervisor that hired and evaluated the teacher and examined the children. Teachers were men and women chosen not for any instructional skills or academic degree, but for their religious background, moral character, and political affinity with the community that hired them. Teachers' wages and working conditions were haphazard, based on what the community could afford. Teachers had no contract, and so could be summarily expelled from their post by a dissatisfied parent or board member, or their employment swiftly cut short when the community ran out of money.

For the most part, the teacher worked alone, under broad and vague administrative directives. In one-room schools across the rural countryside from the colonial period through much of the nineteenth century, individual teachers carried the entire weight of the school. Untrained and poorly supervised in this work, drawing on little more than their own understandings of the purposes of education and their own personal strengths, these early teachers monitored enrollment, maintained the building, disciplined chil-

dren, abided by school board regulations and expectations, and taught whatever curriculum could be gathered and approved of by the local community.

These early educators were isolated and insecure in their positions as
private tutors or struggling heads of a "school" held in a church or private
home. They described their work in universally dark reports of a thankless
and stressful occupation. Soon after the American Revolution, Philip Fre-
neau wrote of his experience as a private tutor as a "wretched state of mean-
ness and servility."[1] Other teachers recounted how their originally inspired
plans of intellectual enlightenment collapsed when they faced recalcitrant
students, decrepit classrooms, contemptuous employers, and social isolation.
In 1788, John Trumbull described how itinerant teachers were treated at the
whim of parents who annually "seek again their school to keep [a teacher]
just as good, and just as cheap."[2]

If the working conditions facing educators were difficult, their image
in the public eye was no more appealing. Most educators were men, and
they were often mocked as pathetic, unmanly creatures who did not have
the physicality for farming or the gumption for the legal profession. They
stood alone in their classroom in a strange community, and on a number
of recorded occasions, they were attacked and chased out of their posts by
rebellious students. In 1820, Washington Irving described the iconographic
educator in his portrayal of Ichabod Crane, the effete, gangly, and sadistic
teacher who carved out a living in rural communities. Crane was the cari-
cature of the mean-spirited teacher who ruled his classroom with corporal
punishment and dulled his students with tedious recitations, a social incompetent who tried to worm his way into the parlors of local elites in order
to secure his own livelihood. Other early Americans described educators
as misfits with no better opportunity in life, crippled by accident, work, or
alcohol addiction and whose disability traversed from physical to mental
to moral, such as this nineteenth-century report of a typical teacher as a

> man who was disabled to such an extent that he could not engage
> in manual labor—who was lame, too fat, too feeble, had. . . . fits
> or was too lazy to work—well, they usually made school masters
> out of these, and thus got work they could out of them.[3]

Such was the image of educational leadership in early America.

As communities grew and stabilized, they expanded their educational
opportunities enough to employ a lead administrator to help manage the
school. Called a preceptor, schoolmaster, head teacher, or principal, these
early school leaders were teacher and school manager combined in one
who symbolized and enacted the cultural authority of the school in the way
that the individual teacher could not. If the school was successful, these

leaders might become the personification of the school and its managerial engine. Yet without any administrative legal scaffold behind them, even the most successful school leader was kept in a position of continual instability and isolation. These early school leaders had no professional affiliation or authorized status, legal precedent, job description, or even an employment contract to protect them from any and all of the demands of the communities that paid their meager salary.

The professional career of Ezekiel Cheever is an example of one of these first versions of a school principal. After his arrival in Boston from England in 1637, Cheever taught for seventy years in virtually every type of educational structure across the New England colonies. He began teaching in a makeshift school in his own home, then temporary school buildings, and later, as his teaching fame spread, in school buildings donated by wealthy citizens. But even Cheever's regional prominence as a schoolmaster could not earn him permanency or status: for over thirty years, he suffered various professional indignities, including low pay, the refusal of the town to repair his school building, and the breech of his contract. Finally, at age fifty-six, Cheever became schoolmaster of the prestigious Boston Latin Grammar School, where he remained for the next thirty-eight years until his death in 1708. Founded in 1635, Boston Latin educated boys who became leading citizens of the new republic, and it continues to this day as one of the oldest public schools in the country. Originally the only teacher in the school, as the school grew in size, Cheever hired and paid for his own assistant. Only in 1699, when Cheever was eighty-five, did the Boston selectmen vote to pay for his assistant.[4] Cheever's notoriety as a schoolmaster eventually earned him professional and economic security, but only as a result of his independent work lobbying for funding and enrollment, and serving as intellectual mentor, cultural figurehead, administrator, instructor, and institution builder. His record of preparing thousands of young men in classical languages, the requirement for acceptance to college and therefore the deciding factor in a young man's future career, earned him the loyalty and endorsement of his former students, many of whom became leading political figures. Unprotected by any form of administrative structure, Cheever was literally a self-made principal.

LEADERSHIP IN ACADEMIES

Until the development of public high schools in the late nineteenth century, the only advanced form of education for boys and girls was in private venture schools, founded with community support and fiscally reliant on endowments and tuition. Far more numerous and accessible than colleges, these seminaries, academies, or high schools often enjoyed more prestige than the community-funded school, even though their quasi-independent status made the school's very existence unpredictable. In an era before children were legally compelled to attend school, academies rose and fell with great alacrity, subject to the economic and cultural tenors of the time, the changing character and demography of the community, and leaders' own abilities to maintain the institution.[5]

Community promoters often saw the establishment of a private venture academy as a way to build up the stature of a new town, and the hiring and naming of a preceptor, or principal, helped to promote the image of both town and gown. The organizational development of the school and the designation of a principal reinforced each other: a school with a principal indicated some institutional stability, and only an institutionally stable school would appoint a principal. Even if the principal was the only educator in the building, that title heralded the cultural status of the school.

A good example of how such community "boosterism" relied on the creation of a school with an administrative leader is the Caledonia Grammar School in Peacham, Vermont. The town was founded in 1776 and within twenty years had a population of two thousand, one of the largest in the state. In 1795, the town debated whether to fund the construction of a courthouse or a high school in order to further the town's growth. The community voted to fund the school and the hiring of a preceptor, and then debated where to locate the school. Reflecting the relative wealth of the town, the school building was the substantial size of thirty by forty feet and two stories high. Students paid tuition fees for the purchasing of firewood, a school record book, and other expenses of the classroom. A young graduate of nearby Dartmouth College was hired as preceptor and, the following year, a woman preceptor was hired to educate newly admitted girl students. As at many academies, staff turnover was high; for its first seventy years of operation, the Caledonia Grammar School had forty principals, serving an average of less than two years each, and most were recent college graduates in their early twenties. Only when Mr. Bunker took over the principalship in 1867 was there administrative stability; he served for thirty years, merging his own professional identity with that of the institution.[6]

Similarly, the first high school in Hartford, Connecticut was founded and funded by leading citizens of the community who in 1847 sought to bolster the city's development as a leading manufacturing town. Prominent Hartford men comprised the board, and they kept a close hand on the management of the school, hiring and housing teachers, directing the curriculum, and monitoring the school's progress. In spite of such care, there was a high turnover rate among teachers and principals, with the exception of Thomas Curtis, principal from 1851–1861, who played a major role in creating an institutional identity and mission. Under Curtis, the school grew from three staff members to thirteen and became known throughout New England for its well-defined curriculum, preparatory academic work for college, and special opportunities for its male and female students including student government and a school newspaper. Curtis' educational values were enacted in the professional development of his teachers and the academic achievement of his students, many of whom went into teaching upon graduation.[7]

Some academies' founding principals embodied the school in their being so that the school and the principal became indistinguishable. Sarah Pierce, who founded and led a female seminary in Litchfield, Connecticut between 1792 and 1833 was just such a principal. Pierce started the school in her family's dining room at the age of twenty-five, challenging the social norm that young women needed little more than a primary education. Within a few years, she had gained enough respect from the local community that they raised money for a schoolhouse, and enrollment grew rapidly to the height of 169 pupils in 1816. As the school gained in national recognition, adolescent female students from across the nation enrolled, boarding in local homes. Pierce led a rigorous academic program that also encompassed social, moral, and religious education, languages, and ornamental subjects. She was the main instructor of all classes, assisted by her sisters, a brother-in-law, and eventually a nephew who shared the leadership with his elderly aunt. Sarah Pierce's commitment to her school was obvious to students, as one recalled Headmistress Pierce publicly announcing that she would lay down her life for them.[8]

So, too, did the two founders of the Round Hill School in Massachusetts commit their professional lives to preparing and shaping a unique academy for boys in the 1820s. Joseph Green Cogswell and George Bancroft spent three years in Europe visiting leading schools and studying with the major educational philosophers of the day before they returned to the United States to raise money for their boarding school. Established in 1823, the Round Hill School in Northampton, Massachusetts was noted for its emphasis on both intellectual and physical education, and its unusually relaxed approach to rewards and punishments. The founders intended to prepare students for college, but also to offer a more holistic education, "to mold children on the pattern of a more ideal type" through athletics, nature study, and community development.[9] Cogswell was a particularly dominant force in the school. One alumni recalled that Cogswell "was the organizer, manager, and father of the community," and was especially a "moral and affectionate influence, besides which he was head farmer, builder, gardener and treasurer of the place."[10]

More typical was the peripatetic career of educators who moved in and out of establishing, teaching, and leading academies, their very employment dependent on student tuition and community approval. Susan Nye

Hutchison's experience as founding principal of the Salisbury School in North Carolina is an example of the instability of academy leaders' lives and careers.

In 1815, Hutchison moved from New York to South Carolina to teach in an academy. After eight years, she left teaching to marry and raise her children, but because of her husband's economic troubles and poor health, she returned to teaching to support her family. For the next twenty years, she lived a transient life, juggling family and economic crises, traveling across the South to teach and lead numerous schools. In 1837, newly widowed, Hutchison left her children with relatives to move to Salisbury, North Carolina where she boarded with a wealthy family and garnered enough community support to endow her school. But within a year, enrollments were well below what she needed to meet institutional expenses, and she closed the school, gathered her children, and moved to Charlotte to teach at an academy there, reporting to her classroom the day after her arrival.[11]

Hutchison's motivation was economic survival, but she was also driven by a missionary zeal to influence young people in Christianity, and by her own intellectual curiosity—as principal of Salisbury School, she found time to teach herself algebra, which "delighted" her (she wrote in her diary that she "got into equations of the 8th degree and felt much rejoiced"), and self-studies of mineralogy, the Old Testament, French, and astronomy.[12]

Such intellectual energy, inspirational vision, and physical perseverance was necessary for academy principals who often acted as school founder, treasurer, development officer, and teacher. Sophia Sawyer, founder of the Fayetteville Female Seminary in Fayetteville, Arkansas in 1839 was a former student of two prominent women's academies in New England. She spent fifteen years as a missionary teacher in Cherokee Native communities in Tennessee, Georgia, and Oklahoma, during which time she became frustrated by the supervising missionary board's regulations and low expectations of Native students. Founding her own school in a frontier town allowed her to shape her institution the way she wanted to, modeling it off of the intellectually rigorous female academies that she had attended. Her strength of character earned her the support of local benefactors who endowed the new school with land and a building. But the school suffered a revolving door of teachers, due in part to Sawyer's notoriously difficult personality, what one teacher called her "spasmodic temperament." Recalled one teacher: "Miss Sawyer was a first-class regulator, and my position with the old lady was either up in the zenith or down in the depths."[13] Yet Sawyer's strong personality secured the school in the end. She was, as one of her former teachers described, "a woman of indomitable energy and perseverance."[14]

African American educators faced particularly difficult obstacles in their goal to establish and lead schools for their community's children. In the antebellum South, where the education of slaves was illegal, enslaved African Americans secretly led schools, and then, upon emancipation, set up private academies to educate freed slaves in the tools of freedom—literacy and self-empowerment. In Mississippi, Lily Grandison taught her fellow slaves by "night and stealth" for many years, and then, once emancipated, she and two other black women opened up a private school for black children in Natchez, charging a monthly fee of one or two dollars. By the end of the war, there were at least six independent schools for black children in Natchez, taught by members of the community's ex-slave and free black citizens.[15] Across the South, these schools were truly community ventures, as ex-slaves collectively purchased and built school facilities, and created independent boards of directors for their goal of universal self-improvement and citizenship. African American civic and educational leaders fought to maintain the independence of these schools, rather than be brought under the controlling umbrella of white-run missionary societies that belittled black leadership and replaced local black educators with white men and women educators from the North.

After the Civil War, white and black educators from the North and South flocked to the southern states to teach in and lead schools for newly freed slaves. More than a third of all teachers who worked with freed slaves in the post–Civil War South were African American, and a large proportion of these were from the North. Many worked within the American Missionary Association, a northern abolitionist Protestant group that founded more than five hundred schools and colleges for freed slaves. Other black educators founded schools on their own. Edmonia Highgate, for example, was born and educated in Syracuse, New York and migrated south right after the South's surrender at Appomattox to teach, found, and lead schools for freed slaves in Maryland, Louisiana, and Mississippi. Her sister, mother, and two brothers followed her, also committing themselves to educate newly freed slaves in the South and developing their own fundraising, recruitment, and promotional practices.[16]

The educational career of Solomon Coles in Texas is another example of this initiative. Coles was born a slave in Virginia in 1844, where he undermined laws that prohibited the education of slaves by gaining his own rudimentary education. Upon earning his freedom at the end of the Civil War, Coles attended night school while working with the Freedman's Bureau in Norfolk, Virginia. He migrated north to Connecticut and enrolled as the first person of color at the Guilford Institute preparatory academy, where he learned the Latin and Greek that qualified him to apply to college. Coles enrolled at the African American Lincoln University in Pennsylvania, and upon graduation in 1872, he enrolled as the first student of color at Yale University's Divinity School.

In 1877, Coles moved to Corpus Christi, Texas to pastor Freedom Congregational Church, founded in 1866 to serve newly freed slaves and black soldiers stationed along the Gulf Coast. Recognizing the lack of education for black children in the city, Coles opened a private school for black children and eventually abandoned his ministry to become a full-time teacher. In 1893, city officials appointed him principal of the city's first African American school.[17]

Like many other black school leaders, Coles' educational work expanded to professional development and advocacy. He helped organize and served as president of the Colored Teachers State Association in 1883, and played a role in the founding of the Texas Colored State Normal School. Coles also joined in the national discourse about race and education, publishing a series of articles in Lincoln University's alumni magazine, including a refutation of African Americans' intellectual inferiority that drew on biblical, theological, and classical references; an argument for the employment of black teachers in black schools; and a critique of white paternalism and racism in black education.[18]

African American school leaders faced similar challenges in the North. In northern states both before and after the Civil War, state "Black Laws" effectively limited African American participation in publicly funded schooling. Northern black communities responded by creating their own educational institutions, raising money and in-kind support to teach elementary and secondary education. Their leaders were often ministers or teachers who drew off of the collective energies of the local African American community and enhanced their educational mission with spiritual and political leadership. In 1863, African Americans in Southeastern Ohio founded Albany Enterprise Academy and hired Thomas Jefferson Ferguson as principal. Ferguson was already a notable educational leader: in 1861, he had helped to organize the Ohio Colored Teachers Association, and in 1866 he published a pamphlet, *Negro Education: The Hope of the Race*, in which he argued that the education of African Americans was more than just "preparation for life"; it was also preparation "for living as full citizens." Further, he argued that African American education would ultimately benefit the white man and the nation at large. Given the minimal supports for the school, Ferguson simultaneously served as principal, president of the school's board of trustees, and teacher. He also extended his leadership into the community, serving as the first African American member of the Albany City Council, president of the Athens County Convention of Colored Voters, and the first African American to serve on a jury in Athens County. Such efforts did not secure the school's future or Ferguson's fame: battered by the local white community's objection to a school run by African Americans, the school closed in 1886, and Ferguson, weighed down by ill-health, died the following year at age fifty-seven.[19]

For all independent venture schools, the absence of legal protection or a bureaucratic framework left their principals subject to the powerful pressures of public opinion. Women educators, in particular, had to conform to the social and cultural rules of the community—many women educators' employment contracts included social prohibitions against marriage or public socializing. The scrutiny on a founding principal was especially high, and a principal's leadership style and social reputation could literally make or break a school. Susan Nye Hutchison, for example, feared for the success of her school after a community member publicly complained about her children's behavior in church: "if I would not govern my own children I would not be fit to manage the children of other people."[20]

In thousands of independent educational ventures across America, teachers, school founders, and principals struggled against economic downturns and the disapproving votes of their school boards in order to keep their schools running. Given the dependent relationships on the community, academy principals shaped their school program along the educational expectations of their local governing boards. That conformity was tested in students' annual examinations that were open to the public and were as much an evaluation of the teachers and principal as the students. In the years before a common curriculum or standardized tests, schools were held accountable to the public in these exhibitions, and an examination session that went badly could lead to the withdrawal of enough students that the school collapsed or the principal was fired. A positive examination revealed a school well managed, and not only for academic accomplishments, as a local newspaper reported on the examination of a female academy in North Carolina in 1835 by praising the principal for her "zeal, her kindness to pupils, her untiring diligence, her acquaintance with polite literature, and the [C]hristian tendency and influence of her counsels and example."[21] Such behavior indicated effective teacher instruction, student learning, and school management and so earned continued community support.

Alternatively, community disapproval could lead to the abrupt end to a principalship and school. In 1867, the citizens of Milford, Connecticut voted to close their newly created high school because it was too expensive, and because they objected to Principal Whittemore's practice of allowing older girl students to teach the young students.[22] Thomas Beecher, principal of Hartford High School in Connecticut between 1848 and 1850, was fired by the board of directors because of his rejection of rote learning and corporal punishment and his advocacy of teaching methods that the governing board found to be "peculiar . . . broad and radical."[23] The school's teachers, who had loved both Principal Beecher and his educational philosophy, effectively chased out the subsequent two principals who they found to be poorly prepared and disrespectful of teachers' values and practices. One of the replacements was "a ninny," scoffed one teacher, and "altogether too small potatoes," and sadly noted that "I do not think the public care very much who heads the school—it is no such matter of life and death as it seems to us."[24]

Many schools were literally dependent upon their founder's personal leadership. The nationally renowned Litchfield Female Seminary closed in 1833, soon after Sarah Pierce's nephew, married and the father of four children, left the school for a more remunerative position. His elderly aunt could only keep the school running for another year. So too did the Round Hill School falter when Bancroft left Cogswell in charge of the school. Although beloved as the emotional force of the school—"the father of the community"—Cogswell was not a good businessman, and the school closed in 1834, after its eleventh year.[25]

In segregated African American schooling, educational leadership was subject to more vicious political winds. Cincinnati African American educator Peter H. Clark was principal of the Western District Colored School in 1857; in 1866, he was promoted to be principal of the Gaines High School, the first African American public high school in the city. Clark remained principal for two decades, during which time he was politically active in state and national politics on behalf of African American civil rights, and in 1885 he was appointed the first African American trustee of the Ohio State University. But Clark's prominence cost him his principalship: the following year, he was fired from his school leadership role.[26]

The career of high school principal William Butler in Kentucky in 1853 is an extreme case of the ongoing struggle for legitimacy of a mid-nineteenth-century school founder and principal. Raised on a farm in southern Indiana, Butler graduated with honors from Hanover College in Indiana, taught in three schools, and tutored the sons of a wealthy Louisville family. In his mid-twenties, he traveled to Europe to improve his language skills and in 1853 returned to Louisville to open a high school with a colleague. The two men offered courses in English, Latin, Greek, modern languages, and civil engineering to forty sons of local professionals in a large well-equipped school building. Among the professional middle class in Louisville, Butler was respected for his intellectual achievements, entrepreneurship, and high moral character; for displaying an egalitarian and professionally courteous manner to all; and for leading a well-disciplined school, using commonly accepted corporal punishment in a fair manner. But such respect only went so far: when one boy misbehaved in class, Butler whipped him according to school rules. The boy went home, picked up a pistol, and came back and shot Butler dead. Antebellum social mores led to the assassin's acquittal: the southern aristocratic code of honor trumped emerging codes of professional authority.[27]

COMMON SCHOOLS, GRADED SCHOOLS, AND SCHOOL LEADERSHIP

It was not school principals who organized to improve their lot. Rather, in the middle of the nineteenth century, a loose collection of government officials and educational reformers developed the outlines of what we now know of as the public school system, then called common schools. Common school reformers promoted a system of publicly funded schools and an administrative system to support them; they introduced the first models of standardized curriculum, teaching practices, and the organization of student learning; and they developed the first administrative guidelines that moved the managerial authority of schools from the local community to the offices of professional educators.

Of the many challenges that faced these common school reformers, one of the greatest was the absence of an organizational system to define and connect the varied educational enterprises that crossed the new nation. Mid-nineteenth-century students attended a range of educational institutions including one-room primary schools that taught basic literacy, grammar schools that taught more advanced academic subjects, and higher-level academies, high schools, and seminaries, none of which had any curricular link to the other, or any means of supervising or coordinating the instruction between institutions. Common school reformers searched for a better way of classifying students by level of instruction for the double purpose of first, standardizing paths of achievement for student learning and second, more clearly defining the organization of schools.[28]

A particularly popular curricular and administrative classification model was the monitorial school, or Lancasterian system, an organizational scheme originating in England that was designed to organize large urban schools at minimal cost. The monitorial system used a large hall for one half of the school's students and smaller classrooms for the other half, each under the supervision of different head teachers, sometimes called principals, who monitored assistant teachers and advanced students who taught smaller sections. In the large classroom, students sat in rows on long benches, grouped roughly by age and ability, and responded en masse to drills. Each grouping followed a prescribed course of study, with advancement dependent on students' passing set examinations. The process set up a clear and standardized path for student advancement across schools and it was economically efficient. It was also socially efficient, as rigid discipline was enforced with a system of rewards and punishments, and students could follow meritocratic paths of achievement. The goal of the entire operation was system and order, which appealed to some educators in increasingly disordered American cities. As the St. Louis Board of Education described it in 1857, "The program of one school shall be the program of all, the same grade shall recite in the same study at the same hour all over the city."[29]

Another attractive aspect of the monitorial school was the division and specialization of teaching labor. Educational reformers admired the organizational model of new factories, in which individuals worked in specific specialized areas. As William T. Harris, superintendent of St. Louis schools in the mid-nineteenth century described it, traditional education was comparable to "the antiquated process by which the gun was made throughout—lock, stock and barrel—by one gunsmith." But the modern system of education relied on a division of labor "where each manipulation has a different workman to perform it."[30]

Inspired by the vision of the factory, mid-nineteenth-century educational reformers adopted the monitorial system into a new, American model of school organization: the graded school. In the first graded school, opened in Quincy, Massachusetts in 1847, classrooms were divided by "grades" of common age or achievement level, with one teacher assigned to each class for the year and a supervising teacher—called a head teacher, or teaching principal—assigned to act as an overarching authority to the whole, organizing the separate courses of study, administering discipline, and supervising the operation of all the classes in order to, as the common school reformer Henry Barnard wrote, "secure the harmonious action and progress of each department."[31] Such graded schools offered the kind of internal uniformity that reformers admired, with the additional attribute of a supervising principal who could maintain some control over the increasingly heterogeneous enrollment. The vision was a hierarchically differentiated school system in which tasks could be divided and supervised by career educators.[32]

While the graded school structure addressed the problem of the internal administration of each school building, the broader management of local districts remained in the hands of locally elected community members, and this permitted continued disunity between schools. To address this problem, reformers promoted a centralized district administrative structure, whereby all local decisions about schooling would be addressed not by elected local parents, teachers, and community members, but by appointed professional school administrators. This organizational change moved the locus of school management from the individual community to the local district office where professional personnel trained in management would deliver policy directives down to the principal at the head of the local school.

An example of how this district structure developed in one district can be seen in the case of Boston, Massachusetts. In 1850, Boston schools were managed by two school committees of one hundred citizens and there was no formal method of teacher supervision; by 1876, the governing committee had been reduced to a twenty-four-member school board that appointed a

superintendent, a six-member board of supervisors, and forty-eight principals of grammar schools who supervised both their own schools and the
local primary schools. In the twenty-six intervening years, the number of
schools had not increased significantly, but the size of those schools and the
number of teachers had more than tripled. And, notably, the control of the
school system had centralized into a central office, an internal hierarchy
had developed with different gradations and salaries for different positions,
and the legal authority of the school system had moved from amateur lay
citizens to career educators.[33]

The appointment of a principal also addressed a critical problem identified by educational reformers: the need for the supervision of teachers. In
1865, Boston superintendent John Philbrick, himself a former principal of
one of the first graded schools in Quincy, appointed grammar school principals as supervising principals over primary schools. The superintendent's
rationale was that primary schools had an increasing number of teachers with
minimal experience, stationed in different classrooms and teaching largely
as they wished. What was needed, argued the superintendent, was a "master
mind" who could connect all these disparate parts. The supervising principal
would be "vested with sufficient authority" to manage school planning and
to "keep all subordinates in their proper place and at their assigned tasks."[34]

The design of a new school building in Memphis, Tennessee in 1872
symbolized the new authority and responsibility of the school principal in
the graded school. Memphis had established its school system in 1848, but
the schools struggled for many years with poorly equipped rental school
buildings and a weak administrative infrastructure that was further undercut by the financial and human losses of the Civil War. The opening of
the Market Street School in 1872 was heralded as the beginning of a new
future for the city. The three-story coeducational graded school had eleven
separate classrooms, running water, washrooms for men and women teachers, a library, and a lecture hall that could be divided into classrooms with
sliding doors. There was also a principal's office built on the first landing off
the staircase, so that while seated at his desk, the principal could "command
a full view" of the hallways and playground. A speaking tube led from the
office to each classroom, offering the principal regular oversight and communication with teachers.[35]

The concern with the supervision of teachers was all the more pressing because of the changed character of the nation's teaching force. In the
early nineteenth century, school reformers identified women as the best
candidates to teach in the new common schools because, first and foremost,
women were a readily available and cheap labor force. Educated in the new
common schools and academies and freed from the most primitive demands

of the household by technical modernization, young white women were an ideal employee pool for low-pay work with children. Women teachers also aligned with the new vision of education as a humane and caring institution since women, it was believed, had a "natural" affinity for children. Caring and cost were happily linked in the eyes of frugal school boards. As Horace Mann, superintendent of Massachusetts schools and one of the most prominent advocates for the reform of American education argued, the fully mature woman had such "a preponderance of affection over intellect" that she would not search for a teaching post for the money or the fame.[36] By 1888, women constituted 63 percent of the nation's teaching force, and over 90 percent of the urban teaching force.[37] Almost all of these women were unmarried, following legal and cultural proscriptions against working women having "two masters"—a husband and an employer.

Women might be more "endowed by nature with stronger parental impulses," as the Boston School Board claimed in 1841, but their expertise and abilities were still questioned by male educators who argued that women teachers needed close supervision.[38] School reformers found an easy and cost-effective solution: women were already accustomed to obeying the commands of men, and since they could be paid less than men teachers, the appointment of a male supervisor over a group of female teachers was efficient in both practice and economics. The quality of education would improve, as the cost would be reduced. Accordingly, when Boston superintendent Philbrick identified candidates for the grammar school principalship who would supervise the largely female primary teacher force, he intentionally appointed "men of large culture and wide practical experience" who could be offered the reward of promotion, recognition, and more compensation.[39] The principal would thus be transformed from a "head teacher"—a teacher with additional administrative responsibilities—to a professional principal—an administrator with authority over teachers.

Philbrick's reform was controversial, in part because grammar school principals were poorly prepared to supervise the teachers of small children, and the additional workload was burdensome. Furthermore, critics charged that the grammar school principals' expanded role gave them too much power, allowing them to act like "a little king" over all teachers.[40] But the point that professional principals, and not untrained lay school board members, should be in charge of teachers' work had been introduced, and superintendents, whose own jobs had increased in size and responsibility, increasingly assigned principals to closely monitor the work of new teachers and to act as virtual on-the-job teacher educators. In 1869, Cleveland's superintendent estimated that no more than a dozen of the 170 teachers in his district had any professional training, and that only the regular supervision of the principal would help those teachers in their work.[41] In St. Louis, Superintendent William Torrey Harris reported in 1871 that good principals could lift "teachers of average ability" through close daily supervision. The goal was efficiency and order: the principal needed to create a corps of teachers that were "uniform in their degree of excellence."[42]

The quest for uniformity extended to the curriculum. Through much of the nineteenth century, there was no common agreement on students' appropriate subjects of study or sequencing. The closest thing to a common textbook was the McGuffey Reader and other reading primers. Given the interest in systematic order and meritocratic development through the grading system, educational reformers called for a common course of study on which to evaluate the accomplishments of students in different grades. Superintendents and school boards developed programs of study that guided children through specific subjects in specific grades, with specific teaching methods in common textbooks. School principals were directed to apply the system to their school and to supervise teachers in their proper instruction.

Individual superintendents took up the charge. William Harvey Wells, Chicago's superintendent between 1856 and 1864, reorganized his city's school system into grades within a primary and secondary grouping and then instituted his own uniform course of study that included both the subjects to study and the specific plan for teachers' methods. Wells published his curriculum text in 1862, and it was widely adopted by other city districts.[43] Portland, Oregon's first superintendent, Samuel King, was equally vigorous in his design and implementation of a uniform curriculum in the 1870s. Like Wells' curriculum, King's curriculum was built around an understanding of sequenced knowledge, both within the curriculum content and in its delivery. Principals were the intermediate inspectors and disciplinarians, instructed by the superintendent to monitor day-to-day behaviors, including both student and teacher behavior. Superintendent King demanded that principals follow his strict guidelines in their supervision of teachers in everything from when to open the windows to what temperature to maintain in classrooms to the number of professional readings to study. Principals were also advised to "cheerfully cooperate with the City Superintendent in executing the prescribed work of the grades."[44] As in other districts, Superintendent King's interest in hierarchy of authority drew on gendered norms: by 1905, all of Portland's elementary teachers were women and twenty-three of the twenty-seven elementary school principals were men. This sex differential, coupled with the low pay, low prestige, and inadequate education of elementary school teachers helped to reinforce the hierarchical structure of the bureaucracy and the central role of the principal in enacting that bureaucracy.

DEFINING THE NEW PRINCIPAL

The new administrative structure of the graded school in mid-nineteenth-century America created a hierarchical relationship between district and school leadership as each accomplished its own cleanly defined tasks. The newly authorized position of the principal thus served the goal of both the internal and external reorganization of schools: the principal was a stabilizing ballast to a school building filled with multiple teachers and classrooms and acted as an administrative agent to a centralized office. The new principal stood between and connected the two, acting as the local implementer of the educational vision as articulated by the superintendent and school reformers.

The vision was clean, but the reality was not. The principal's office in the middle of the new school organization experienced great growing pains across the nineteenth century, primarily because superintendents and boards of education were unclear about how to distribute their authority. Although the principal's job was to coordinate the different classrooms of the graded school into "one system of government," that job was originally quite limited in scope and centered primarily on tasks of maintaining order and discipline.[45] For example, in 1841, school trustees in Cincinnati, Ohio, one of the first cities to appoint principals to their schools, gave the principal the responsibility of monitoring examinations and seeing that the bell was rung for school to begin; seven years later the principal's authority had expanded only to the ringing of the bell for recess, the suspension of pupils for profane language, and the monitoring of students' attendance record.[46] School district leaders in Providence, Rhode Island gave principals similarly limited authority in 1845: they could enroll new pupils, keep the daily attendance rosters, eject students for "gross misbehavior," employ a person to make the school fire, sweep and clean the school house, report on tardiness or absences of teachers, and keep track of books and supplies.[47] In 1854, during his first year as superintendent of Chicago schools, John Dore glumly described the role of that city's principals as little more than governing "the filing in and out of classes."[48] There was virtually no conception of the principal's role as a community or intellectual leader; the principal served as a functional manager only, with specific responsibilities only for addressing student registration and discipline.

Furthermore, through the nineteenth century, there was continued duplication of principals' and superintendents' responsibilities, and there was ongoing conflict between the two positions as they both jostled for professional authority over their different pieces of the educational enterprise. Nineteenth-century district office and school building administrators argued over jurisdiction of the transfer and appointment of teachers, what books and how many to purchase, and the examination and promotion of students. In New York City in 1859, for example, principals accused the superintendent of enforcing an examination that intruded into the daily curriculum and that gave the superintendent "despotic power" to rate a class on the basis of a mechanical test.[49] From superintendents' perspective, such complaints were evidence that principals were unprofessionally wedded to their own authority and were resistant to the enlightened reform ideas of the district.

A notorious example of such a conflict occurred in 1840 in Massachusetts over the topic of corporal punishment. Horace Mann, the state superintendent of education, was newly returned from a trip to Europe where he had observed the progressive educational practices of Prussian schools where teachers encouraged students' curiosity about learning rather than enforced memorization and recitation. Also notable among Prussian schools was the replacement of corporal punishment with more nurturing and developmental processes of discipline. When Mann ordered the institution of such practices, Boston school principals protested, arguing that student learning only happened with disciplined memorization. "Duty should come first and pleasure should grow out of the discharge of it," the principals argued in a lengthy response to Mann's call for reform. Mann responded by charging the principals with privileged self-interest, and when advocates of the new philosophy of education gained the majority on the Boston school committee, the principals who advocated their traditionalist practices were dismissed or transferred out of the district.[50]

More common than this face-off between opposing offices were the blurred reporting lines of overlapping administrative positions. In smaller towns and rural communities there was often little distinction between the principal and the superintendent and few consistencies in job description. In mid-nineteenth-century Iowa, for example, the town of Muscatine had a "principal" of the city schools, while nearby Tipton's lead administrator was called a "superintendent." Dubuque had ward principals only, with no central superintendent; and Des Moines had a "supervisor" although the entire school system consisted of only a single building with four teachers. In Iowa City, the superintendent was also the high school principal whose functions included meeting parents and examining pupils every Saturday afternoon in his office. In Clinton, a superintendent supervised a single teacher in the city's sole school. In addition to this confusion, there was high turnover of administrators and irregular growth and demise of schools. Between 1897 and 1903, alone, three quarters of the school administrators of Iowa's county seat towns changed jobs.[51] Because it was not immediately clear to taxpayers what a principal did, or where the role's function began or ended, many school boards simply bypassed the hiring of a school principal and assigned a teacher the title of "head teacher" or "principal teacher." Nor was there a systematic process to the authorization of these first school principals. Particularly in rural communities, increased enrollment might lead to the addition of classrooms and the appointment of a head teacher, if the community decided to allocate the funding. The appointed head teacher might be the longest-serving teacher, or the teacher most liked by the school board, or the only teacher willing to take on extra responsibilities.[52]

HA HA!

Although principals in the nineteenth century were slightly more secure in their employment than in earlier years when a disapproving parent could simply fire the local school head, there was no common system of professional development or job security. Different districts set different requirements for a school head, including a high school or college degree, teaching experience, and examinations that might cover a wide variety of topics, although not necessarily the topics of teaching method, curriculum, or administration. In mid-century San Francisco, the principal's certificate was valid for only one year, and renewal was not permitted. The principal's examination was more of an endurance test than an evaluation of educational leadership skills or philosophy. The geography component of the exam included naming all the bays, gulfs, seas, lakes, and other bodies of water on the globe; all the cities in the world; and all the countries in the world. The time set for answering the questions was one hour. In one exam period, by the end of the hour, one candidate had quit, one had reached the fifth question, and one had reached the fourth question. Nonetheless, all candidates were marked exactly the same: 60 percent.[53]

Chester Dodge's and John Swett's experiences exemplify the erratic and makeshift character of the mid-nineteenth-century school principal. Dodge was first hired as principal in 1873 in a district outside of Chicago on the recommendation of the head of the local teachers' college from which he had just graduated. At age twenty-one with only two weeks' experience teaching, he became principal of a school with seven teachers in the main building and three teachers in two branch schools. Within a year, Dodge was offered a principalship at another school with a 20 percent increase in salary (from $800 to $1,000). The following year, he lost that position due to his promotion of a new method of reading that community members objected to. Dodge's third school was in a community that was divided in half by a railroad, poor on one side, wealthy on the other, and a deep tradition of conflict between the two sides, which contributed to Dodge's removal at the end of the year. In ten years, Dodge had led seven different schools, including rural, urban, elementary, and high school.[54]

John Swett's experience as a teacher and principal in mid-nineteenth-century California is another example of the irregular processes of principal appointment and work. Newly arrived in San Francisco in 1853, Swett applied for a job as a teacher in the new city school system, but was instead appointed principal to replace a school head who had resigned after only sixty days because of discipline problems with students. Swett's school enrolled sixty boys and girls, half of whom were in the primary division, headed by a woman teacher. School was held in a small rented house, what Swett called a "shanty" with a "shed-like addition" for the primary children. There were no blackboards, maps, or curriculum, and furniture consisted of one water pail, a small table for the teacher, and one rickety chair. Children brought their own ink, pens, and paper to school. Swett gained control at the school by expelling the misbehaving students and by organizing parents to fund the construction of new school facilities, including a principal's office. Indeed, a large part of Swett's success as principal, which later led to his promotion to state superintendent of schools, was his ability to motivate the community to support education. Principal Swett adapted the traditional public examination sessions into a community event where students exhibited their knowledge in academic competitions with awards. The examination was followed by a festival that doubled as a school fundraising drive. Adopting new educational ideas, Swett took students out on walks in the hills, promoted athletics, and gave lectures on discipline, honor, courage, politeness, and other virtues. His pedagogical and community strategies echoed his educational vision that education was the mechanism that would unify the rapidly expanding west into a common civic body. As administrator, Swett recalled his struggles with "overbearing and conceited men" on his board who "played the part of petty tyrants over school teachers," but he also downplayed his work as a school principal as very similar to that of "the routine work common to all teachers," including "the monotony of school life."[55]

Community support, of course, only worked when communities approved of local educational efforts. The history of the African American school in late nineteenth-century Oxford, Ohio highlights the ongoing public debate over new educational laws and policies that disrupted community norms and power relations. Black laws in the state required racially segregated schools until 1887 when the Ohio legislature repealed the separate school provision to allow for racially mixed schooling—a decision made primarily to cut the expenses of local districts that complained about the cost of even their minimal support of black schools in addition to white schools. In some districts, primarily in northern Ohio, integration occurred quickly and peacefully, but there was violent resistance in other districts where white parents and educators physically prevented black children from entering local schools, closed schools to prevent integration, and gerrymandered school districts to create racially distinct districts.

In 1887, the small university town of Oxford in southern Ohio had a newly constructed white school and an old and overcrowded black school.

Black parents petitioned to have the schools merged under the new state law, but the white town and school leadership refused. Denied their rights, Oxford's black residents filed a state lawsuit against the Board of Education and won. Significantly, the court made no special claim to equal rights for African Americans, judging only that a local school board was required to abide by the state legislature's ruling. The board had the obligation to provide for all of Oxford's school-aged children and "to permit them to enjoy, without distinction on account of race or color, any and all benefits" of the local public schools. Most black students transferred to the Oxford Public School that winter, although some stayed in the old black school. Indeed, across the country some African Americans opposed racially integrated schools, well aware that black teachers would not be hired by white school boards to teach white children. This was the case in Oxford. Mr. Grennan, the white teacher who had taught in the black school since 1866, was transferred to the mixed school, while the black teacher, Mr. East, stayed as principal of the black school until it closed in 1892, whereupon Mr. East lost his job.[56]

In the American South, reform initiatives for the expansion of state school systems, graded schooling, and centralized administrative bureaucracy were delayed due to the disruption of the Civil War and Reconstruction, and ongoing racial, class, and religious divisions. In the early 1900s, reformers promoted the construction of modern school systems as part of the modernization of the Southern economy and society, but it was not until the 1930s that most Southern states built state and county educational infrastructures with curriculum and attendance laws and civil service policies for educators.[57] And upon completion, these were racially divided school systems for white and black, offering significantly less funding, organization, and support for black schools and educators.

CONCLUSION

Through the late nineteenth century, school founders and leaders were largely solitary figures who fended for themselves in their ventures. Unprotected by any matrix of school structure, dismissed by community members as social outsiders who had only marginal cultural claim on their children's lives, and overburdened by their overlapping roles as school founder, teacher, fundraiser, and manager, those who undertook school leadership did so as a broad and poorly defined practice. Early school leaders' freedom from a larger administrative structure allowed them the liberty to shape the school's educational mission as they wanted—Round Hill's notable emphasis on physical education and nature is a good example. But that independence could also be their downfall, as there was no larger organizational structure to support or defend the principal in times of conflict with the community. Principals' ability to enact their educational philosophy was sharply circumscribed by their school's direct dependence on the community. While the absence of administrative structure might allow for individual initiative in educational practices, it also undercut the potential for stability and continuity in schools.

Common school reformers' administrative innovation—the graded school—provided some form and function to schools and began to clarify the role of the school head or principal. Yet even by the end of the nineteenth century, the system was hardly well formed. In his 1893 expose of American urban schools, Joseph Rice described a variety of different responsibilities for principals, from Philadelphia where they were "lords and masters of their own schools" to Indianapolis where each school had a principal, but the duties barely extended beyond teaching and general supervision over the building. In some cities, one principal was in charge of a number of schools; in others, the principal was little more than a clerk whose main job was to keep attendance.[58] In elementary schools in particular, the principal's office remained a far more tentative, undefined position than in secondary schools where the principal often took on a more official public role in the community. For women and people of color who led schools, school leadership was an even more unstable enterprise. And even among the schools of the wealthy, the preceptor or principal was an iconoclastic figure, part teacher to be pitied and looked down upon and part administrator with marginal authority who was still beholden to the community.

The very notion of school leadership remained poorly defined, primarily because American citizens and educators alike were uncertain of who should be in charge of schools: community or church leaders, parents, teachers, a district leader, or a building leader. Nor was there any clarity on the nature or authority of such leadership work: was it the mechanical management of children at recess, the examination of student academic work and the disciplining of their behavior, or the authority to purchase equipment and hire teachers? Common school reformers struggled to address these questions by creating educational policy and law that would guide school leaders in acting out their newly conceived regulations. But the structure was hardly secure, and at the end of the nineteenth century, the public school principal was still a liminal creature, neither fish nor fowl, with no perceptible or permanent job description, holding multiple job responsibilities and no clear directive for improving children's education.

CHAPTER TWO

THE MAKING OF THE
PRINCIPAL'S OFFICE, 1890–1940

In September 1925, when Roald Campbell became principal and teacher of the seventh and eighth grades at Wilson School in Bingham County, Idaho, he was nineteen years old and freshly graduated from Idaho Technical Institute, with one semester of experience practice teaching. To prepare for his new position, Campbell borrowed a friend's Model T Ford and drove forty miles to visit his former teacher for advice, then twenty-five miles to visit the county superintendent to gather information about books and supplies, then eight miles to visit with each of the three school board trustees to secure approval to order the needed books and supplies, then to the school to review the status of the facilities. When school started, Campbell was in charge of three other teachers, all women, with tenure that varied from two to ten years. The county superintendent visited the school a few times during the year and led a one-day workshop for teachers. Campbell attended the rare school trustees' meetings and, when he needed approval for the purchase of instructional material or equipment, he again visited each trustee at his home. In addition, as teacher, Campbell taught eight subjects to the seventh- and eighth-grade classes and coached the boys' sports teams. After five years, Campbell was appointed superintendent in Moore, Idaho, a job that included the role of school principal, where he stayed for three years until he was appointed superintendent and high school principal of Preston, Idaho, a larger community. He was twenty-seven years old. Campbell described the way that his different roles blurred together, recalling how as superintendent he was referred to as a "schoolmaster," which meant colloquially both principal and superintendent.[1]

The expansive nature of Campbell's administrative role was typical of early twentieth-century educational administration. As one of the few men in the school room, he was a target for promotion simply because of his gender, and not because of any extra experience or ability. In some districts, principals were little more than teachers with extra administrative responsibilities; in others, the principal was also the superintendent, and in still others, the school principal was not even identified as an administrator. A national study of elementary principals in 1926 tried to differentiate between the different roles of principals who were called head teacher, teaching principal, building principal, and supervisory principal, but admitted that in many cases it was difficult to tell "where one stage ceased and the next began."[2] In small cities and communities, the principal acted as the lead policy maker, curriculum designer, public relations director, and finance officer, which could lead to conflicts over authority during a superintendent's infrequent visits.[3] The elementary principalship was particularly noted for its multiple job demands, teaching responsibilities, and, given the lower number of men in elementary education, the continued appointment of women to the role. According to one observer in 1926, the elementary principalship was not a professional position but merely "a function" that varied "with varying situations."[4]

Roles were particularly confused in rural communities where there was only a small degree of separation between superintendent and principal, both of whom taught, undertook clerical and janitorial work, and acted as community liaisons. Many principals continued to spend the bulk of their work days in the classroom—much like their nineteenth-century predecessors, a teacher with extra administrative responsibilities. Typical was a principal in a small high school in rural Pennsylvania in the mid-1920s who spent thirty-three periods of a forty-period week teaching seven different subjects ranging from Algebra to European History to Civics. As the head of the local system he was also held responsible for directing instruction in the elementary school.[5] Typical too was that teaching was one of only a myriad of activities that principals were expected to undertake, including athletic coaching, directing plays, supervising clubs, and participating in local church and community events, and professional associations.[6] Even in larger communities, the distinction between teacher and principal remained blurred. Elementary principals in Washington, D.C. in the spring of 1921 complained about their burdens; most were eighth-grade teachers as well as principals who were busy preparing their students for high school, even though "every year adds to the number of reports we are required to make."[7] "I am principal, and all else," admitted Susie Watkins of Battle Hill School on the edge of Atlanta in 1935, where she was the sole instructor of all subjects and manager of thirty-nine children, boys and girls, ranging in age from five to seventeen.[8]

In addition to unclear professional distinctions, the principalship suffered from low salaries. A 1905 survey of almost five hundred city school systems found that men elementary principals earned an average annual salary of $1,542; women elementary principals' average was $970.[9] High school principals, virtually all of whom were men, earned more than their elementary peers, most of whom were women, but even at the secondary level, principals' salaries were comparatively low, particularly in rural communities where all educators earned less than in the cities. Granted, in a period when the average working man's annual salary was $600, and the average teacher's was under $500, principals were not as poverty-stricken as they claimed. But compared to the salary of the high-status occupations with which principals aspired to be associated, they had some reason to be concerned. In 1905, the average college professor earned $1,700 a year, physicians earned between $1,000 and $2,000, and lawyers and engineers between $2,000 and $4,000. Principals took little comfort in the fact that they earned only slightly more than the humble minister or the uneducated and unionized building-trade worker.[10]

Educational reformers of the late nineteenth and early twentieth century saw the professional improvement of the principal as a necessary task for the construction of a modern school system. Across the country, officials in state education offices and professors in newly founded education colleges argued that the only way to turn the great ship of public schooling into the modern age was a more empowered principalship that would have the authority to translate central office policy to schools. Accordingly, educational administration reformers developed four strategies for clarifying and enhancing the principal's role. First, they argued for reshaping the regular responsibilities of the principal away from the classroom toward specific administrative work housed in a separate principal's office. Second, they reinforced the authority of the principal as a supervisor over teachers. Third, they promoted a competitive credentialing process for the principalship through universities and state agencies. Finally, they developed a campaign to increase the number of men in educational administration. This chapter examines the initiation and marginal success of these four overlapping reform processes in the late nineteenth and first half of the twentieth century. First, I introduce the context of educational reform of the period.

THE ADMINISTRATIVE PROGRESSIVE
EDUCATIONAL REFORM MOVEMENT

The move to improve principals' status and job description came not from within the ranks of principals but from a new cohort of educational reformers who continued the momentum of past reformers to improve American education. These reformers were part of a wider social reform movement at the turn of the century, commonly called the progressive movement. The educational wing of progressive reformers was a diverse collection of social

and educational reformers: some turned their attention to improving pedagogical practices in the classroom, others saw improved school organization
as the key to improved learning. Historians have called this latter group of
educational reformers "administrative progressives," because they believed
that improved administrative structure would improve educational practice.[11]
Administrative-progressive reformers' vision was to reorient public education from an eclectic, local operation run by community-elected citizens
to a more systemic bureaucracy run by trained managers. They promoted
a centralized administrative structure whereby all decisions about schooling
would be addressed not by local parents, teachers, and community members whom reformers saw as ill-informed about new educational ideas, but
by professional school administrators who understood how to design and
implement modern practices of standardization and cost efficiency to the
burgeoning educational enterprise. The application of scientific principles
in the development of cool rational processes would lead to social efficiency in school and nation: an absence of waste, a clarity of purpose, and
the efficient direction of students and educators toward their mutual goals.
Indeed, many of these reformers adopted the term "social efficiency" as the
way to describe their initiatives to improve student learning and the entire
apparatus of school administration.

A strengthened principal's role was seen as the lynchpin to social
efficiency–oriented reform, because the principal would be the local professional agent who would implement central office policies in the local school.
The conception of the principal as a middle manager perfectly suited the
visions of educational administration reformers who conceived of the modern school system as a corporate enterprise, led by descending hierarchies
of trained leadership originating in state and district offices and cascading
down to building leaders. Educational administration reformers increasingly
distinguished administrative and pedagogical areas of research and divided
educational administrators into specialty groups—principals separated from
superintendents and assistant superintendents, and from the panoply of
other administrative experts in school finance, law, building management,
and curriculum.[12] Between 1890 and 1920, the number of such "supervisory officers" increased dramatically in major urban districts: in Baltimore,
supervising administrators jumped from 9 to 144, in Boston from 7 to 159,
in Cleveland from 10 to 159.[13] Administrators dreamed that with these
increases in specialized personnel, school districts would become well-oiled
hierarchical organizations with expert decisions emanating from distinct
professional offices. Such a structure, reformers believed, would educate all
children equitably and efficiently.

A more systematic organization of student learning was all the more
necessary because of the growth in enrollment in public schooling in the

late nineteenth century. Between 1890 and 1918, high school attendance increased over 700 percent, while the total population increased only 68 percent.[14] Educational reformers puzzled over how to design curricula that would efficiently address the different needs and interests of this expanding student cohort that was increasingly diverse in family and class background, ethnicity, race, and gender and that had an increasing array of vocational and professional options ahead of them. Their concerns were echoed by higher education leaders who demanded more systematic preparation of high school students, and by high school educators who demanded the same of elementary students. Just as insistent were the captains of late nineteenth-century industry, business, government, and the new medical, engineering, and legal professions, who demanded specific skill sets and attitudes of their future employees. Administrative progressive reformers sought to develop an organizational system that would efficiently channel modern students into this wide array of adult roles.

The life and work of Ellwood P. Cubberley exemplifies the ideas and practices of administrative progressive reformers. The first dean of Stanford University's School of Education, Cubberley shared with other emerging professionals a faith in the cool hand of disinterested science and objective administration to improve society. He promoted hierarchical systems of school management that replaced community voice with the centralized administrative authority of educational experts, well trained in graduate degree programs like those he developed at Stanford.

Cubberley's original scholarly interest was in geology, and he was throughout his life a meticulous note-taker and data collector who was fascinated by problems of cause and effect. Born in 1868 in a small town in northern Indiana, Cubberley earned a bachelor's degree at Indiana University and spent the next few years in an upward trajectory from one-room county school teacher to college professor to, at age twenty-three, college president of Vincennes University in Indiana. At age twenty-eight, he moved to California for the position of superintendent of San Diego schools. The political infighting in the San Diego Board of Education reinforced Cubberley's emerging belief that education should be managed scientifically, and not by strong personalities or local biases. Within two years, he moved to Stanford University where he spent the remainder of his professional life developing just such a science of educational administration.

In his hundreds of investigative studies of school districts around the country and his instruction of thousands of school administrators, Cubberley developed his theories of school management. He saw education as one of the nation's most important political problems of governmental management, and he believed that the solution to inadequate schools was to strengthen methods of educational delivery, which he referred to as "school machinery."[15] This quest led him to conduct extensive studies of school and district organizational structures. Cubberley was particularly bothered by administrative leadership practices that were inconsistent across communities and mired in clerical routine. He was especially concerned with the role of school principals, who, he argued, needed to clarify and assert their own authority as well as to align with district administration. Drawing on metaphors from the burgeoning industrial and managerial professions, Cubberley described the ideal relationship of the principal to the district office as:

> analogous in the business world to that of the manager of a town branch of a public utility to the general superintendent of the business; to that of the manager of a single department to the general manager of a department store; to that of the superintendent of a division of a railroad to the president of the company; or that of the colonel of a regiment to the commanding general of an army.[16]

In spite of his sterile metaphors, Cubberley and his peer school reformers were zealous in their faith that improved delivery systems would improve the rapidly growing educational system. Facing a literal tidal wave of student enrollment and financial cost increases, they addressed the technical problems of school organization and student learning with evangelical passion. Clarifying the responsibilities and skill required of local administrators played a major part of their reorganization of education.

North Carolinian and journalist Walter Hines Page took up the reform of his state's education system with similar verve in the early 1900s, arguing that an advanced school system was the only way to pull the defeated, rural South into the modern industrial age. In his 1901 address delivered at the commencement of the Georgia State Normal School, Page offered an imaginary portrait of how a single new high school could serve as the catalyst for change in a small Southern community that was still mired in old-time rural dysfunction, including the presence of old-fashioned private academies led by "a cultivated old lady" and a "sturdy old master," each of which rose and fell with the school founder. Such educational unreliability undermined the economic stability of the town, Page insisted, thereby keeping the South isolated, backward, and ignorant. The single best way to sweep away these old cultural cobwebs was to hire a new high school principal. Drawing on the popular imagery of the efficient economically oriented reformer, Page described the new principal as "a man who knew how to manage men," who would begin his work with a careful scientific study of the town's needs that would fill "a book almost as big as a banker's ledger." This school leader would single-handedly modernize the community by leading the construction of a modern new public school building, hiring trained teachers, recruiting the best citizens to serve on the school board, developing an active and progressive curriculum, and fundraising for a new gymnasium and library. Such advances would ripple out to the community, leading to the construction of new factories, new roads, and new city infrastructure. In the old days, the town was weighed down by the charitable burden of the schools; in the modern day, the school would build the town, and the principal would be the driving force behind it all.[17]

THE PRINCIPAL'S OFFICE

According to educational reformers like Cubberley and Page, the first step in the professionalization of the school leader was to physically separate the principal into a distinct administrative office. With the development of the graded school in the late nineteenth century, the head teacher had moved physically from the podium at the front of the monitorial classroom into a separate, non-classroom space. Educational administration reformers argued that the enhancement of this enclosed space into a formal principal's office would further the school leader's professional authority. From the principal's office, the modern principal would be able to supervise the school in modern ways—by paperwork, reports, and standardized assessments, all accommodated in an office with special cabinets for filing records, a secretary to help file those records, and a waiting room for people to meet with the principal to talk about the content of those filed records. The authority of the principal working from the office would move from direct to indirect, from literal to representational power, making a symbolic break between the classroom and educational administration. In a great irony, principals could better control teachers and students the farther away from them that they were.[18]

The construction of a principal's office thus became a central strategy for enhancing the role. A 1928 yearbook of the national elementary principals' association described the principal's office as "a physical device used in the management of the school just as the blackboard is a device used in the instruction of children."[19] Architectural designs included the construction of not just an office but a protective space around the office, including an outer area used as a waiting room with a desk for a secretary, two entryways so that the principal could have a public and private entrance, and a private toilet, coat closet, and telephone extension.[20] In later years, public address systems linked the principal's office with classrooms, emphasizing how the principal was both apart from and constantly overseeing teachers. The burgeoning school supply industry offered additional office equipment, such as the Dictaphone, mimeograph, ditto, and accounting machines, all of which promised to help the principal create systematized office procedures and "channels of routine." The goal was to make the principal "a directing educational engineer instead of a head teacher and clerk."[21]

But for all the enthusiasm over the professionalization of the office, its message was contradictory; school principals were told to become administrative bureaucrats of a school "plant" even as their school curriculum encouraged the active engagement of all educators in students' development. At the same time that principals were assigned their own office, they were then criticized for spending too much time in that office, which many educational reformers saw as the last place that the truly inspired principal should be. In 1924, Chicago's superintendent urged principals to get "out of the office chairs and into the work area."[22] A Brooklyn superintendent accused the "tyranny of business custom" as the reason why so many principals wasted their time of "morning freshness" in their offices reading the daily mail instead of out in the hallways and classrooms inspiring teachers and students.[23] Cubberley himself applauded the work of an elementary principal in Salt Lake City who was always "somewhere in the rooms, busy with his work, instead of sitting on his chair in his office."[24] Similarly, educational administrators who assigned principals mountains of paperwork now criticized principals for being a "Director of Routine" rather than leading "educational engineering and generalship."[25]

The very topic of what principals should do in their new office raised contradictory admonitions. Principals were advised to clear their offices of excessive communication and other entanglements with "non-educational" organizations that might clutter their day and bias their professional expertise. Indeed, some educators argued that the very best principals should use their office as a sanctuary from the tiresome trivia of school life and spend their time at their desk developing significant leadership strategies. In Wilmington, Delaware in 1921, for example, principals were urged to cut off communication with the outside world through "evil telephones" and to use the office as a buffer and the secretary as a bulwark against parents, teachers, and community members who believed, incorrectly, that they had the right to bother the principal at all hours, often with matters of "little consequence."[26]

Although the principal's desk in the office was the ideal space to complete administrative paperwork, some reformers urged principals to delegate those tasks to secretaries and assistants. As Chicago superintendent Ella Flagg Young argued in 1915: "something besides routine work should occupy the mind and time of principals . . . if they are to lead, encourage, and inspire a school."[27] "Principals are to be more than makers of schedules, keepers of books, and enforcers of rules," agreed a 1944 report on Pennsylvania schools.[28] In their defense, principals responded to the swirl of advice about the office by noting that it didn't matter so much *where* the principal was, as *what* work the principal was engaged in, and that the real question was about the type of administrative support the principal had to free up time for more important work.[29]

But the hiring of clerical help was inconsistent, depending on districts' ability to afford the extra costs. One 1927 study found that only one-third of American elementary principals had a full-time clerk, another fraction had part-time clerks, and fully half of all elementary principals had no clerical assistance at all.[30] Principals who did have staff carried the additional responsibility of supervising that staff. As school buildings increased in size and complexity, custodial services were hired to monitor heating, cleaning, and ventilation systems. This relieved the principal of such menial labor but replaced it with supervision of other workers. In Chicago, in 1905, for example, the Board of Education wrote in excruciating detail about whose responsibility it was to open the school, keep the keys, and supervise heating apparatus.[31] The problem seemed to be which of the two—principal or janitor—would supervise and be responsible for cleaning. If a superintendent found a school dirty, whose fault was it? Such confusing job descriptions undercut the idealized image of the authoritarian building administrator with clearly defined roles.

Nonetheless, the creation of the principal's office, a separate, clearly identified location in the school for non-classroom work, was effective in furthering the popular understanding of the principal as a distinct authority figure. Even as the office removed principals from the classroom, it enhanced their authority over it. Separated in their offices, their assumed presence expanded throughout the school.

SUPERVISORY LEADERSHIP

Having extracted the principal from the classroom, the next step toward the professionalization of the principal was to create a clear supervisory line of authority over teachers. In his influential critique of American schools in 1893, Joseph Rice identified as a main problem in schools the haphazard system of training and evaluating teachers through inconsistent, misdirected, and infrequent supervision. Rice's critique was both a dismissal of teachers' skills—"teachers are as a rule too weak to stand alone, and therefore need constantly to be propped up by the supervisory staff"—and a negative assessment of principals, who clearly were not providing such necessary props.[32] Since Superintendent Philbrick's innovative appointment of grammar school principals as supervisors in mid-nineteenth-century Boston, principals' supervision of teachers was seen as the cornerstone of effective school management. Supervision of classroom teachers, reformers advised, was the crux of the organization of the complex new school system, as it was the only way

A GRAPHIC INTERPRETATION OF
THE MANNER IN WHICH THE PUB-
LIC ADDRESS SYSTEM UNITES A
SCHOOL AS IF ALL CLASSROOMS
WERE ONE

Figure 1. "A Graphic Interpretation," *The American School and University*, 1928–1929: 263.

by which central administrators could guarantee teachers' adherence to new standards, including punctuality, obedience, and other behaviors that would bring "order to a chaotic and backward school system."[33]

School reformers emphasized the role of the principal as supervisor not only to improve classroom instruction, but also to enhance the cultural authority of the school building leader, expanding the position beyond mundane administrative tasks into higher level instructional responsibilities. The first, observed one reformer, "is mere shop keeping; the second is educational statesmanship."[34] Such statesmanship could come only with the exercise of explicit authority over teachers. Metaphors of principals' supervisory leadership often relied on popular imagery of modern industrial society. As Seattle's superintendent promised in 1933, all education would be improved by the principal's "well lubricated, frictionless operation of the machinery."[35] Some years later, a popular textbook used for principal preparation specifically referred to the principal as "a kind of foreman who through close supervision helped to compensate for ignorance and lack of skill of his subordinates."[36] Others were more explicit in their insistence on the principal's authority as a supervisor. In Chicago in the early 1920s, the superintendent informed newly appointed principals that: "You have the hand of iron. Use it. If teachers or a wild bunch of citizens. . . . try to run the schools, put a stop to it with the power that you have."[37]

Such authority was especially necessary given the gender dynamic in schools. Many male educational reformers upheld an undocumented belief that most women teachers had only minimum training and that they were likely to teach for only a few years before marriage. (In fact, women teachers were no less prepared than men, and in some cases might have had more preparation in female dominated Normal Schools, and their tenure in schools was often longer than men's.[38]) A Minnesota superintendent saw the rural school problem starkly as one of "too much femininity," the solution to which was the appointment of "men of the highest type" as principals and superintendents.[39] Dean Ellwood P. Cubberley argued that the average rural teacher was "a mere slip of a girl, often almost too young to have formed as yet any conception of the problem of rural life and needs." This young girl, "almost entirely ignorant of the great and important fields of science," and "lacking in those qualities of leadership so essential in rural progress," needed supervision from men of "adequate preparation, deep social and professional insight, and large executive skill and personal power."[40]

The principal's application of *both* executive skill and personal power drew on the combination of both traditional bureaucratic and individual charismatic authority. Supervision was not merely the task of directing individual teachers to improve their classroom work; supervision also entailed instilling uniform adherence of all teachers to the educational enterprise. Effective supervision would thus both improve learning and it would enforce bureaucratic role relationships in schools.[41] Thus, the division was not just between a principal and a teacher, but between an entire conceptual understanding of the different roles played by the two in schools. In 1908, Washington, D.C.'s superintendent of schools described the ideal configuration this way: There should be a class of school directors, administrators, and supervisors, whose function is management rather than instruction. These school managers see the schools from a point of view different from that of the instructors. The subject is defined not as the instruction and control of individual pupils, but as the organization, maintenance, administration, direction, and supervision of schools.[42]

The creation of this separate class and the transfer of supervisory authority to the principal required the disentangling of the principal from the work inside the classroom and moving that work outside and over the classroom.

But a number of variables worked against this seemingly mechanical realignment of roles. Reformers, administrators, and teachers disagreed on the purpose of supervision: was it to serve as an evaluative process for teachers, thereby providing a bureaucratic function? Or was supervision a mechanism for instructional improvement, thereby serving an educational goal? Administrators at the building and district level quarreled over who should supervise teachers and what was the goal of supervision, and their disagreements were played out in the creation of a confusing maze of supervisory identities and responsibilities.[43]

One problem was that although the principal was heralded as the cornerstone to effective teaching, through the mid-twentieth century, supervision remained under the purview of the superintendent's office, often the responsibility of an assistant superintendent or district-level supervisors. District supervisors came in two forms: a "general supervisor" reviewed the instruction of general subjects; that position eventually merged into the assistant principalship with additional administrative duties. "Special supervisors" were itinerant staff, charged with supervising the instruction of subjects requiring special expertise, such as music, art, penmanship, physical education, health instruction, and children with special needs. The status of special supervisors varied: some were teachers with special responsibilities, others served as quasi-administrators across the district.[44]

For example, William H. Lebo, who taught music in Hamilton, Ohio city schools between 1900 and 1933, was identified as both a teacher and a supervisor. In function, he resembled a special supervisor with special expertise as a musician. But his work was more like that of a district administrator. In his three decades in the district, Lebo built up the music program across the district to include boys' and girls' chorus, band, and orchestra. He was also the citywide music director, developing and leading music activities outside of the school district. Although Lebo was described as a "supervisor" as early as 1911, there were no other music teachers in the district whom he supervised. This type of special supervisor acted as somewhat of an independent expert, given broad discretionary power

Figure 2. "The Super-Vision Demanded," from *Childhood Education* 4, no. 7 (March 1928): 312.

around the district and in some cases holding more authority than the school building principal.[45]

Because supervisors reported to a district officer and not to the principal, relations between supervisors and principals could often be strained. Principals complained about the inability to integrate the large numbers of supervisory experts into the school, about conflicts with teachers over who was the ultimate authority, and about the way that their own work could be undercut by supervisors who ignored the principal's building authority. Alternatively, visiting supervisors might be dismissed or undermined by building staff. A woman supervisor could face a tense gender dynamic when as a district supervisor she was ostensibly superior to a man building principal. Such was the situation in Gary, Indiana in 1913 when Assistant Superintendent Annie Klingensmith found herself treated as a "rank outsider" and her supervisory advice flatly dismissed by the long-tenured male principal of a school.[46] Furthering the status confusion was that there were no set qualifications or eligibility requirements to be a supervisor beyond experience or perceived ability to evaluate. Supervisors who were based in the district office might be paid more than teachers, and some were paid on parity with elementary principals, even though they might have less educational background and less experience than many teachers or principals.[47]

Visiting supervisors also added to the confusion of the school day. In the town of Albert Lea, Minnesota in 1928, elementary teachers reported to at least seven different supervisors "all of whom visit classes, offer suggestions on teaching, or in other ways attempt direction or guidance."[48] In a Chicago elementary school in 1922, teachers objected to the authoritative role of the music supervisor who required that every teacher conduct singing at the assembly. Teachers complained that because of this requirement, the entire school schedule was disrupted, and, because they did not have training in music, many were put in the humiliating positions of making a "pitiable spectacle of herself before an assembly of children." The supervisor had told teachers that the decision was the principal's, but the principal, who was "greatly beloved" by teachers, said that the demand had been sent to her and she was forced to do it. The teachers appealed to the superintendent for relief.[49]

Further complicating matters was that with district supervisors moving in and out of their building, the principal was still responsible for the evaluation of teachers. But in fact, most principals were simply too overburdened by their other duties to regularly evaluate their teachers. In Albert Lea, where supervisors literally swarmed around the building, the principal's job remained so complex that a 1928 survey flatly stated that "in no sense can it be said that their duties are merely supervisory or administrative. All of these officers supervise. They all do clerical work. They all hold conferences, and attend to administrative matters and, no doubt, a legion of other minor duties."[50] The definitional problem concerned black elementary principals in Washington, D.C. as they sought to form a union in early 1920. The president of the new group sought advice from the American Federation of Teachers (AFT) on whether "supervising principals" could be in an elementary principal's union, given that such principals had authority *over* regular principals who were "primarily" classroom teachers. Elementary principals were "responsible for all property on the school reservations, for the discipline of the buildings, and for certain administrative work," but they had no power to evaluate teachers. Were supervisory principals thus administrators or teachers? The president of the AFT provided an answer, but probably not a solution to this definitional quagmire: according to the AFT constitution, "supervising officers except superintendents" were eligible.[51] This phrase ultimately justified the affiliation of dozens of principal unions with the AFT, ostensibly a union for teachers.

Distracted by their other responsibilities, and untrained in supervisory techniques, principals often proved to be inadequate supervisors. A 1927 survey of principals in Concord, Massachusetts may have described a typical scenario: the principal visited teachers with "no objective in view other than the very general and usually rather hazy purpose of 'helping teachers where they need it.'"[52] Relations between administrators and teachers were desultory and mechanical, with administrative memos addressed to clerical and scheduling issues. Leadership was characterized by "arbitrary administrative fiat, rather than by cooperative discussion of important problems on the part of teachers and supervisors together."[53] Educators regularly observed and bemoaned such inadequate supervision. Apparently, concluded one educational reformer gloomily, "public school principals have an idea that the mere presence of their observing faces in a classroom will inspire and improve the instruction."[54]

Indeed, the prominent image of the new principal was not that of an inspiring observer at all, but rather a rule-bound and distant bureaucrat, delivering orders and rigid evaluations from the office. Cubberley observed the way in which principals in Portland, Oregon "vivisected" the curriculum "with mechanical accuracy into fifty-four dead pieces."[55] Other popular reports of schools described principals as drill sergeants who ordered teachers to maintain mindless rules of neatness or behavior, making dictatorial demands such as requiring teachers to make students hold their books "in their right hands, with the toes pointing at an angle of forty-five degrees, the head held straight and high, the eyes looking directly ahead."[56] Teachers described principals' major impact as a disciplinary figure, located in a distant office, physically and culturally separate from the life of the classroom, and charged with maintaining order in the school. Clearly, educational administration reformers observed, principals needed to learn how to diversify and enlighten their professional activities.

CREDENTIALING PROFESSIONALS

In their goal of developing the professional legitimacy of principals, educational administration reformers identified a process of required academic preparation and credentialing. The objective was both to make entry to school administration positions a competitive endeavor and to prepare aspiring educational leaders in a common body of knowledge. Trained in accredited universities and authorized by state officials, the newly credentialed school principal would have the intellectual cache of higher education and the political legitimacy of the state, paralleling the type of cultural authority that characterized other professionals like doctors and lawyers. Such academic preparation and credentialing in the principalship would, reformers hoped, improve both principals' practice and professional status.

The process of certifying educators had begun in colonial New England when schoolmasters were "licensed" by local selectmen or clergy. The rationale for these legal guidelines was usually worded in such as a way as to prevent certain people from teaching children; for example, according to the licensing act of 1654, selectmen were warned not to appoint any person who had "shown themselves unsound in the faith or scandalous in their lives, and not giving due satisfaction according to the rules of Christ."[57] By the turn of the nineteenth century, educators continued to be concerned about their impact on children, but there was an additional concern about the status of the profession.

Early twentieth-century reformers argued that the creation of a cohesive academic body of knowledge was a critical step in the professionalization of educational administration. With the development of sequenced graduate coursework and endorsement by the state, the school principalship would cease to be an accidental occupation tagged on to the end of a teaching career. Instead principals would be identified and mentored by the leaders of the field—professors of education in newly authorized graduate schools of education. Carefully selected out of a competitive pool and trained by experts in the field, the principal would then be skilled at the work and publicly recognized as a professional. As one reformer asserted in 1924, advanced training and graduate degrees would become the "passports to principalships of greater responsibility."[58]

There was great room for improvement in this area. Well through the 1920s in many states, barely half of all elementary principals had graduated from college.[59] As late as 1937, twelve states still did not require a bachelor's degree for elementary principals.[60] Although high school principals tended to have more academic training, including college education, through the 1930s, about a quarter of all high school principals around the country still did not hold a bachelor's degree.[61] Most principals at all levels had no professional training or coursework in educational theory or psychology, testing, administration, or supervision. In-service professional development was also inconsistent: some principals might have attended some kind of summer training or professional meeting at some point in their career, but such activities were rarely a prerequisite for the position.[62]

The requirement of academic coursework furthered the goal of professionalization by identifying educational administration as an intellectual field of study, not just a technical position of management. In the early twentieth century, faculty in newly founded education schools developed a knowledge base that increasingly distinguished administrative and pedagogical areas of expertise in school law, finance, testing, supervision, and building management.[63] The academic preparation of school principals in these topics would teach more than the educational "technique" of managerial skills, but would also develop a "habit of thoughtful analysis of situations and problems."[64] Underlying all of the arguments for a principal preparation program was the idea that educational practices were changing and principal preparation needed to keep up: thorough preparation in both liberal and professional studies was particularly imperative in 1930 because "no longer" was the principal expected to be "a figurehead of autocratic leadership; rather he is concerned with the adjustment of the school in its aspects to the needs of a democratic society."[65]

Many of the advocates of advanced educational credentialing were themselves professors in schools of education who were recruiting for their new degree programs. As dean at Stanford University's new School of Education, for example, Ellwood P. Cubberley transformed school administration from an informal field built on experience to a professional field requiring specific coursework in empirical studies of school finance, organization, and leadership, many of which Cubberley conducted himself with his students. At Harvard University, education professor Paul Hanus developed special degree programs for school administrators as a way to bolster the academic stature of his university's new educational program that had been the target of criticism from the arts and science faculty. Gender was part of the problem: at Harvard as in other educational programs, the bulk of education students were young women, a situation that furthered the downward spiral of the new school's prestige. Hanus designed advanced graduate courses for administrators that were separate from the teachers' courses and that were targeted toward male high school teachers and administrators. The administrative coursework at Harvard allowed ambitious male high school teachers a speedier track to the principal's office than the traditional path of a few years of teaching experience in the schools.[66]

Academic credentials were not enough to build a true profession of educational administration. Like the new medical and law professions, aspiring school administrators also requested professional endorsement through state certification. Between 1923 and 1934, the number of American states that distinguished teacher from administrator certificates more than tripled from seven to twenty-seven.[67] The state of California offers a good model of this gradual expansion of credentialing. In 1925, California required school administrators to hold a teaching license, a two-year education school degree or four-year bachelor's degree, have a minimum of one year of teaching experience, and have completed fifteen semester hours of college work in school administration. Eleven years later, California required distinct state certification in administrative specialties, the first state to do so.[68] Required courses included school administration and supervision, child development, history and philosophy of education, educational tests and measurements, and specialized courses in the organization and administration of vocational education, junior high schools or high schools, schoolhouse hygiene and construction, statistics, and school surveys.[69]

Yet in spite of these efforts, the proposed equation that academic credentialing plus state certification would lead to principals' professionalization did not play out as expected. Through the 1920s, a number of national and state studies reported that the content of professional courses for principals was too superficial and that they rarely involved specific application of concepts to actual practice.[70] Even with increased requirements designed to "protect the profession and the public against the untrained and unskilled—the shyster and the quack," a review of educational programs in 1925 found that "to an appalling degree, the leadership of our public schools and educational institutions is entrusted to untrained and unskillful administrators."[71]

Furthermore, even as aspiring principals were increasingly required to take written tests and submit academic credentials, their experience as teachers remained the prominent qualification. At the dawn of World War II, the most common requirement for the hiring of a principal was two to five years' teaching experience and a bachelor's degree, with less than a quarter of all states requiring a certification exam or any courses in educational administration.[72] In the checklist of qualifications for the principalship that was devised by the Chicago Board of Examiners in 1930, for example, an applicant's experience as a teacher was valued twice as much as a bachelor's and master's degree.[73] Even in the high schools, where principals were more likely to hold advanced degrees, experience still held priority over professional training in hiring and promotion. By the 1950s only one-third of all states stipulated specific academic requirements for the principalship.[74]

THE MAN IN THE PRINCIPAL'S OFFICE

Reformers' ambivalence about the professional status of the principal's office was accompanied by concerns about who sat in that office, and much of the efforts of the professionalization movement in educational administration centered on the recruitment of a select group of people who, it was believed, would enhance the professional status of the principal's office. Having developed the technical mechanisms for enhancing principals' professional status through the creation of the office, the development of supervisory lines of authority, and the establishment of a credentialing system, reformers turned to the problem of who should be recruited to the job.

Most troubling to reformers was that the bulk of elementary principals were women. The elementary school had long been considered both the domain of women and an institution that resisted formal bureaucratic order. Compared to the secondary school with its subject areas, curriculum aligned toward vocational or collegiate preparation, and college-educated teachers, the elementary school was a disordered mass of small children, integrated curricula, and women teachers with insignificant certificates and normal school degrees. Women appeared to be the natural leaders of such a domestic organization, and well through World War II, the elementary principalship offered women the greatest opportunity for administrative leadership in public education.

Between 1900 and 1950, over two-thirds of American elementary schools were led by women principals. Most of these positions were in rural schools, but women were also prominent in city schools, holding over three-fourths of elementary principalships in cities under thirty thousand and well over half in many of the largest American cities.[75] In some communities, women principals were not only numerically but culturally dominant, holding a kind of matriarchal lineage. In some Southern cities after the Civil War, the combination of the loss of so many white Southern men during the war and the expansion of public school systems led to a significant increase in white middle-class women's long-term employment in public schools.[76] In Memphis Tennessee, Annie Christine Reudelhuber was the respected head of the Smith Elementary School for thirty-eight years, between 1882 and 1920, and the school was re-named the Christine School in her honor upon her death. A women teacher in the school followed her as principal for the next twenty years, and Reudelhuber's sister was also long-time principal of another Memphis school.[77] In Seattle, Washington, Superintendent Frank

Figure 3. Brownsville, Texas. A woman teacher and a male administrator, Brownsville Grammar School, 1902, from the collection of the author.

Figure 4. Mrs. Dame, teacher, and Mr. Dawthus, principal, Durham, North Carolina, circa 1910–1912. Courtesy of the Pauli Murray Papers, The Arthur and Elizabeth Schlesinger Library on the History of Women in America, Radcliffe Institute.

Figure 5. An unknown woman teacher and a male administrator, n.d. Courtesy of the Smith Library of Regional History, Oxford, Ohio.

Cooper made a practice of hiring and supporting a large number of women principals, so that in 1938, over three-fourths of the district's twenty-three women elementary principals had nineteen years' tenure.[78] Such longevity was notable because in most districts, even in the elementary schools, women principals tended to have less job security and shorter tenures than men. For example, in Milwaukee between 1900 and 1930, the average tenure for women elementary principals was only five years, while half of the male secondary principals held their positions for over twenty-five years.[79] Still, even with such turnover rates, in most early twentieth-century communities, the majority of elementary principals were women.

While dominating elementary principals' offices, women were virtually excluded from the more prestigious and higher-paying secondary school principal's office, except in all-girls' schools. Through the 1920s, less than 10 percent of all high school principals were women, and in some regions of the south, they barely existed. In Alabama in the 1920s, for example, only 4 out of the state's 289 white high school principals, or 1.4 percent, were women.[80]

Gendered differences in elementary and secondary school principalships were embedded in the structure of the two positions. Through the mid-twentieth century, educators at the elementary and secondary level were on different salary scales, with elementary principals earning between two-thirds and three-fourths of secondary principals.[81] In the segregated white schools of Augusta, Georgia in 1929, for example, elementary principals earned the same average salary as male secondary teachers and two-thirds of secondary school principals. (Elementary principals in the black schools earned less than half of white elementary principals.)[82] Even within elementary schools, women principals were disadvantaged by the creation of separate boys' and girls' departments. In turn-of-the-century New York City, Katherine Devereaux Blake was principal of the girls' department of PS 6, earning 70 percent of the salary of the male principal of the same school's boys' department. In 1911, the boys' and girls' departments merged as the result of an equal pay act that prohibited different pay scales for men and women educators, and Blake became the school's sole principal. But even then, because of the continuing separate salary scale between elementary and secondary educators, Blake's salary remained below that of her peers in the high schools. New York did not eliminate salary discrimination between elementary and high school educators until 1947.[83]

The differences between elementary and secondary principals played out in other ways. Early twentieth-century architectural plans represented the occupational difference in material terms: the high school principal's office was often positioned on the first floor at the entrance to the school building to symbolize the principal as the public face of the school. In the elementary school, the principal's office was often on the second floor, embedded in the core of the classroom area. High school principals were more likely than their peers in the elementary schools to have clerical help, separate conference rooms, and assistant principals; one 1929 study reported the suggestive finding that high school principals were three times more likely to dictate letters than were elementary principals, indicating that secondary principals were three times more likely to have a secretary to whom to dictate. Elementary principals were also more likely than secondary principals to teach classes and to be involved with children on the playground and lunchroom, and in community organizations.[84]

Women were also de facto excluded from the principal's office in secondary schools by common employment prerequisites for the job. A secondary school principalship that required a bachelor's degree effectively limited the number of eligible women, who had only limited access to universities.[85] In comparison, most elementary principals had only a two-year degree from a normal school or teacher training institution, historically the domain of women educators. In Ohio in 1925, for example, 25 percent of men elementary principals and 10 percent of women elementary principals

Figure 6. Principal M. Effie Kellum, in her ninth year as principal, middle front row, wearing glasses. Allen Street School teaching staff, Lansing, Michigan, 1931. Courtesy of the Tedd Levy Collection.

FACULTY AND CLASS OF 1916

Figure 7. Principal Charlotte Hawkins Brown, center, wearing glasses, with teachers, Palmer Memorial Institute, Sedalia, North Carolina, 1916. Courtesy of the Charlotte Hawkins Brown Papers, The Arthur and Elizabeth Schlesinger Library on the History of Women in America, Radcliffe Institute.

had graduated from college.[86] Educational attainment directly affected salary: the salaries of college-educated principals were higher than those without a bachelor's degree, even though college graduates tended to be younger and have less experience than other principals.

Further excluding women from the secondary principalship was that both teaching and administrative experience in the elementary school was considered less favorably than their counterpart in secondary schools. In turn-of-the-century New York City, elementary principals were denied the opportunity even to apply for secondary principal positions because, according to the school superintendent, the experience of managing an elementary school was simply not enough of a qualification for leading "a great city high school."[87] In many districts, only high school principals could qualify for the additional position of supervising other schools, which earned extra pay.[88] In Chicago in the 1930s, elementary teachers required two years more of teaching experience than secondary teachers to qualify for any principalship, although working against that policy was an "age penalty" that subtracted points for any principal applicant over the age of fifty-four.[89] The work of elementary teaching and administration, done primarily by women, was flatly counted as less significant for school leadership than similar work in the secondary school.[90]

To early twentieth-century reformers, the low status, expansive job description, and continued feminization of the elementary principalship gave the position a decidedly unprofessional character, contributing to the popular anxiety that the numerical domination of women educators undermined young boys' masculinity. As one educator argued in 1908, an "effeminizing and softening influence of women teachers on boys" led to an "unnatural condition."[91] Critics discouraged women from the principalship because it would cause women too much anxiety and because it seemed obvious that women teachers would prefer to work under male principals, whose "superior executive gift" led them to be "more just, patient, and sympathetic" as school leaders.[92]

Such ideology led to the redesign of elementary principals' job description, qualifications, and credentialing processes with the goal of attracting more men to the position. The development of academic and credentialing requirements played a significant role in this process because access to these programs was explicitly limited to men through recruitment norms and common admissions quotas in graduate programs. In addition, American male veterans returning from the First and Second World Wars received preferential tuition waivers for graduate courses.[93] The new priorities were hardly a secret, and women educators were quick to point out the increasing gender disparity in principals' offices. As early as 1897, New Jersey principal Elizabeth Almira Allen argued that experience was the proving ground for both teachers and administrators, and that the requirement of university degrees inevitably worked against women principals who, Allen observed, were "fast becoming obsolete in New Jersey."[94] Teachers saw this shift in principals' background as a loss of teachers' influence in the increasingly hierarchically organized school. Margaret Haley, founding leader of the first teachers union, the Chicago Teachers' Federation in early twentieth-century Chicago, criticized principals whose "sole claim to fitness for the position is that of having written an examination on academic subjects with particular emphasis on theory and method of teaching."[95]

Another professionalization process that effectively reorganized women out of the elementary principalship was school consolidation that replaced small elementary schools where women had been principals with large schools. Early twentieth-century educational reformers advocated for the replacement of small rural schools with larger, consolidated schools as a solution to a perceived "rural school problem." The one-, two-, and three-teacher schools of rural communities were criticized for having limited equipment and resources, poorly trained teachers, and administrators who were too burdened with teaching and management to promote visionary educational programs.[96] The principals of the new consolidated schools were overwhelmingly men who were younger and had less experience than the former women principals who were reassigned to classroom teaching. During the consolidation process in two rural counties in California between 1930 and 1950, for example, the number of women principals declined from almost twice the number of men principals, to one-quarter.[97]

CONCLUSION

Bessie Kidder Thomas was in many ways an unusual principal. Head of the Woodstock High School in rural Vermont between 1918 and 1932, she was one of only a few women to lead a secondary school in a time when only 14 percent of other high school principals in the state and less than 10 percent in the nation were women.[98] Holding a bachelor's degree from Wellesley College, she was one of less than 10% percent of all educators in Vermont who had a college degree.[99] In a time period when women teachers were often forced to resign upon marriage, Thomas was married and her husband was active in his wife's work, serving as a kind of first husband, attending school parties and mentoring the high school boys.

As principal, Thomas adopted a familial leadership style. She was known by the entire community as "Aunt B," and she made a point of knowing every student in the school personally. Well respected throughout the community, in 1923 Thomas was appointed supervising principal, authorizing her to supervise teachers in all elementary schools in the district, even while she continued to teach her own classes. In addition to her own teaching and administrative leadership, Thomas connected with students through dramatics, dancing, and particularly athletics, which she supported by serving as the bus driver for school teams and by promoting sportsmanship as a way of life to be applied in sports, the classroom, and at home. Thomas' ethic of sportsmanship was not merely about individual achievement and competition: sportsmanship was also about furthering the collective good through teamwork. About her own role as principal, Thomas felt she had "an optimistic view" and that, as in the functioning of an effective team, "if everyone feels his or her responsibility, peace will finally be gained."[100]

However unique, Thomas' principalship was typical of most principals' roles at the time, and this fact frustrated early twentieth-century educational reformers. Thomas was a vestige of the nineteenth-century head teacher with multiple roles as teacher, principal, coach, and supervisor. She had no formal professional training in educational administration, and she developed her own unique leadership style that maintained her identity as a classroom teacher. Typical of thousands of other principals across the country in the early twentieth century, the job description of the principal of Woodstock High School was expansive and flexible, allowing for an informal feminine identity as the neighborhood aunt.

Educational reformers condemned the model presented by Bessie Kidder Thomas, recommending instead a male principal with a well-defined position that was distinct from that of the teacher, a leader who came to the job with training at the feet of experts in educational administration, and with the authority to effectively translate district policies to the school. Educational administration reformers in the early twentieth century campaigned for these changes, arguing for the professional benefits of constructing a separate principal's office, for supervisory responsibilities, standardized credentialing process, and the recruitment of men. Their goal was the creation of a clearly defined administrative structure with a distinct professional position for school principals in the middle of the educational organization.

But the struggle to create a professional school principal seemed to be thwarted at every turn. In 1925, a professor in the educational administration department at Teachers College in New York City bemoaned that nobody really knew

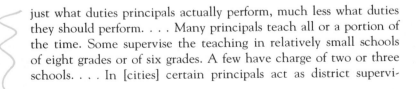

just what duties principals actually perform, much less what duties they should perform. . . . Many principals teach all or a portion of the time. Some supervise the teaching in relatively small schools of eight grades or of six grades. A few have charge of two or three schools. . . . In [cities] certain principals act as district supervisors, having oversight of twelve or more schools. In small towns and in outlying districts of large towns, one person frequently has charge of the work in both grades and high school. The majority of principals have no assistance. Some have clerks or assistants or both. Obviously, there is no such thing as the elementary school principalship but a function varying with varying situations.101

In 1938, a national study of American schools found that the nature of the principal, especially in the elementary school, remained "unsettled."102

In one way, the professionalization movement of the early twentieth century was successful, but this success carried the seeds of its own destruction. One goal of the educational administration credentialing movement was to replace the inconsistent and partisan meddling of local communities with a professional body of educators. But the new authority of academically based educational leaders introduced a new provincial body of decision makers, what historians David Tyack and Elisabeth Hansot called "the educational trust"—an interlocking directorate of university professors, state superintendents, and other officials who formed a powerful network that served the interests of chosen insiders. The old community nepotism that had favored a local grammar school graduate over a university-accredited educator was now replaced by a closed community of white male educational and political leaders who maneuvered their own into similar positions. Such professional networks would shape the nature of the principalship through the twentieth century, sharply limiting the number of women school leaders and creating a professional job description that emphasized administrative loyalty over educational innovation.

For all the visions of a standard hierarchical organizational system of an educational profession, through the early twentieth century, school principals' work remained a very hands-on, immediate job, requiring individual leadership strategies and no small amount of energy and creative thinking. Ironically, the very efforts to clarify the principal's role expanded the responsibilities of the position to such an extent that there was little time for professional development. Even as principals were assigned professional stature in the new school administrative hierarchy, their original day-to-day work remained, leaving them "so busily engaged by a vast swarm of petty details" that they had little time for professional development.103 In addition, the professionalization movement increasingly distanced the principal from the classroom and student learning, creating an administrative culture of authority and discipline and not educational and community engagement.

As we will see in the next chapter, some principals resisted the demands of this bureaucratic model by offering alternative models of the principalship.

CHAPTER THREE

OUTSIDE THE PRINCIPAL'S OFFICE

Principals, Democratic Leadership,
and Community Change

Ethel Thompson Overby, the first black woman principal in Richmond, Virginia, believed that, above all else, the school principal was a community educator. As principal of two racially segregated elementary schools in Richmond between 1933 and 1958, Overby employed literacy and citizenship education for her school's students, teachers, and parents with the explicit purpose of empowering her community to resist racist city policies. The daughter of a domestic servant and a freed slave, Overby began her activism as a teacher in segregated black schools in the 1920s where she raised money to create a school library, since African Americans were prohibited from using the Richmond public library. As principal, Overby intensified her civic engagement work, developing a critical literacy curriculum in which students were taught to question the structure of the society in which they lived, including why they had to sit in the back of the city bus, and how to respond to racial insults. She provided books from the Association for the Study of Negro Life and History and encouraged her teachers to teach black history and literature. She required that all of her teachers register to vote, and she organized students to register their parents, while raising money to set up a citizenship loan fund from which parents could borrow the $3 poll tax. As a result, voter registration in Overby's school district was the highest of all black districts in the city. Overby used the public press to publicize the cramped physical conditions in her school, and she organized parents and students to speak to City Council for a new school. She kept

the Richmond community informed of students' achievement through persistent public press releases and her sheer physical presence in church and
community events. In this way, Overby incorporated academic with civic
education, linking school and community.[1]

In the early twentieth century, educational administration reformers
argued that school principals' attention should be realigned from the classroom to the boardroom and from community responsiveness to administrative authority. But not all educators bought into that movement. Some
African American principals in segregated schools and progressive white

principals saw democratic leadership and community engagement as a central tenet of their work, and they shaped their role as principal into an
advocacy position for civic activism, student and teacher leadership, and
labor unity. This chapter examines the work of some of these early and
mid-twentieth-century principals who saw their professional identity differently from the hierarchical model proposed by educational administration
reformers.

DEMOCRACY IN SCHOOL ADMINISTRATION
AND COMMUNITY LEADERSHIP

Educational historians have traditionally divided the educational reform
movement of the late nineteenth and early twentieth century into two
camps: administrative progressives who advocated for the development
of school systems driven by values of fiscal economy and organizational
accountability, and pedagogical progressives who promoted a child centered,
humanistic approach to education. While Ellwood P. Cubberley and other
administrative leaders introduced in the previous chapter represent the work
of the first group, "pedagogical progressives," such as the educational philosopher John Dewey and progressive school founders Lucy Sprague Mitchell
and Elizabeth Irwin, promoted a child-centered curriculum that was based
on students' needs and interests. These educators argued for the expansion
of the school curriculum from traditional academic subjects to more socially
oriented learning in such classes as physical education, home economics,
vocational education, the arts, and after-school clubs and activities. Following the guiding philosophy of John Dewey, pedagogical progressives held that
the school was a microcosm of society and that only through the development of thoughtful, democratic practices in school would students develop
an understanding of how to be democratic citizens.

Pedagogical progressives' attention was primarily on classroom practice, although some also examined the administrative organization of educational institutions, arguing that a school could not be fully democratic unless
its leading administrators also behaved democratically. As Dewey argued in

one of his few writings on this topic, "every member of the school system, from the first-grade teacher to the principal of the high school," must be involved in educational decision making. School leadership, Dewey wrote in 1903, should not consist of "one expert dictating educational methods and subject matter to a body of passive, recipient teachers, but the adoption of intellectual initiative, discussion, and decision making throughout the entire corps." He concluded that "no matter how wise, expert, or benevolent the head of the school system, the one-man principle is autocracy."[2]

In his call for democracy in educational administration, Dewey identified the school principal as an "administrative statesman" whose leadership involved engaging in intellectual and professional problems of education, the development of cooperative community relationships, and the skilled delivery of administrative functions. Recognizing the demands of school bureaucracies, Dewey cautioned administrators against becoming focused on the "mass of ritualistic exercises called school administration."[3] Rather, principals needed to carefully reflect upon and construct their vision of the community purpose of their schools. To do this, school administrators first needed to decide if their school mission was to "perpetuate existing conditions or to take a part in their transformation." Administrators then had to develop methods of treating the school as a cooperative intellectual community and not to act as "an aloof official imposing, authoritatively, educational ends and methods." Finally, administrators needed to take part in what Dewey called "adult education": the ongoing engagement of the public by inspiring and leading the community toward social transformation. Central to all of this work was democratic leadership and the inclusion of all members of the school community in educational decision making.[4] The foundation of democracy, Dewey insisted, was "faith in the capacities of human nature; faith in human intelligence, and in the power of pooled and cooperative experience."[5] A democratically led school would prepare children to lead a democratic society.

Dewey's call for democratic educational leadership influenced a number of educators, particularly in the dark days of the economic depression of the 1930s. In 1932, educator George Counts asked Americans to reconstruct their society from the ground up, asking if schools dared to "build a new social order." Following New Deal proposals to rebuild the nation economically and socially, a number of educators promoted alternative education programs that charged schools with engagement in social change in the community. One of these, the Community School movement of the 1930s, reinforced the links between the school and the local community by encouraging administrators to go beyond mere institutional management. According to Samuel Everett, the author of the 1938 leading text on the topic, *The Community School*, "the responsibility of educational administration is to demonstrate realistically its ability to participate in the formulation of broad social policies."[6] The principal needed to play a major role in this activity, creating a comprehensive plan for school usage and making the school building available day and night for community events, adult education, recreational activities, parent-teacher groups, and local community organizations. The principal of the "many-sided social institution," the community school, would be responsible for "the dynamic leadership of the community's educational activities."[7]

In the 1930s and '40s, even educators who did not identify as progressive emphasized the themes of democracy and community engagement in schools, contrasting the ideal American educational organization with the international specter of totalitarianism. According to reviewers of the Pittsburgh, Pennsylvania system in the 1940s, "good administration does not consist of the activities of supermen and women who hold high administrative posts and who dictate the program to be carried out by teachers in the school system."[8] In Newark, New Jersey in the early 1940s, the principal was advised to shift from the "principal teacher of the school to principal educational leader" of the community.[9] Educational surveyors in Lincoln, Nebraska agreed, arguing that "the principal should be the leader and co-ordinator within the individual school. . . . The school is a co-operative enterprise; it can be most effective only when teachers share in its administration."[10]

Set in the context of the new educational administration professionalization movement, however, these dicta were rarely designed to create "a new social order." In educational administration manuals, the language and priorities of democracy were tempered by the language and priorities of educational management: modeling democracy in schools was well and good, but the principal still needed to retain the responsibility for creating democratic conditions and behaviors. Democracy, yes, but final decisions remained in the principal's office.[11]

Furthermore, as with much of the advice delivered to principals, community engagement often came only in the form of additional responsibilities added to their daily calendar. Principals were liberally given advice to develop community-oriented activities, such as connecting with local businessmen's groups, recruiting the efforts of local women's advocacy clubs, supporting the parent teacher association, and developing a publicity program to keep the school in the public's eye. Principals were advised to maintain regular contact with a broad array of social welfare and civic agencies, including the Boy Scouts and Girl Scouts, local Red Cross, YWCA and YMCA, the chamber of commerce, and business and professional clubs. These admonitions added to an already overloaded table of responsibilities, and principals struggled, understandably, to accomplish them all. A 1924 survey of large high schools in California found that principals spent only 5 percent of their time, or barely four hours a week, on community activities.[12] A 1928 national study of 614 elementary principals found that most spent only about two hours a week in such work.[13]

EDUCATIONAL STATESMANSHIP IN SECONDARY SCHOOLS

Secondary school principals were better positioned than their elementary peers to adopt Dewey's call for educational statesmanship. American secondary education underwent radical changes in both size and content in the first decades of the twentieth century. In 1900, there were barely 300,000 high school students in the United States; by the 1920s there were two million, and in 1929, over three million. This growth was due in part to the expanded purview of public education occasioned by child labor and compulsory education laws that both increased and diversified high school enrollment. The expansion furthered a change in the traditional secondary school program from a classical academic curriculum to comprehensive programs that addressed the diverse needs and interests of students, including vocational, technical, and agricultural education. Progressive education advocates also

Figure 8. Principal Leonard Covello with Friends and Neighbors Club, circa 1939. Courtesy of The Historical Society of Pennsylvania.

expanded the role of schools from the delivery of academic content to social service, health, cultural, and civic education. The Cardinal Principles Report of 1918, issued by the Commission on the Reorganization of Secondary Education of the National Education Association, captured the heart of these changes by declaring that American secondary education should take into account students' individual differences, goals, attitudes, and abilities as well as broad social and civic objectives. The seven principles of the report charged secondary schools with developing healthy life practices, the command of fundamental processes of mathematics, writing, reading, oral and written expression, "worthy home membership," vocational preparation, civics, physical education, and ethical practices of personal responsibility and initiative. The expansive view of education promoted by the report, combined with the rapid changes of secondary school enrollments, opened up the possibility for a new type of secondary school principal who would promote an agenda broader than the college preparatory role of traditional secondary education.[14]

Principals in private schools were in the best position to adopt progressive curricula and practices for their schools, as they were free from state regulations and worked with a select school community that might support

Figure 9. Progressive principal Rae Logan and the faculty of Skokie Junior High School, 1930s. Courtesy of the Archives and Special Collections, Mansfield Library, the University of Montana-Missoula.

innovation.[15] In the 1930s and '40s, the Progressive Education Association's Eight-Year Study project encapsulated the spirit of innovation in secondary school curriculum that flourished in these years and that was particularly successful at private or university-affiliated schools, which comprised the majority of the thirty involved institutions. Of the few public school participants, the teachers, administrators, and students in Tulsa, Oklahoma and Des Moines, Iowa were notable for their redesign of school curricula, teaching practices, and student life to include experimental programs in human development, interdisciplinary studies, student involvement in curriculum planning, and community engagement.[16]

Pockets of progressive practice were also implemented in other public schools around the nation, often initiated and furthered by particularly dynamic school principals. Leonard Covello is one example of a high school principal who took up the call for educational reform in a community-oriented high school. In 1934, Covello, an Italian immigrant who was educated in the New York City school system, was appointed principal of the newly founded Benjamin Franklin High School in East Harlem, then the heart of the Italian immigrant community. Benjamin Franklin was conceived with Covello's input as a school that would specifically address the needs of adolescent immigrant boys in that community. Covello was both practitioner and scholar (he earned his PhD in sociology of education from New York University in 1944) and he applied his deep understanding of Italian immigrants and community development to his work as principal. Throughout his career, he worked with school and city officials to develop schools into more sensitive and proactive agencies for poor immigrant communities.

Covello identified the community school as a place where students engaged in community service as part of a broader educational goal of teaching participatory citizenship. The community outreach programs at Benjamin Franklin High School included local research projects, intercultural and citizenship education in the school and the community, and campaigns to improve local housing and health facilities. Covello took considerable pains to forge a link between community improvement and student academic achievement, arguing that by centering the school in the local community, traditional academic goals would be advanced by "attaching a sense of importance to the individual himself as well as to his education for a larger responsibility." Typical among such initiatives was the Friends and Neighbors Club in which students worked with local residents to beautify their tenement apartments.[17] While Covello introduced student-centered pedagogy in the community activities, his reform interest tended to emphasize the community over the school, which ultimately undermined the academic program. The school suffered from a high dropout and course failure rate. As a leader, Covello may have turned his focus to the demands of the local urban community at the expense of the academic agenda of the principal's office.[18]

In rural school districts, too, progressive community change could be inspired by the effective leadership of the principal who acted as motivator, facilitator, and communicator between school and community. For example, in the small rural community of Holtville, Alabama in the 1930s, high school principal James Chreitzberg and his teachers were frustrated at the disconnection between their classroom work and the great economic and social needs of the local agricultural community. In 1937, Chreitzberg joined his school with a reform project sponsored by the Southern Association of Colleges and Secondary Schools, which led to a schoolwide curriculum revision designed collaboratively by teachers, students, and community members. After identifying antiquated agricultural practices in the region, the school developed collective partnerships with farmers on irrigation, crop rotation, and diversified farming. After observing problems in diet and health, students led the community in the creation of a refrigeration facility to preserve fresh foods. Noting the lack of local entertainment in the community, the students set up a weekly movie night and student band. Students developed their own independent study and professional goal plans in coordination with teachers, guided by the principal's vision that students could be constructive members of a democratic community if allowed to do so. Principal Chreitzberg stood at the center of the community change, facilitating curriculum reform, maintaining relationships with the community, identifying support around the state, and supervising teachers and students.[19] For all its creativity, however, the school and project remained racially segregated, according to the legal and cultural norms of the white community.

One thousand miles to the north in the same period, in the rural community of Floodwood, Minnesota, the high school principal led another community-based school reform. As in Alabama, Principal Kenneth Hovet worked with teachers, local merchants, and farmers to develop curriculum projects that taught students practices of democratic citizenship, intellectual problem solving, and community improvement. As a result, through the 1930s and '40s, students and teachers at Floodwood High School ran a cooperative creamery, adult education study clubs, health and music programs, and conducted surveys of community problems. In 1943, Hovet, now superintendent, invited University of Minnesota progressive educational philosopher Theodore Brameld to design a one-semester curriculum project called "Design for America" in which students critically examined current American society and designed new social, economic, and governmental structures to reconstruct society for a more democratic future. As in Alabama, a critical part of the Floodwood project was the positive relationships between the school and community and the local origins of the reform, led by a long-term and trusted school leader who maintained a professional balance between change and familiarity, community and school.[20]

Other progressive principals focused more directly on the school, developing pedagogically progressive curricular and student activities programs. In the middle-class suburb of Winnetka, Illinois in the 1920s and '30s, junior high school principal S. R. (Rae) Logan led a curricular reform that was nationally heralded as an ideal progressive program. A western populist who valued egalitarianism and democracy, Logan came to Illinois in 1926 from Montana, where as a local superintendent, he had integrated schools in two Indian reservations and fought to equalize school funding through a reform of state taxation. Upon his arrival in Illinois, Logan held a joint position as assistant superintendent and principal of Skokie Junior High School. It was in this latter capacity that Logan made his mark, supported by the Winnetka superintendent's districtwide progressive curriculum reform movement that blossomed in this liberal and highly educated suburban district. Principal Logan's Skokie Junior High School offered students experiences in social and economic activities that they created and led at the school, discussion and debate about current issues, and field trips to community organizations.[21]

Like Dewey, Logan believed that democratic citizenship could only be taught by allowing children to practice it—the embodiment of the progressive principle of learning by doing. Logan developed what became known as the Skokie miniature community in which students created and managed their own society inside the school. The school government system involved faculty, staff, and students in a constitution that students wrote and published with a student printing press. To learn about economics, students developed their own corporations with student shareholders and cooperatives to support the raising of pet rabbits, tropical fish, and a beehive for making honey. Skokie Junior High also created a credit union for students, housed a nursery that functioned as a laboratory for family life, and created and ran a number of committees throughout the school, such as the Motion Picture Operators Committee that trained students to run the film projector for teachers, a Courtesy Committee that welcomed visitors to the school, and a Lunch Room Committee that taught fellow students how to behave and clean up in the cafeteria and that consulted with cafeteria staff on menus. Students wrote a bicycle safety ordinance that was passed by the City Council and took on service projects in the community.

Democracy was central to Logan's understanding of his role as principal: "Children should participate in making all decisions affecting their school life," he stated decisively. "They should be encouraged to analyze and criticize any existing administrative procedure" and school administrators should act only "in the capacity of helpers, specialists, and interpreters between faculties and boards of education."[22] Logan's collegial relationships with teachers and his engaging personality helped him in his goal, as did his promotion of a program that was amenable to the progressive Winnetka school district, including moderate values that he described as "friendly helpfulness, courteous candor, public service, social inventiveness, and the habit of seeking common ground for cooperative action."[23] Logan gently supervised student activities, providing dialogic questions that encouraged student exploration and strategically offering technical support, such as when he helped the Biology Bureau of Bees in their effort to move a beehive by personally climbing a tree and suffering multiple stings.[24]

In times of conflict, as when a group of students were caught shoplifting, Logan led peaceful problem-solving sessions, encouraging students to reflect on the impact of their actions on outside communities. With teachers, Logan unobtrusively initiated a daily after-school discussion group, what the teachers called the Skokie Koffee Klatch, where they gathered in the lounge after school to talk about educational issues. Logan was known as a good listener who fostered in teachers an inquiring frame of mind about their teaching; he regularly advocated the work of the school as a collective quest to address the problems of student learning, schools, and society itself.[25]

Behind his affable personality, Rae Logan was a strong intellectual leader who saw schools as central to the maintenance and improvement of society. A teacher who worked with Logan described him as "essentially a philosopher" whose "basic interest in education was in the development of institutions in the schools through which children could learn to live together peacefully in a spirit of helpfulness for each other, with the constant goal of improving the conditions under which they and their fellow man lived and would live." To teachers, students, and the school community, Logan's spirit was "contagious."[26]

Four thousand miles to the west, a principal in Honolulu, Hawaii was also engaged in the development of a progressive and democratically run school organization. Miles Cary, born and educated in Washington State, was principal of McKinley High School in Honolulu from 1924–1948. McKinley was one of the most multicultural high schools in the American system (in 1928, students came from 155 different ethnic and racial backgrounds).[27] In 1929, the territorial governor recommended expanding the curriculum in Hawaii's secondary schools, and Cary responded by introducing a "core studies" program to McKinley. At the heart of the program was an interdisciplinary core class that combined the subjects of English and social studies and that served as the homeroom and democratic forum for the high school government. As at Skokie Junior High School, students in their homeroom worked in committees to address particular school issues and problems. To Cary, the goal of the core studies program was to have the high school make "a more positive contribution toward the development of citizens for a democratic society" by giving students the opportunity to think about the real problems of society, work cooperatively in their study, and participate in school management.[28] Students and teachers determined the content area of their core studies class, and worked collaboratively on their assignments. Cary believed that the high school curriculum should involve students in examining issues that were central to their lives and interests, and that at the same time were socially useful and "rich with connections in many directions."[29]

Cary's leadership as school principal was based on his belief that final authority for school decision making rested not in any single individual but in the democratic process.[30] Students remembered that Principal Cary always encouraged them to be active, contributing members of their communities, and he gave students a sense of dignity in their work, talking about the values of "brotherhood," responsibility, honesty, and democracy. Such values, he argued, could not be learned intellectually, but only by experience. "The only way children learn how to play baseball," he reasoned, "is through playing baseball."[31]

As with many progressive educational practices, the development of the core studies program was very time consuming. During the first year, Cary and his teachers met every Saturday and over the summer to develop the curriculum. In later years, he met with teachers in weekly meetings, and developed with them a handbook on the program that they repeatedly revised. Students, too, were involved in working groups to review the curriculum, and they took on leadership roles in planning school assemblies, supervising campus cleanup, creating a mutual-aid fund to pay for medical expenses for students injured in school-related activities, coordinating with the PTA in the hiring of a health director, and publishing a daily high school newspaper.[32] Recognizing the importance of explaining the radical new program to the public, Cary regularly issued press releases, spoke publicly to groups and served in leadership positions in the Hawaii Educational Association and community groups.[33]

Cary's commitment to democracy and equity expanded into his public actions: in 1942 and 1943, he became education director at a Japanese internment camp in Arizona where he implemented core studies curriculum and an on-the-job training program, struggling with the poor classroom facilities and supplies in the camps. Upon his return to Hawaii, he publicly criticized the internment camps and race-baiting of Japanese Americans and encouraged his students to think critically about racism. He later advocated for statehood as a way for Hawaii citizens to have a voice in their government. In the late 1940s, Cary's leadership and program came increasingly under attack, but Cary refused to compromise his commitments, thus limiting the trajectory of his professional career.[34]

It is ironic that the head of the school so often took the pivotal role of developing shared governance practices for teachers and students in the Community School movement. But, as these principals recognized, they were usually in the best position to champion such work. According to Principal Cary, his strategic role was one of "calling all manner of people together to work on all manner of problems," including parents, teachers, and students.[35]

CULTURALLY RESPONSIVE PRINCIPALS

For principals of schools with dominant ethnic and minority populations, community engagement was a driving force of school leadership. Educational historian Lauri Johnson has described the work of some African American principals in the early to mid-twentieth century as "culturally responsive leadership." Such school leaders, Johnson argues, were notable for their role as public intellectuals, curriculum innovators, and social activists.[36] Biographical studies of black school principals in the early to mid-twentieth century identify a fairly consistent leadership style of institutional caring and professional and intellectual excellence that can be described as culturally responsive leadership, or what has also been called "servant leadership."[37] Such principals resisted racist policies and expectations by galvanizing their school communities into social justice activism and academic achievement.

Most American educational administration reformers ignored the plight of black principals who worked in almost complete isolation from whites, whether in legally segregated schools in the South or in de facto segregated schools in the North. Black educators tended to come to the attention of mainstream white educators only in a crisis. In response to the 1935 Harlem race riots, for example, New York City mayor Fiorello LaGuardia commissioned an investigation of the community's living conditions and found dilapidated school buildings, overcrowded classrooms, and racist behavior by white teachers. In one school, the principal's office was furnished with only an old desk and two chairs, one of which was broken. Tellingly, the report chronicled only the deficits of the Harlem schools and described principals' work as cleaning up messes and struggling with students' disciplinary problems.[38] Rarely mentioned by contemporary white educators was that although predominantly black schools were fiscally impoverished, they were rich in community support. For example, the previous year, six hundred Harlem parents had mobilized to improve their children's schooling by signing a petition to remove the white principal at PS 90 whom parents charged as being racially prejudiced.[39]

In the South, the unintended consequences of white neglect was that black schools built their own communities of academic excellence, commit-

Figure 10. Gertrude Ayer, the first African American principal in New York City, 1940. Courtesy of Hudson River Museum, Yonkers, N.Y.

ment to students, and neighborhood support that were a beacon of achievement for African Americans. Chief among the assets of the Southern black school was the principal.[40]

In the years before the legal mandate to desegregate Southern schools that was initiated by the Supreme Court's 1954 decision, *Brown v. Board of Education*, black principals led the closed system of segregated schooling. Acting as more than just a school building leader, black principals in racially segregated schools of the South were important role models and respected leaders in their communities, often comprising the bulk of the black middle class and serving as central liaisons between the school and the family. The commonly used title for a black school principal, "professor," indicated the cultural authority held by black communities toward their school leader.[41] Black principals also mediated between black and white segments of society, advocating for the black community to the white power structure. Ironically, black principals often held significantly more authority and autonomy than their white counterparts, due to the neglect of all-white school boards. This allowed the black principal to be the ultimate decision maker in the school and to have authority to shape personnel, implement programs, and raise money for needed resources. Of course, this authority was only over a closed

system; black principals had no real power or access to resources outside
the school beyond what they could negotiate or cajole out of white central
administrators. Furthermore, their working conditions and compensation
were significantly inferior to their white counterparts. Across the South,
black schools averaged one-third of the district funding allocated to white
schools; in 1936, the NEA reported a disparity of 250 percent between
pupil expenditures in white and black schools in the South.[42] Principals'
and teachers' salaries reflected this disparity: in Columbus, Georgia in 1929,
black teachers and principals earned less than half of their white peers.[43]

Black principals stood in a particularly high-stakes middle ground
between the white education officers who actively resisted black education
and the black community who fought for their children's academic achievement. Strong black principals adopted creative strategies to maneuver, foil,
and deceive white leadership into supporting black education, a process that
educational historian Vanessa Siddle Walker describes as a strategy of duplic-
ity and deception with the goal of increasing resources for black schools.
The unwritten rules of the black principalship "required a combination of
deceit, communicative skills, and educational expertise in the interaction
with the superintendent."[44]

The principalship of N. Longworth Dillard at the Caswell County
Training School in North Carolina is an example of such exceptional, and
exceptionally creative, school leadership in a segregated black school. In
1930, Dillard became teacher-principal of a small segregated school in rural
Yanceyville, North Carolina. He was twenty-four years old and had two
years' teaching experience when he became principal over three women
and eighty pupils, grades 1–7. Almost immediately Dillard expanded the
public presence of the school, promoting school activities through a local
newspaper, invigorating the PTA, and publicly honoring students for their
achievements. Under his leadership, he opened a high school department
and increased enrollment and graduation rates; of the thirty-two students
in the graduating class of 1937, nine continued on to college. Dillard's
major goal was the construction of a new high school building, a project
that would take twenty years to accomplish due to an intransigent white
county school board that resisted virtually any support of black education.
Dillard's strategy was to circumvent the local board and go straight to the
state, to recruit students from across the county, and to rely on parents to
support school programs.

In his goal of developing students' civic and academic abilities Dillard introduced homerooms to provide ongoing interaction between teachers
and students and extracurricular activities to provide what Dillard called
"opportunities for practicing the qualities desired in good citizens."[45] He
mentored teachers' professional development, so that by 1954, well over

half of the seventeen high school teachers were enrolled in graduate course-work. Dillard infused a social role into the monthly PTA meetings, which he developed as the main site for the exchange of important information about the school budget, development, and activities. Dillard also called on parents for meaningful contributions to the school, and maintained connections with the community with his continual presence in students' homes and churches. Leading all of Dillard's work was the importance of seeing that children were educated, a goal that worked against the major cultural, political, and economic institutions of the white South.[46]

In the North too, black principals worked for community engagement and educational excellence. Gertrude Ayer, the first African American principal in New York City, followed a similar agenda of curricular innovation, intellectual work, and social activism. Ayer graduated from New York's Girls Technical High School in 1903, the first African American graduate of the school, the president of her class, and, against public objections, the graduation speaker. After earning her teaching certificate, she taught for a number of years in the city, left teaching to marry and raise two children, and in 1916 began a twenty-year career as a labor activist and vocational guidance counselor, working in city schools with the Women's Trade Union League, YWCA, and Urban League. In 1935, at age fifty, Ayer was appointed temporary principal of PS 24 in Harlem, a predominantly African American school of eight hundred pupils, with twenty-five teachers, most of them white. In the midst of the Depression, the school community was wracked with poverty: Harlem suffered a 60 percent unemployment rate and the Harlem Riots of 1935 reflected the frustration of black residents.

As principal, Ayer earned the trust of parents by revitalizing the curriculum and adding additional relief services to the school. She initiated an activity program at the school that incorporated intercultural curriculum and the work of Harlem artists to address the diverse backgrounds of native-born African American and Caribbean students. Her curriculum drew both on progressive ideas of students' engagement and on economic and community uplift: students tended community gardens, developed school businesses and managed savings accounts, and participated in student government activities that included judges, sanitation squads, and election inspectors. She linked the school with the community, leading students out into the cultural life of Harlem and inviting neighborhood workers and community leaders into the school. Ayer also opened up her school to community support agencies, including a child guidance center, a health and dental clinic, and the first school cafeteria in Harlem. Ayer maintained a public intellectual presence, authoring journal articles and investigative reports for local newspapers, writing a regular column in the *New York Amsterdam News*, organizing community forums, and raising money for after-school programs and summer camps.[47] Ayer saw this curricular work as part of her larger civic mission: she believed that black educators had the responsibility to teach black youth "to maintain a critical attitude toward what he learns, rather than to lay emphasis on stuffing and inflating him only with the thoughts of others."[48]

The types of challenges faced by black principals can be seen in one educational initiative of Hazel Mountain Walker, who in 1936 became the first black principal in Cleveland, Ohio. A graduate of Cleveland Normal Training School, Walker began teaching elementary school in 1909 and within ten years had earned a master's degree in education and a law degree. She became the first black member of the city's women's club, was active in city politics, and eventually served on the Ohio State Board of Education. A central core of Walker's life's work was her engagement in Karamu House, an interracial settlement house founded in 1915 that promoted African American arts and theater. Walker was one of Karamu's earliest members, playing leading roles in plays and radio skits, and she was credited with finding a name for the community theater, Karamu, a Swahili word for "place of joy and entertainment."[49]

Between 1936 and 1954 Walker was principal of Rutherford B. Hayes Elementary School in a poor Cleveland neighborhood. The school had an enrollment of a thousand students, virtually all of whom were black, poor, and from migrant families from the South. Of all Cleveland schools, Hayes had the most over-aged students and the most students with below-average scores on city reading and intelligence tests. Hayes was located only two blocks away from Karamu House, and in 1939, Walker spearheaded an afternoon school activity program with Karamu for the least successful students in the school (identified by the city as the "z group") for cultural and academic enrichment to improve academic skills. Four afternoons a week, forty-two students met at Karamu House to engage in intensive projects in the arts, civic education, and geography. Included in the curriculum were trips to local cultural, public, and commercial sites, the study of African American history and culture, hands-on projects, and group performances to improve students' self-confidence and verbal ability. Walker met regularly with the supervising teacher and the director of Karamu House, carefully coordinating the joint work and evaluating the project.

Funded by a local foundation, the joint project had mixed results, due in part to an uninspired teacher, a revolving and untrained group of staff, and an early curriculum that underemphasized the education of basic content material. Walker also recognized a "terrible feeling of futility" that haunted the children who were never able to believe that their lives would change.[50] Although the group leaders tried to engage families in the project, parents were only marginally involved, due to their own pressing life demands. In retrospect, Walker may well have had her own education in futility, as the results of the project revealed the real barriers that could undercut even the best-funded and well-intentioned project. Walker's own practiced skills in tutoring poor students in reading were overwhelmed by students' needs for medical and psychiatric help and by families' economic troubles. The project was not repeated after the first year.[51]

As a privately funded initiative, Principal Walker's Karamu project suffered in part from the absence of broader district support. On the other side of the state some years earlier, another black woman principal struggled against the complicated political dynamics of her city district to support her community. Beginning in 1911, Cincinnati black educator Jennie Porter had lobbied against the state's twenty-four-year-old law that prohibited racially segregated schooling. Porter well understood that although the 1887 law had supported black parents' efforts to integrate the white schools in nearby Oxford, Ohio, as described in chapter 1, it had also allowed for continuing racist practices, including the virtual exclusion of black educators from public schools and what amounted to de facto segregation due to residential and economic segregation. In a number of northern cities, black residents petitioned for separate schools, arguing that black children would be better served in schools led by black educators, free from the racial denigration of white educators and students. So argued Porter, who lobbied for ten years to create a black school in Cincinnati, ultimately founding the Harriet Beecher Stowe School in 1921 with Porter as the first black woman principal in Cincinnati. In her two-decade tenure as principal, Porter hired dozens of black teachers and developed community outreach initiatives. But complicating her work was the opposition from the NAACP, which publicly criticized Porter as a tool for segregationists. In her work supporting Cincinnati's black children and teachers, Principal Porter, a native Cincinnatian who held a PhD and over thirty years' experience as a local educator, became identified as an accommodationist who abandoned African American rights to the interests of white racists.[52]

Other cultural and political landmines undermined progressive reform efforts in impoverished schools. In New York City in 1935, black and white radical teachers, teacher union members, and members of both the NAACP and the Communist Party, organized the Harlem Committee for Better Schools to lobby the city for improvements in public education. Their work sparked a wave of progressive educational activism in the community, including workshops on black history for Harlem teachers, the removal of racist textbooks from schools, and lobbying for the construction of new school buildings.[53] But the incident that gave the committee the most attention was a fourteen-year-old black boy's accusation that his white principal had beaten him in his Harlem school. The Committee for Better Schools mobilized, setting up picket lines at the school and organizing

demonstrations to force Principal Gustav Shoenchen's expulsion from the
school system. The protests attracted thousands of participants and publicity
from the black community and culminated in a trial by a special committee
of the Board of Education.[54] Schoenchen was found innocent of wrongdo-
ing and then transferred outside of Harlem after the angry public reaction
to the decision.

But the case was more complicated than it initially seemed. Principal Schoenchen was an unlikely candidate for such a charge, having just
completed his PhD in education at New York University and published his
dissertation study on the Activity School, a progressive model of school
organization which that year had been installed in seventy city schools,
including Principal Gertrude Ayer's Harlem school.[55] A second-generation
German Jewish immigrant, Schoenchen was himself targeted by German
Nazis, and he held the support of the white teachers in his school who
objected to the intrusion of the Teachers Union and black activists to their
school. Schoenchen defended himself by criticizing the assumption that as
a principal, he was automatically assumed to be authoritarian. In an open
letter to New York teachers, he criticized the union leadership, "supposedly
composed of intelligent people," for condemning "without hearing one of
their own colleagues because he happens to be a supervisor and hence one
of the 'bosses' in the Communist ideology."[56] Whatever happened, the toxic
mix of political activism, race, ethnicity, and publicity turned this case of
one school into an explosive community event, with the principal at the
center of the crisis.

Troubles with principals could allow district offices the opportunity to
play their own political card, as evidenced in the case of Owen Duncan,
black principal of the segregated black high school in Charlottesville, Virginia. In spring 1945, all eighteen teachers, plus the librarian and school
clerk at Jefferson High School, stood at a public community meeting and
denounced Principal Duncan, accusing him of "dictatorial leadership" and
of acting toward his staff in ways that were threatening, sarcastic, belittling,
and offensive. The all black staff reported that Duncan fired teachers who
disagreed with him and that teachers had no idea how they were evaluated.
Most upsetting to the community was that students disrespected the principal to such an extent that when he spoke at assemblies, students "booed and
hissed." The black community demanded that the white board of education
investigate the case, which they did, interviewing the teachers on location
at the white high school. In their finding, the board noted that the black
PTA supported the principal and they minimized the conflict as the complaints of a few radical teachers. Given the racial context of the biracial
school system, the white board abdicated any responsibility for the principal
who was their employee, and by effectively blocking any increase in black

teachers' political power, they kept the black community divided. By keeping a controversial and ineffective black educator in control of the school, the white board furthered its own goals of undermining black agency.[57]

TEACHER AND PRINCIPAL UNITY

The Charlottesville teachers' antipathy to their principal was not unusual. Many other teachers found it impossible to believe that any principal might have progressive or democratic attributes. By the mid-twentieth century, most teachers felt the negative impact of the emerging model of administrative hierarchy in American schools. Where principals had previously been little more than a lead teacher in a building who instructed teachers in the wishes of the school board, modern principals were increasingly distanced from teachers, embedded in the middle of a dense bureaucracy that bounded them with regulations to impose on those below them in the hierarchy. If not already personally inclined to authoritarian attributes, principals were encouraged to develop them. The intensified power of the principal concerned many teachers who reported abuses by their local administrator, what one teachers' council in Chicago in 1921 called the assumption on the part of some principals that their office carried with it "the right to be an autocrat, a boss, or a czar, instead of a leader in educational ideals."[58]

Early teacher unions and associations vehemently objected to the new professionalized model of a school principal who stood above and apart from the classroom teacher. In 1913, an anonymous writer to the journal *The American Teacher* lambasted "this pernicious doctrine that there is virtue in the humility of the servant" and argued that teachers must "refuse to bend the knee, and to look to the men and women higher up as the bootblack looks to the patron." Teachers "are not in schools to serve the principals and superintendents, although we are under their direction. We are in school to serve the public and the children of the public."[59] Even some educational professors, whose very work was used to justify the rationalization and streamlining of educational administration, despaired of the new "factory" plan of school administration, under which "the status of the classroom teacher is becoming more and more akin to that of the "hands" in a factory, working under foremen and superintendents who assume the real responsibility."[60] Driven by such a politic, some of the early teacher associations, leagues, and unions excluded all school administrators, furthering the distance that was growing between them. Other political, ethnic, and class issues exacerbated the rift, such as in Principal Schoenchen's case noted earlier.

But in an era when teachers' associations and unions were politically weak and often divided by gender, race, and class, teachers' antipathy to

building principals was not universal. Even as unions articulated a growing
distance between teachers and administrators, many teachers expressed alle-
giance to their school head, appreciating the relief from administrative and
disciplinary responsibilities that their principal assumed.[61] Because principals
were generally required to have experience in the classroom, teachers' loyalty
to principals was often rooted in that shared experience. Women teachers, in
particular, were more likely to support the leadership of a woman colleague.
In 1895, women teachers in an elementary school in New York City objected
to the appointment as principal of their school of a male grammar school
teacher who had less experience than their own head teacher. The teachers argued that because their own Miss Egbert had been in their school for
many years, she was "imbued with the atmosphere of the school" and best
knew its needs and interests.[62] Because of shared experiences and working
conditions, women elementary principals often aligned with women teachers' political struggles for pensions for women educators, equity in salary
scales between the male-dominated secondary school and female-dominated
elementary school staffs, access to educational decision making, and critique
of hierarchical administrative structures.

   In 1928, for example, a Minneapolis principal penned in rhyme her
thoughts on the current trend in supervision to the popular tune of "Over
There" and presented them to the annual meeting of the Chicago Teachers'
Federation, a group of primarily women elementary school teachers who
clearly welcomed the cynical opinions of a woman principal about current
educational reform initiatives.

>   Supervise, supervise,
>   Don't let up, don't let up,
>   If you're wise,
>   For the day is coming, you see it coming
>   When principals must supervise.
>   So beware! Leave that chair!
>   Visit 'round. Visit 'round everywhere.
>   Be a rover, and put it over,
>   Supervise, look wise, and be sure to criticize.
>
>   Analyze! Scrutinize!
>   Don't be slow. It's a go, realize
>   You must stop your stalling,
>   Or quit this calling.
>   We've no time to idealize,
>   Take your chart. Make a start,
>   Draw a graph. Be a whiz on the staff.

Put it over, or leave the clover,
Supervise all the day if you want to get more pay.

Get your card. Rate 'em hard.
Diagnose. Diagnose. Diagnose.
It must be objective,
To be effective,
A thing that everybody knows.
Evaluate, prognosticate,
Be first rate—'tis your fate.
Don't be late.
Supervise, then; oh, supervise then.
Play the game, make a name, it's the way to get to fame.[63]

Progressively minded principals, male and female, noted the discrepancy between their vision of school leadership and the entrenched culture of divisive hierarchy. As a new principal in an early twentieth-century New York City elementary school, Angelo Patri vividly felt the shock of how he was perceived as a school leader. In one of his first walks through the hallways, Patri recalled:

> I passed the open door of a classroom and saw a teacher smiling down at a little boy. . . . I was glad and walked towards the teacher. Instantly the smile disappeared, her body grew tense, the little boy sat down and all the other little boys sat up stiff and straight and put their hands behind them. . . . I tried to say something pleasant but I saw they were afraid of me and I went away.

When Patri sought the counsel of the previous school principal, he explained, "I've tried to have the teachers and children feel that I'm their friend, that I'm eager to help them but I don't seem to be able to get them to speak or act freely in my presence. They are afraid of me!" As well they should be, responded the former principal: "The teachers and children are all right. You'll find them well trained. Take my advice—if you want any peace of mind, keep them under your thumb."[64] To Patri and other critics, the professionalization of the supervisory function of the principal had created a monster in the principal's office.

The tension of the principal's changing role was the topic of a former Chicago teacher's 1915 autobiographical novel, *The Crayon Clue*, in which the teacher heroine described her elementary school principal, Miss Forrest, as "a splendid principal . . . a jewel to us, every teacher in the building loves her." But then teachers were forced to use textbooks they didn't like and cheap chalk that left greasy remnants on the blackboard. The combined difficulties made it impossible to teach, led the students to misbehave, and drove one teacher literally insane and shrieking down the hallways. Why had the jewel of the principal let the school deteriorate to such chaos? The teacher heroine suspected that Miss Forrest had caved in to authority: "when it came to standing out for some things, we've felt that Miss Forrest wasn't reliable; that she was trying to stand in with the powers that be. We thought she lacked moral fiber." As it turned out, Miss Forrest was caught in the middle of a corrupt purchasing deal between the district and a school supply company. The school board threatened to demote her if she did not agree to purchase the textbooks and the greasy chalk. Significantly, it was the feisty teacher and not the cowed principal who publicized the scheme and solved the problem.[65]

Although burdened by competing pressures from their position in the middle of the educational system, some principals maintained their own identity as educators by supporting classroom teachers. Some principals played a leading role in the formation and leadership of local teachers' associations and joined with teachers in efforts to improve school funding, class size, and local autonomy. In some small communities, where the lines between teachers and principals were usually blurred, principals led the unionization efforts of the local teacher corps, perhaps because they held more job security, pay, or a wider understanding of the problems facing schools than their fellow teachers. In 1930, the United Brotherhood of Carpenters and Joiners of America in Waycross, Georgia identified a number of "teachers" who wanted to organize a union in that city. Five of the seven recommended teachers were school principals.[66]

And in cities, too, teachers and principals intersected their political organizations. Two New York City principals were among the leadership of the radical American Federation of Teachers, founded in 1916, and in 1920 the segregated white Grade Teachers Union in Washington, D.C. unanimously voted to grant a union charter to their principals.[67] In Atlanta, Georgia, the vibrant (albeit all-white) Atlanta Public School Teachers Association (APSTA) incorporated principals among its ranks and leadership from its founding in 1905 well through the 1960s. The association identified school principals to recruit members in their school and collect dues, organize association educational and political events, and support new union efforts in the region in coordination with the American Federation of Teachers and the Georgia Federation of Labor. Over 90 percent of Atlanta's educators were members of the association, and a number of school superintendents were former members. The association constitution specifically permitted administrators and supervisors to be members, and the APSTA president in 1927 noted the unique Atlanta situation where "all of the principals have come up from the ranks and we do not have the friction that exists in some places between the principal and the teaching force."[68] Such understandings of unity were not always unanimous, however. In Chicago in the 1930s, a joint committee of principals and teachers did not include the activist Chicago Teachers' Federation, which had for years worked only for elementary teachers.[69]

Many women principals combined their earlier careers as teacher activists with their new understanding of school administration, using their professional leverage, improved status, and higher salary to fight for their women teacher colleagues. Elizabeth Almira Allen's educational activist work from the 1890s to her death in 1919 is an example of how one woman principal was able to cross the then still-permeable barriers between teacher and principal politics. While principal in Hoboken, New Jersey, Allen served as president of the New Jersey Teachers Federation. Across her career, Allen actively organized for women educators' pensions and tenure laws and for more democratic decision making in schools, calling for a "Teachers' Congress" where teachers could debate educational issues.[70] Although a principal, Allen often sounded more like a teacher activist. She opposed efforts to centralize educational management and critiqued the new administrative hierarchy as "autocrats" who worked against the purpose of education in a democracy. She argued that supervisors' role of imposing central office procedures created an oppressive layer of oversight on teachers, forcing the teacher to perform like "a machine, to do specified lines of work in a specified way and on a time schedule."[71] Allen argued: "You cannot treat the teachers like slaves without bringing up a race of slaves."[72] In 1904, Principal Allen refused to enforce a Board of Education policy for promoting teachers through exams. Arguing against the hierarchy that divided teachers and administrators, Allen insisted that since administrators were largely promoted on experience and not examinations, so too should teachers. In response, the board suspended her, but she challenged the suspension in court, won her case, and was ultimately reinstated as principal.[73]

In Atlanta, Georgia, two women principals served as leaders of the local teachers federation. Julia Riordan, principal of Atlanta's Davis Street School from 1909–1921, was a founding member of the Atlanta Public School Teachers Association (APSTA) and held leadership positions in the association while it ejected a popularly disliked superintendent, fought for teachers' salary increase, and affiliated with local, state, and national labor unions.[74] Riordan was fired in 1921 by a newly elected Board of Education that included two Klan members who objected to both Riordan's Catholicism and her political activism.[75] Riordan's successor was Mary C. Barker, a

principal in two Atlanta schools between 1921 and 1944 and also a charter member of the APSTA. Barker faced opposition in the central office
and among teachers, who resisted her efforts to engage them in socially
progressive activities, including the support of black teachers, child labor
laws, and teacher participation in school governance. Such activism alienated Barker from her teachers whose interest centered on improving their
pay and working conditions. Barker's career struggles also suggest that her
wider understanding of district organization that she gained as a principal
distanced her from her school-based teachers.[76]

Career principals who engaged in such activism ran professional risks.
A principal who advocated too independently for teachers or for the community might earn the disapproval of district leaders who expected mid-
level managers to follow central office policy. In Buffalo, New York between
1918 and 1920, educator Mary O'Connor, who founded that city's teachers
federation, led a valiant battle against a domineering superintendent who
used the language of efficiency and professionalism to centralize administrative control over teachers. The superintendent first courted Buffalo's
teacher militants to win their loyalty, promoting O'Connor to principal.
When O'Connor resisted the superintendent's policies, he dismissed her
from that position, replacing her with a less-experienced educator at a higher
salary.[77] Similar obstructions faced elementary principal Olive Jones when
she applied to be associate superintendent in New York City in 1922, a
position that the president of the Board of Education had publicly promised to a woman. Women's groups and teachers' associations around the
city actively campaign for Jones, who had a long career in New York City
schools as a teacher, supervisor, elementary principal, and president of the
city's Principal's Association. More than that, Jones had a record of political
allegiances with teachers, having advocated for increased teacher salaries
and improved evaluations processes, for a state teachers' pension plan, and
for the creation of retirement homes for teachers. Jones' political activism
worked against her in her quest for the associate superintendent position:
the board appointed another woman, with less experience and credentials,
whose brother was a local political leader.[78]

Principals also formed their own clubs and unions that functioned as
a combination of a social group and a professional organization for principals with shared interest in progressive education, community improvement,
and their own professional development. Members studied education law,
investigated salary raises and benefits, and became involved in school board
elections and school funding campaigns. In the mid-1920s, the Cincinnati Elementary School Principals' Club organized around the topic of low
salaries for elementary principals, arguing that some elementary principals'

salaries were lower than those of high school teachers. The club recommended minimum qualifications for elementary principals and a salary scale determined by both academic training and years of experience.[79]

Reflecting their overlapping identities, principals sometimes maintained membership in both teachers' and administrative unions. In Vallejo, California in 1920, principals formed a union while retaining their membership in the local teachers' union. According to one of the founders of the principals' union, the intention of the group was "to work chiefly *with* and *through* rather than supplementary to the classroom teachers organization."[80]

But principals' unions tended to be small and short-lived. Membership in the American Federation of Teachers (AFT) involved annual dues, and many principals did not see the value, or did not have the time, for membership. Many groups struggled with maintaining the membership of principals who were also full-time teachers with double work and double loyalties. Other principals' unions suffered declining membership as principals left the profession or advanced to the superintendency. And in Southern cities, principals were divided by race; in Washington, D.C., elementary principals organized separate white and black principals' unions in the 1920s.[81]

If not in unions, principals organized in less formal clubs for professional development. In Seattle, women school administrators banded together, encouraged by the city's progressive superintendent, Frank Cooper, who was famous for appointing women to principalship positions. In 1910, elementary principal Adelaide Pollock founded what became the School Women's League, a group that later expanded to the state level and in 1915 became the National Council for Administrative Women in Education.[82] Similar clubs were created across the country, organized for both social networking and to assist women administrators in identifying other talented women for administrative positions.

Such women's groups stood in opposition to the larger number of men principals' associations, and schoolmasters' "clubs," constituted to consolidate male principals' authority often in opposition to progressive reform movements. In Los Angeles in the early 1920s, for example, the city teachers' organization and liberal school board members battled against the established male principals' association and local business leaders over teachers' campaign for higher salaries and more involvement in school policy decision making.[83] Such male principals' clubs capitalized on the professionalization movement that aligned school leadership with district leadership in opposition to teachers.

While principals organized local, city, and state principals' clubs and organizations, they lacked a comparable presence in the National Education Association (NEA). Founded in the mid-nineteenth century as a forum for

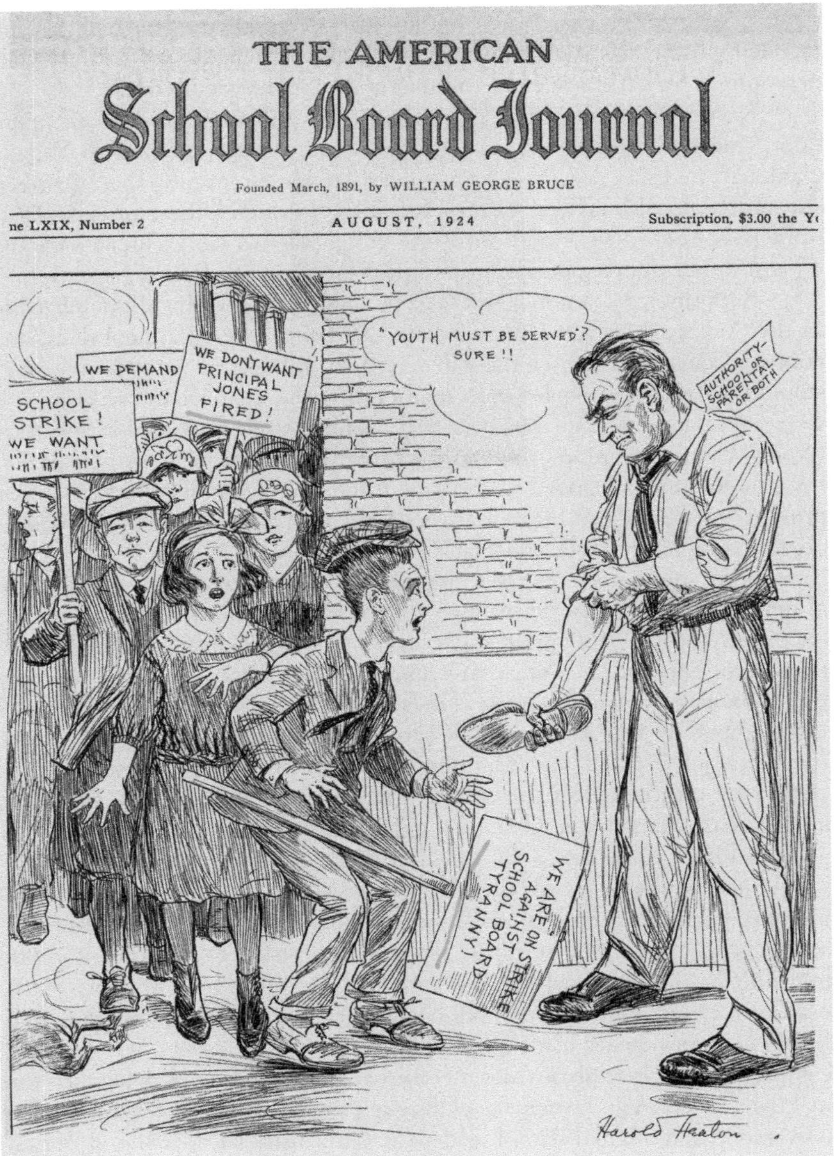

Figure 11. School strike. The lingering distinction between principals and district leadership, 1924. *American School Board Journal* 49, no. 2 (August 1924): 35.

"school men" to discuss educational issues, the NEA had functioned primarily as an organizational hub for superintendents. Teachers' concerns about salaries and working conditions were largely ignored until women classroom teachers organized for the formation of the Department of Classroom Teachers in 1913. Principals were also sidelined by the NEA's emphasis on district and state leadership until 1916, when they founded the National Association of Secondary School Principals and in 1921 the Department of Elementary Principals, both under the NEA umbrella. Although seemingly a male-dominated and conservative continuation of the old schoolmasters' clubs, the NEA's Department of Elementary Principals sponsored the career development of a number of women principals who served as officers and speakers and, from 1918 through 1960s, elected women presidents in alternating years.[84]

In segregated black schools, principals relied on professional networks perhaps more than their white peers. Excluded from white national and regional professional organizations and from work with neighboring white educators, black principals connected within their own to provide professional development and to design political strategies to challenge Jim Crow laws and economic policies that undercut their schools.[85] Black principals were included in black state teachers associations, such as the Virginia and the Mississippi Teachers Associations, where educators collected data to use as evidence against racist school boards and state legislators, raised money for legal defense funds for civil rights cases, and invited NAACP attorneys to instruct members about the use of litigation to address educational inequities. In Georgia, the School Masters Club provided the organizational structure for principals of segregated black schools to mentor each other, share professional ideas, and collectively research school data for use in lobbying white school boards for educational improvements.[86]

CONCLUSION

Many principals expanded their work outside of the confines of their professionally defined office, challenging the educational bureaucracy that had created that office. Even as the goal of educational administration professionalization movements was to narrow the role and identity of the school principal, many school leaders moved outside of those professional lines, developing democratic educational practices, connecting with communities, and leading political movements that maintained links between teachers, principals, and communities.

These progressive and activist ventures were primarily locally based, initiated by individual principals in their schools, either with approval of like-minded superintendents or conducted surreptitiously out of sight of district offices. Through the mid-twentieth century, principals could do this because of their relative legal and cultural independence in their schools. All this would change in the second half of the twentieth century, when school administration became more embedded in national legal and policy agendas and school principals entered the middle of even denser layers of administration.

CHAPTER FOUR

CRACKS IN THE SYSTEM

School Leadership, 1945–1980

In 1952, an elementary principal in rural southern New Jersey described the challenges of his job in a period of rapid educational change. In his four years as principal of the Woodstown Elementary School, Howard Morris had seen the enrollment increase from 423 to 639 students, had overseen the construction of a new school building, and had incorporated staff and students from the former racially segregated black school. All of this had come to a head when school opened in September 1950, primarily because the construction was not yet finished, and principal Morris struggled with the continuing presence of contractors, a faulty door frame clogged with mud, windows that didn't lock, cracked walls behind the steam pipes, missing toilet paper holders, bulletin boards that were too hard to put tacks into, and so on. By the end of the school year, the school still needed sidewalks and a few bookshelves, and the new drainage system in the front yard was still unfinished.[1]

The integration of the black school was relatively more successful: there was "only one complaint concerning assignment of white pupils to Negro teacher," the principal noted with some relief, and the students seemed to get along, particularly the boys in sports, although Principal Morris believed that the African American students were "having real trouble keeping up in their lessons," and, he ominously added, "this appears to be a long range problem."

But Principal Morris was distracted with more immediate problems, including planning a first aid clinic for teachers and transportation to the upcoming county spelling bee; addressing a problem of traffic safety;

evaluating the textbook budget; supervising a new janitor; reviewing students' standardized and psychological tests; evaluating the new insurance plan; investigating the vexing problem of Bus Route #3, which for some reason was making the local residents along the route very unhappy; assuring the superintendent about Miss Mathis' annual presentation of "The Story of Menstruation" to the seventh- and eighth-grade girls and securing the film projector for that event; and keeping track of newly enrolled students, teachers who called in sick, a teacher who was called up for military duty, and the installation of the Jungle Jim purchased by the Parent Teacher Association.

Due to what Principal Morris described as "various administrative activities, adjustments, moving etc." during the fall, he noted to his superintendent that he found himself "spread very thinly" and he knew that this would need to change "or the supervisory program will sag." In the spring, he was able to return to supervision, and in April, he reported that he had made twenty-eight visits that month to eighteen teachers' classrooms, for anywhere between twenty minutes to two class periods, and he had met with most of those teachers in a conference. But he admitted that he could not remember the gist of all of his conferences. He was more successful at holding individual meetings with teachers in his office to discuss specific problems with student achievement or behavior.

Principal Morris' account of his work as an elementary school principal encapsulates many of the challenges facing school leaders in the years immediately following the Second World War. In this period, schools experienced an unprecedented increase in the complexity of administrative operations with additional challenges introduced by postwar legal and policy restrictions, student and parent dynamics, and curriculum development. Most notable among these changes was the increased external influences on the school, as postwar American public schools opened up to outside scrutiny and governance. The principal, positioned in the middle of the educational system, faced both the impact of modern cultural changes in the student and school community and the intensification of modern educational policy developments. These double pressures pulled the school leader in opposite directions: increased cultural pressure pulled the principal out into the hallways and classrooms while more administrative demands from the educational bureaucracy tied the principal to the office desk. As Principal Morris reported on his typical workday, for example, he juggled the administrative and legal requirements around issues of employment, transportation, facility construction, curriculum development, community engagement, field trips, racial integration, standardized testing, traffic safety, textbooks, janitorial services, sex education, and insurance policies. And his day was also busy with personal interactions with teachers, staff, students, and parents.[2]

Late twentieth-century schools experienced an unprecedented increase in the complexity of administrative operations caused by a radically changed educational landscape. In the four decades after the Second World War, American public schools were turned upside down by the intervention of state and federal government in schools; organized teachers; activist parents; an oppositional youth popular culture; increased racial, ethnic, and class conflict; and the expanded bureaucratic procedures developed to address all of these modern circumstances. As the broader context of education changed, the core purpose of the school principal remained stably embedded in the center of the school, and the position maintained many of the organizational problems that had frustrated educators over the previous century, including competing demands of administrative work over educational supervision, low status, and an unclear professional identity. What changed was that the intensity of principals' work increased, as late twentieth-century schools took on larger social issues and adapted schools to new legal and organizational expectations. The best school principals faced these changes in their school buildings and offices head on, balancing their responses between the demands of the school community and the central office. Many principals, raised and experienced in a prior era, were confused by the changed context and reacted by continuing earlier strategies to build up the traditional professional authority and stature of their position. All principals saw the ground shift beneath their feet more dramatically than ever before in the history of the principalship.

This chapter sets the context of the postwar era and describes its impact on principals and how educational administrators responded, in part by clinging to their professional status and in part by designing new leadership strategies for a new climate.

THE EDUCATIONAL CONTEXT OF THE
LATE TWENTIETH CENTURY

At the immediate close of the Second World War, American public schools resembled their predecessors in form and content. A typical American school in 1950 emphasized discipline, social conformity, and academic studies as most important, carefully guided by an established administrative hierarchy. Racially segregated by practice and by law, the bulk of American public schools were homogeneous in enrollments; the typical curriculum balanced between academic and vocational coursework with some compensatory or remedial education, while students' social development was nurtured in athletics and extracurricular club work. Watching over it all was the principal who governed with unquestioned authority, who understood the consensus of community expectations of the school, and who enjoyed wide discretion in interpreting and enforcing rules on student and teacher behavior. The principal's emphasis was on building management and public leadership, maintaining order in fiscal, educational, and administrative matters, and acknowledging local community concerns. The principal's goal was to maintain equilibrium among all the functioning parts of the school, and the largely unquestioned authority of the principal's office assured this.[3]

All this was to change by the mid-1950s. The first challenge to schools was the student enrollment explosion of the postwar "baby boom": total school enrollment increased by two-thirds between 1945 and 1965. Secondary schools grew particularly rapidly: whereas in 1920, less than a third of teenagers attended high school, by 1940 three-quarters were enrolled, and in 1960, almost 90 percent.[4] Enrollment growth impacted everything about schools, from the shape and size of school buildings to the behavior and beliefs of students. A particularly new and challenging youth culture arose in the 1950s and '60s, emerging from the large cohort of baby boomers, postwar affluence, changed family structure, and a newly mediated popular culture. Teenagers from diverse ethnic and class backgrounds met in schools that served as a rich petri dish of social interaction, nurturing a popular youth culture that challenged the traditional authority structure of schools.

The increased accessibility of schools to a more diverse group of students led to proposals to reform the function and curricular emphasis of public education. James Bryant Conant's 1959 study of American high schools argued that the expansion of modern education demanded what he called a comprehensive high school that would offer a range of courses addressing the different needs and interests of students with structures to channel students of different abilities. A decade later, Charles Silberman's popular 1970 book, *Crisis in the Classroom*, argued that the problem with traditional secondary education was its authoritarian structure that taught students only a vapid "mindlessness" and social alienation. To deepen students' connection with education, Silberman recommended the relaxation of traditional academic requirements and the expansion of electives and interdisciplinary courses, more unscheduled time, the abolition of dress codes, and the awarding of credits for out-of-school activities. These initiatives led to what some educators disparagingly described as the "shopping mall high school," referring to consumer-oriented elective coursework and an emphasis on addressing student pleasures over academic rigor.[5]

Postwar politics also impacted schools. A national preoccupation with the Cold War led to the first significant federal intervention in schools. In October 1957, the Soviet Union launched *Sputnik*, the first satellite into space, intensifying the competition over technology between the United States and the Soviets. The *Sputnik* crisis led immediately to the passage of the National Defense Education Act (NDEA) in 1958, which provided federal funding for science and technology education, foreign language education, and other educational topics that contributed to the improvement of American military and economic strength. Of particular importance in the NDEA were improved school testing, guidance counseling and vocational education, and funding for teacher education in these areas. These programs set a precedent for federal funding of and intervention in public education in subsequent years, including the monumental Elementary and Secondary School Act of 1965, which instituted federal funding for social enrichment programs for poor children.[6] Later federal legislation and Supreme Court decisions further expanded the responsibility of schools to provide special aid for children with limited English proficiency in the Bilingual Education Act of 1968 and the 1974 Supreme Court decision, *Lau v. Nichols*, and for the education of children with disabilities in the 1975 Education for All Handicapped Children Act. These policies acknowledged the arrival of whole new populations of children into schools, requiring the development of new personnel and programs, while formally yoking local schools to the federal government.

These social changes led to a national panic about juvenile delinquency, adding to the popular perception that the American education system was failing in its mission. In 1958, FBI director J. Edgar Hoover cautioned against rebellious youth culture as a "menacing cloud, mushrooming across the nation."[7] In response, educators implemented more aggressive discipline policies. Los Angeles developed the first districtwide discipline policy in the nation in 1959; by 1975, discipline policies were in 75 percent of American schools. Simultaneously, the federal government and local school districts began to fund new collaborations between law enforcement and schools, designating school police officers and surveillance devices in schools.[8] These policies were supported by teachers and parents, in large part because now disciplinary responsibility was taken off their shoulders and assigned to administrators. When Gallup polls of the 1970s and '80s continued to rank "lack of discipline" as the worst problem in education, administrators took the blame.[9]

The most contentious federal intervention in education came from the United States Supreme Court with its 1954 decision, *Brown v. Board of Education*. The *Brown* case, in which the court famously, and unanimously, ruled that "separate educational facilities are inherently unequal," was the culmination of decades of work by civil rights groups to make racial segregation in schools illegal. In *Brown II* in 1955, the court laid out a plan of action for dismantling the long-standing dual system of education in the South and mandated that this be done "with all deliberate speed." Nevertheless, compliance with the ruling was a long and contentious process. A dozen years after the *Brown* decision, 80 percent of white students attended schools that were 90–100 percent white, and black students were equally isolated in virtually all black schools.[10] In a context of increasing racial hostility and controversy, the Civil Rights Act of 1964 allowed federal funds to be withheld from school districts that had not complied with the desegregation goals of *Brown*, thus extending federal oversight of local school management.

Simultaneously, working relationships within school districts were radically changed with the emerging teacher union movement. Teachers had first organized in the early twentieth century, and there were fledging union efforts through the 1950s. The legal authorization of public-sector unions in the early 1960s fueled the expansion of two major teacher unions—the National Education Association (NEA) and the American Federation of Teachers (AFT)—so that by the end of the 1970s, the majority of teachers were in unions, bargaining collectively over issues of wages, hours, and working conditions.[11] Teacher unions increasingly demanded a role in district policy making, and collective bargaining contracts introduced proceduralism and legalism into employee relations.

Accompanying such changes were storm clouds of doubt and critique. Given the increased enrollment in the postwar era and the social tensions caused by increased diversity in schools, educators in the 1960s worried about the differential achievement of different groups of students. The most notable research of this genre was the 1966 report, *Equality of Educational Opportunity* (commonly called the Coleman Report after its lead author, James Coleman), that fueled debate about "school effects." The report provided evidence that students' background and socioeconomic status were more significant in determining educational outcomes than were measured differences in school resources. The troubling implication of this finding was that no improvement in educational funding, preparation, curriculum, or professionalization would have any significant impact on students, thus undercutting educational reformers' efforts to increase funding and support for schools.[12] In response to the study, scholars began to explore other variables that might impact student success.

Parents and communities, too, became involved in increasingly litigious and conflictual ways. In the expanding suburbs of the postwar era, organized parent groups lobbied school boards about budgets, curriculum, racial integration, and social programming in schools. Suburban school parents' tensions were exacerbated by skyrocketing enrollments, intensifying housing market dynamics, and increasing property taxes to fund the growing schools.[13] Among the most notorious parents' rights events was an explosive controversy over textbook adoption in Kanawah County, West Virginia in 1974. Spearheaded by a board member, parents and community members charged that the Board of Education–approved curriculum was anti-American, anti-Christian, and obscene. Through the fall of 1974, parents, community members, and activists boycotted and picketed schools and led increasingly violent rallies, marked by gunshots, vandalism, arson, and bombs that temporarily shut down three schools and damaged the Board of Education building. In January, the frenzy culminated with the arrival of national Ku Klux Klan leaders on the steps of the West Virginia capitol in downtown Charleston.[14] School principals stood in the middle of the raging battle between the school board, protestors, lawyers, and police. It was principals who managed students and schools through a disruptive fall semester and who felt the brunt of parent activists who identified the principal as the first school officer to lobby before approaching more entrenched boards of education and state legislatures.[15] As the public and media portrayal of schools repeatedly criticized the mediocrity and bureaucracy of modern institutional education, principals felt the force of these accusations directly.

CRISIS IN THE PRINCIPAL'S OFFICE

The mid-twentieth-century competition between the United States and the Soviet Union raised a profound national panic about American competencies that intensified the scrutiny on American schools. A strong undercurrent of these critiques was the complaint that public educational leadership was dysfunctional in operations and disconnected from real educational needs. A barrage of complaints from both the left and the right set in motion a culture of suspicion against educators both in the classroom and in administrative offices, a popular tone that undermined the legitimacy of public schools and further eroded public support.

Critics from the left attacked school administrators as defenders of an entrenched hierarchy of educational leaders. Jonathan Kozol's 1967 account of his teaching experience in inner-city Boston, *Death at an Early Age*, described racist and autocratic principals in urban schools, while Ivan Illich's 1971 book, *Deschooling Society*, critiqued institutionalized education and called for the abolition of formal schooling. From the right, critics complained that principals had become too bureaucratic, too distant from community values, and too controlled by what was seen as an interlocking directorate of education professors, school administrators, and professional educators, derisively termed the "Educracy."[16] They ridiculed professional educators for their adoption of progressive education that, they claimed, diminished traditional academic learning and emphasized social activities over academics. In his 1953 charge that contemporary American schooling was an "educational wasteland," University of Illinois history professor Arthur Bestor cited with outrage the comments of a junior high school principal who argued that the truly advanced educational system should not assume academic competence on the part of all students. According to this

Differentiated Expect.

principal, "We shall some day accept the thought that it is just as illogical to assume that every boy must be able to read as it is that each one must be able to perform on a violin, that it is no more reasonable to require that each girl shall spell well than it is that each one shall bake a good cherry pie."[17] Such thinking on the part of school administrators, charged critics, was leading the nation to ruin.[18]

The popular articulation of this dynamic appeared in a lurid front-page article on the "Crisis in Education" in the March 1958 issue of *Life Magazine*. Sloan Wilson, the author of the popular 1955 book *The Man in the Gray Flannel Suit*, which criticized the conformity of modern bureaucracy, wrote a scathing article on American education called "It's Time to Close Our Carnival." "To revitalize America's educational dream, we must stop kowtowing to the mediocre," asserted Wilson, the author of the most popular book about mediocrity of the day. Wilson cited a principal of a junior high school in New York City who admitted that when he signed diplomas, he suffered "great pangs of pedagogical conscience" because, although many of his students could barely read, he had, "with the connivance of the duly constituted authorities helped to perpetuate the fiction" that they had become literate. Such misgivings were contrasted with the work of a woman principal of a Soviet school, who, in a companion article, was described as a "stern disciplinarian" who held multiple national honors and who was photographed in the midst of delivering a history lecture.[19]

The Soviet reference was not accidental. In 1952, Senator Joseph McCarthy began the investigation of what he identified as a communist threat in the United States. Through the 1950s "Red Scare," educators were scrutinized for implementing a leftist political agenda into schools. This, it was argued, led to the undermining of American strength in the face of Soviet resurgence and proved the great discrepancy between "what Ivan knows that Johnny doesn't."[20] Although some school administrators were suspect, for the most part, the investigations focused on classroom teachers, while principals were assigned the task of ferreting out the offending teachers. For example, under the New York State Feinberg Law, in September 1949, principals were required to survey all the teachers in their school on their political beliefs; by that May the superintendent suspended eight teachers, who were then tried, found guilty, and dismissed.[21] Worse than the firing, noted some educators, was the shiver of fear and paranoia that swept schools, including the self-censorship that educators underwent to avoid public suspicion.[22] Out of self-protection, school administrators who did not enjoy tracking down disloyal teachers were all the more encouraged to do so.

Exacerbating the public perception of political crisis among American school teachers was that of a disciplinary crisis among American school children. Popular culture of the postwar period offered an alternative youth culture that made school less central to students' lives, even as their attendance rates far outpaced that of their parents. Combined with the increased enrollment of students from diverse backgrounds, the American public school student took on a new and notably more rebellious character.

Under traditional models of school management, principals had assumed the disciplinary role of parents, *in loco parentis,* and maintained order through methods that linked students' classroom behavior with broader goals of social order, community norms, and civic obedience. But diverse school enrollments made consensus and trust more difficult to achieve and presented greater opportunities for conflict, as previously silenced groups sought recognition in legal and civil rights procedures.[23] Federal Supreme Court decisions of the 1960s and '70s granted students procedural and substantive rights to student privacy and due process, culminating in the 1969 Supreme Court decision *Tinker v. Des Moines,* which ruled that neither "students nor teachers shed their constitutional rights to freedom of speech and expression at the school house gate." Further, the court added that disagreements and disorder in schools were acceptable, as they prepared students for a world of conflict and debate.[24] The legal recognition of civil liberties and due process for students, and the public recognition that education could include conflict and difference, contrasted with earlier concepts of schools as places of order, hierarchy, and consensus. That students had constitutional rights echoed lessons from popular culture that students had their own values, politics, and desires—all of which challenged the traditional purpose of education as the agency that assumed the responsibility for instilling such values.

Such assumptions were bitterly contested through the 1970s, as courts reversed earlier civil rights rulings in favor of school administrations. In the 1977 Supreme Court Case *Ingraham v. Wright,* for example, a divided court found that a Florida junior high school principal was justified in forcibly restraining and paddling a student because he did not leave the school auditorium when asked to by a teacher. Part of the argument by the court majority was that for the school to follow due process for the student, the school administration would suffer increased "fiscal and administrative burdens."[25] Under this argument, administrators' obligations were one reason to justify a retraction of students' civil rights. Yet public opinion and court rulings on discipline remained wide and discrepant, reflecting conflicting public views about schools and youth. Other instances of consensus and homogeneity were obviated by courts in the 1960s, most notably the 1962 U.S. Supreme Court decision *Engel v. Vitale* that prayer in the public schools was unconstitutional, a ruling that mirrored the loosening of other social norms for young people.

Indeed, the 1960s and '70s were most noted for the increase in student activism, organized initially as part of the wider civil rights and anti-Vietnam

War movements and merging swiftly with larger social movements for freedom from traditional social customs and relations. High school students
joined and in some cases preceded university students' activism, sending a
chill of panic through secondary school systems. In a national survey of all
American secondary schools in the 1969 school year, the National Association of Secondary Principals found that 59 percent of high schools and 56
percent of junior high schools reported some type of student protest. Coun-
tering a public perception that urban high schools were the source of trouble,
the study found that suburban high schools experienced student-led protests
at a slightly higher rate than city high schools. In their public protests, high
school students tended to focus on local and social issues impacting their
lives as teenagers, such as district and school regulations on dress codes,
personal grooming, smoking, and censorship, more so than national issues
such as race relations or the Vietnam War.[26] This last finding was debated,
however, by the congressional subcommittee organized to investigate student
activism at the college level, which made a special investigation in response
to the 1969 decision of the Student for a Democratic Society (SDS) to
expand their work from colleges to high schools. The subcommittee con-
curred with FBI director J. Edgar Hoover who sent an alarming report on
"student extremism" to the national PTA, warning that the SDS's efforts to
establish a foothold in high schools was a significant problem of national
defense, given that the agenda of SDS was one of "extremism, violence and
revolution, promoting "Marxism, hatred against all facets of our society,"
and "blind destruction."[27]

Principals had more immediate concerns to worry about, including
how to respond to student boycotts and sit-ins at their office door or in the
cafeteria. School administrators scrambled to respond with both legal and
organizational strategies to "man the barricades," warning principals that
even if they assumed that "it can't happen here," they should know that
student disruption was happening everywhere. Principals were advised to
create emergency plans with clear procedures and lines of command between
staff, parents, and the police, following legal guidelines. Early detection of
the problem was key, but critical questions remained: should the principal
meet with students or address them over the PA system? How to manage
staff when students organized a sit-in in the school building? Should principals acquiesce to student demands or hold the line? What to do in cases
of violence? How to handle public relations and the press?[28]

Other questions plagued the principal. How to address the explosive
rates of unmarried high school girls' pregnancies, the infiltration of drugs
into schools and reports that over a third of all high school students had
tried marijuana at least once, and the virus of teenagers' disrespectful and
mocking behavior toward adults in authority?[29] It was clear that schools

had changed from protector of traditional values to a cauldron of dynamic and experimental youth culture, and according to popular opinion and the law, principals were responsible for channeling and controlling that culture.

In other ways, the public impression of principals was unpromising, as the late 1970s witnessed episodes of principals being publicly lambasted, derided, and physically assaulted by students, parents and community groups. Such incidents heightened principals' perception that they were, as a 1970 *Wall Street Journal* article described it, "losing the reins" of control to students, teachers, and parents.[30] In their defense, principals began to fight back. In March 1972, a front-page story in the *New York Times* titled "Crime and Violence Rise in City Schools" led the president of that city's High School Principals' Association to call for more power to principals to suspend misbehaving students. In March 1976, Principal Howard Hurwitz of Long Island City High School barricaded himself in his office to defy the district chancellor's order to readmit a student whom the principal had suspended. Known as a strict disciplinarian and opponent of the chancellor, Principal Hurwitz announced that "[t]hey will have to carry me out piece by piece."[31] And he kept largely to his word, staying in his office for three days until negotiations with district officials led to a compromise in which he would face only a potential fine for insubordination. When he retired the following spring, Hurwitz used his address at graduation to condemn the intrusion into school management of groups like the American Civil Liberties Union, minority parent groups, and federal antipoverty programs. A decade later, he published his memoir about his experience, appropriately titled *The Last Angry Principal.* Hurwitz defiantly fought for "a vanishing conception of the principal as an unassailable school leader and final arbiter of educational justice."[32]

The popular perception that principals were both responsible for causing disorderly schools and capable of "fixing" a school did little to clarify the expectations of school leaders. It remained uncertain who was responsible for school discipline, curriculum, personnel, and facilities, and principals repeatedly turned on their superiors for acquiescing too quickly to the demands of community and civil rights groups. Principal Hurwitz railed against exactly this in his refusal to print a student article in the school newspaper, without having followed or shared with students the board guidelines on students' rights and responsibilities.[33] The community pressure on principals to solve social problems by fixing the local school often conflicted with legal and administrative policy, leaving principals stranded between the public and the district lawyer. Worse, the issues that principals identified as mattering to a school were harder to gain support for. In 1961, Elliott Shapiro, elementary principal in New York City, placed an inflammatory advertisement in a city newspaper to force the school board to address the pressing issues at his school, which included rats and roaches, a leaking roof, unsanitary children's toilets, and numerous fire hazard notifications.[34]

Through the 1970s, school administrators faced what appeared like an imploding profession. "These are hard times for the urban school principal" opened a 1971 *New York Times* article. "Caught in a crossfire of demands by students, parents and unions for new answers to old problems," principals were still "confined by an inflexible system." As city school systems decentralized their governance structure to allow for more parental involvement, principals became "exposed to community pressures without the protective cover of central school headquarters," they worked with teacher union contracts that they did not negotiate, and in a bureaucratic system that was not able to respond to the diversity of demands of modern schools.[35] Principals reported feeling unsure of their role, and "on the defensive, confronting an educational world they neither made nor anticipated."[36] Particularly in urban districts, wrote one commentary in the mid-1970s,

> the popular picture of the urban principal is that of the man in the middle, caught up in the storm of angry and frequently contradictory demands. Besieged by noisy delegations of students, parents, teachers, or community residents, he finds himself simultaneously to blame for poor facilities, too much homework, insufficient time for faculty planning, and students' misconduct on the way to school.[37]

The assumption of this author that the principal was a man reflected yet another challenge to the principalship in this period.

SEX AND THE MODERN PRINCIPAL

Part of the critique of educational administration was fueled by a broader national anxiety about masculinity among all white-collar male workers. Since the late nineteenth century, advocates for the professionalization of educational administration had argued for the recruitment of men into the principal's office. The assignment of men in administration to supervise women in the classroom offered the same professional hierarchy and prestige found in other executive offices. The hiring of male administrators also addressed a long-standing social anxiety that the preponderance of women teachers had a "feminizing" impact on children, especially young boys, creating what one early twentieth-century pundit called "a woman peril in American education" that led to "a feminized manhood, emotional, illogical, non-combative against public evils."[38]

The mid-twentieth-century crisis in American masculinity was also spurred by questions about the nature of modern men's work. During the

1950s, the number of blue-collar workers declined while the number of white-collar salaried managers and administrators doubled.[39] Although representing the best of postwar prosperity, the increase in middle management raised a number of questions about gender roles. Modern corporate capitalism seemed to have transformed the independent masculine entrepreneur into a passive cog in the bureaucratic machine, a company man who conformed to organizational hierarchy in a windowless office. The modern corporate manager, as portrayed in film, fiction, and popular commentary, was a strangely emasculated, disempowered, and soulless being, neither skilled worker nor professional, but merely an "organization man."[40] The popular writer Norman Mailer warned that this manager "faced a slow death by conformity with every creative and rebellious instinct stifled."[41]

Exacerbating the impact of workplace conformity was the charge that young men were being demasculinized by the modern school curriculum. School leaders were criticized for offering anti-intellectual progressive curriculum that had "too many trimmings" and "wasteful frills."[42] American schools were charged with being "soft" in testing, curriculum, and standards, and the inclusion of family-oriented curriculum such as sex education, psychology, and life skills furthered the image that the modern school mirrored the domestic world.[43] A popular 1969 book, The Feminized Male exemplified this concern, arguing that an "overexposure to feminine norms" at home and school was turning boys into sissies, noting that the most intellectual boys scored the lowest on masculinity scales.[44]

Popular culture images of the principal reflected this national anxiety about the masculinity of school leadership. Norman Rockwell's painting from the May 23, 1953 cover of the popular Saturday Evening Post is a good example: a young white male principal is interrupted from his desk work by his officious woman secretary who stands above him, describing the problem outside his office: a young girl who has clearly been in a fight. The girl—defiant, rumpled, and proudly sporting a black eye—has more confidence and has clearly been involved in more physical activity than the startled young principal at his desk. Surrounded by females and papers, this young man hardly betrays the assured masculinity of the ideal principal— thus showing the ironic poignancy and humor of the scene. Similarly, in the first modern popular media about education, Our Miss Brooks, broadcast on radio from 1948 to 1957 and on television from 1952 to 1956, the principal Osgood Conklin is a blustering, crotchety, and dishonest man, who constantly annoys his faculty and students and serves as the antithesis of the self-confident English teacher Connie Brooks. The trope of the incompetent male principal as foil to the savvy woman teacher was also played out in Archie comics, first appearing in 1942, where the rotund and bumbling principal, Mr. Weatherbee, is consistently outsmarted by teenagers and bossed around by the elderly spinster teacher Miss Grundy.[45] Male administrators, it was clear, were fumbling, flabby creatures who were inadequate role models for young men.

Cold War critiques of educators' politics segued with popular anxiety about gender identity in the persecution of homosexual educators through the 1950s. Indeed, the persecution of gays and lesbians proved to be the backbone of the anticommunist paranoia: the number of government employees fired on the basis of sexuality far outnumbered the number of alleged communists who were dismissed.[46] In schools, too, paranoia about the infiltration of deviant sexuality mirrored the persecution of political radicals with charges that gays and lesbians had "formed cells in the public schools and were corrupting the unwitting into Communism and lesbianism."[47]

In such a climate, educators struggled to defend and promote the masculinity of school teachers and administrators. In a 1946 description of a professional search for a school principal, the superintendent "was very cautious and discriminate in his male appointment. The man selected could not be labeled as an effeminate being. He was a former collegiate athletic hero. His physique was comparable to any of the mythical Greek gods. He was truly the ultimate in manliness." Last, but not least, he was married.[48] When a board of education employs a school administrator, noted a writer in the same journal in 1963, "it is also bringing the man's wife and family into the community."[49] In a national postwar campaign to recruit men into teaching, educators cautioned male teachers from becoming so consumed by their work that they would lose their masculinity by not participating "in the virile activities that make up the life of any other man" such as participation in sports and men's clubs. Education needed an injection of masculinity, argued one advocate, who concluded enthusiastically: "Move aside, sissies, we are on our way!"[50]

That accusations of both political and sexual deviance were directed overwhelmingly at teachers, not principals, is further evidence of the growing divide between the two employee groups. The assignment of educational administrators to persecute allegedly deviant and radical teachers reinforced those administrators' own assumed identity as safely heterosexual and conservative. By the 1960s, the campaign to replace women elementary principals with men had succeeded to such an extent that the image, if not the reality, of the school principal was a married male who was aligned with the normative social and political views of the community. It was not conceivable that a school principal could be radical in any way, politically or personally. And school principals had good reasons to maintain this image, as they had no union protection, no tenure, and they served at the mercy of their school board.[51] Furthermore, the persecution of others could help bolster their own protective shield. So effective was the assumption of principal identity that through the 1990s, there was virtually no research, support groups, or advocacy for gay and lesbian school administrators. As gay and lesbian school teachers and students began to claim rights and gain recognition, for example through the NEA inclusion of sexual preference in their nondiscrimination statement in 1974, gay school administrators remained virtually invisible.[52]

That women continued to remain a majority of principals in the elementary school through the 1950s furthered the popular concern about the state of the principalship. A full-force attack on the "feminizing" influence of schools led to the aggressive promotion of men into and demotion of women out of the principal's office in the years after the Second World War. Three policy developments spearheaded this change. First, men's access to the principalship was furthered through the Servicemen's Readjustment Act of 1944, commonly called the GI Bill, which covered the costs of higher education for returning veterans, the vast majority of whom were men. Men flooded the previously female-dominated field of education, particularly at the graduate level so that in the mid-1960s, 37 percent of men teachers held a master's degree, while only 18 percent of women teachers did.[53] By the early 1970s, while 75 percent of bachelor's degrees in education were earned by women, proportionally twice as many men as women earned master's degrees in education. The discrepancy increased at the doctoral level where women earned less than 10 percent of the doctorates in educational administration, even though they constituted 20 percent of doctoral graduates in general education areas.[54] Women were notably absent from faculties of graduate programs in educational administration: In 1970, less than 1 percent of educational administration faculty in public universities were women, although slightly more (6.4 percent) were faculty in private institutions leading to, not surprisingly, a greater number of women students in private institutions than public.[55]

Men's increased presence in graduate programs in education accompanied the second policy that furthered the masculinization of the field after the war: increased graduate requirements for administrative licensure and a changed intellectual tenor of the field. Between 1950 and the mid-1960s, the number of states that stipulated graduate degree requirements for the principalship more than doubled, from one-third to two-thirds of all states, or 39 out of 50 states.[56] With more men earning graduate degrees, more men held the qualifications for the principal's license. The changing character of the field also improved men's access to school leadership positions. In the 1950s, educational administration reformers began to promote school administration as a scientifically based body of knowledge, informed by sociological and political theories. Leading the movement to revise administration preparation was the founding of two new professional associations—the

National Conference of Professors of Educational Administration (NCPEA) in 1947 and the University Council of Educational Administrators (UCEA) in 1956.[57] Both groups focused on the application of research to develop a more sophisticated and scientifically rooted profession of educational administration, and both attracted significant private foundation funding to do so.[58] For example, at one regional center, housed at George Peabody College of Education in Nashville, Tennessee, scholars' examination of criteria for predicting success in school administration candidates led to the development of a "competency approach," which clearly identified the behavioral, social, and intellectual components of effective school administrators.[59] The adoption of such an assessment tool with the approval of national foundations created a clear professional pathway toward school administration, one that worked, perhaps unconsciously but also clearly, to alter the gender balance in the principalship. Continuing the professionalization trend begun earlier in the century, school administration shaped itself as a competitive, rigorous, and selective field. As one reformer argued in 1954, "less and less will school administrators just happen," rather they will be "discovered and selected and will undergo long periods of systematic pre-service training with internships."[60] With few senior women to advocate for change in the field, the promotion of women into educational administration was less likely to "just happen."

A third way men were recruited into the principalship was to develop alternative pathways and rewards for men to enter education, a traditionally feminized field with salaries lower than those in other professions that required a college degree. School districts encouraged men teachers to move swiftly into administration, which had a higher pay scale than that of teachers. New degree requirements obviated the need for extensive teaching experience as a prerequisite and allowed for speedier ascents into administration by young men. A 1968 study found that most men principals had a median of five years' classroom experience, while women principals had a median of fifteen years. Women principals were also older than men: over 75 percent were over fifty years old, while barely a third of men principals were that old.[61]

One particular strategy for recruiting younger men into school administration was through athletic coaching. Boys' physical education in schools expanded quickly after the First World War, when draft statistics revealed that the soft underbelly of the American military was physical fitness: One-quarter to one-third of American recruits were found physically unfit. Increased physical education requirements in schools functioned as a valuable socializing force, instructing boys in admirable masculine and competitive attributes. Between 1919 and 1921, seventeen states adopted physical education requirements in schools; by 1930, thirty-six states had done so.[62]

As boys' sports became more central to schools, and more popular with school communities, coaches became a critical piece of school public relations, positioned at the forefront of the school's public image. The additional position of coaching sports offered men teachers extra pay at a higher rate than female coaches who earned significantly less than male coaches. In the academic year 1969–1970, when the average teachers' salary was $12,000, high school head coaches for boys made an average of $1,000 additional pay per year. Some football coaches made significantly more, such as the head high school football coach in Corpus Christi, Texas who earned $4,000 extra. At the Michigan City, Indiana senior high school, the head football coach earned $3,865 supplemental salary while the cheerleading coach, director of the school play, and advisor to the yearbook and newspaper each earned $300 for their work. Most advisors of clubs, debating teams, and smaller sports made nothing.[63]

The work of athletic coaching—communication, authority, disciplinary training of students, and public relations—aligned with the emerging professional identity of the new principal and, in a happy coincidence, provided the masculine image that appealed to both the public and to school reformers. An aspiring male principal who had a background in athletic coaching was automatically identified with a physicality that excluded women, people with disabilities, and men whose masculinity might be questioned by their sexuality. Professional associations of school administrators took pains to describe the great variety and physical mobility of the job, emphasizing athletic activities and sportsmanship in their professional meetings. The message was that school principals were not only responsible for bureaucratic paper-pushing but also for such physical work as supervising fire drills, breaking up playground fights, disciplining adolescent boys, and providing a virile and stabilizing presence in the school.

Because of the dominance in boys' sports—a situation that only began to be redressed by the passage of Title IX in 1972—coaching institutionalized a career ladder that was virtually blocked for women. When the standard prerequisite for the superintendency was experience as a school principal, a 1971 study of school superintendents found that almost 80 percent had coached athletic teams earlier in their career.[64] A national survey of school principals between 1987 and 2000 revealed that one-fifth of elementary principals and half of secondary school principals had been an athletic coach before taking on the principalship.[65]

The combined impact of the GI Bill that supported the advanced academic study of male veterans, the increased administrative requirements earned in male-dominated university departments, and the male-dominated coaching pipeline to administration significantly narrowed women's opportunities to be school administrators. Not surprisingly the number of women in

GENDER

school and district administration offices plummeted in the years after the Second World War. Between 1939 and 1962, the number of women superintendents declined by 70 percent. Women elementary principals declined from a high of 55 percent in 1928 to 20 percent in 1973.[66] In that year, only 3 percent of junior high school principals and 1 percent of senior high school principals were women.[67]

In the entire state of New York in 1972, women constituted only 1.7 percent of high school principals, 20 percent of elementary principals, and 8 percent of all middle and junior high school principals.[68] In the state of New Mexico in 1975, only 4 of the state's 164 high school principals and only 37 of the 315 elementary school principals were women.[69] Even in New York City, popularly considered a seat of liberal progressivism, less a quarter of the system's five hundred elementary principals were women in the mid-1970s.[70] Since most districts offered different salaries for elementary, junior high, and high school principals, these differentials had a financial impact, with elementary principals earning about 86 percent of secondary principals through the 1960s and '70s.[71]

Changes in the cultural and structural aspects of the principal's office since the early twentieth century had made the increase of men into administration seem almost natural. In education, as in other fields and in society at large, masculinity had become associated with technical mastery, confidence, economic wisdom, cultural authority, and physical strength—all attributes that aligned with the new understanding of school leaders as managers in a hierarchical educational business. By the 1960s, the very structure of the principalship was designed along that masculine archetype, and this only intensified with the increasing popular concern about school discipline. In schools, it now seemed to be the natural order of things that women taught and men managed.[72] The National Council of Administrative Women in Education fought this trend by advocating for an increase of girls' opportunities in education and leadership. But the group was not optimistic: At their 1965 annual meeting, one NCAWE speaker commented that given the 93 percent increase of men into education in the previous decade, and the common assumption that "the goals of most of these men is to become school administrators," the group's objectives had become increasingly difficult to obtain.[73]

EDUCATOR UNITY AND DISUNITY

Even as the principalship changed within itself after the war, its relations with other educators changed as well. In particular, the development of collective bargaining in educational unions in the 1950s and 1960s had a major impact on the principalship. To a great extent, the unionization of teach-

ers followed the trajectory of educational division that had begun decades
before. The driving goal of educational administration reformers earlier in
the twentieth century had been to realign school leadership away from the
old head teacher model to a more authoritative administrator who supervised
teachers. By the mid-twentieth century, this campaign was so successful
that teachers and principals worked in separate orbits. Teachers described
the principal as a "distant presence" who had little interaction with teachers and students. "I was lucky if I saw the principal three or four times a
year," recalled a Pittsburgh teacher who taught through the mid-twentieth
century. "He just waved passing the door and that was all I'd see of him."[74]
A Chicago teacher in the late 1940s described the principal this way:

> I would say in general that the principal doesn't make too much of
> a difference. They don't really add anything to the actual teaching.
> They have no pedagogical value. They're just administrators. They
> see that the school runs smoothly. But as far as teaching, they don't
> add a thing. They are just minus quantities.[75]

Figure 12. St. Paul strike. Principal Helen Conway and striking teachers, St. Paul,
Minnesota, 1946. Courtesy of the Minnesota Historical Society.

If not known for their "minus quantities," principals were known for their domineering authority, leading with the message that, as a Chicago elementary teacher remembered of her principal in the 1950s, "we are in control, you do as you are told, if you don't like it you leave."[76] The emergence of teacher unions formalized the deteriorating relationship between teachers and principals. For teachers, unionization offered the clarity of set job descriptions, secure salary and benefits, a sense of professional control over their work, and civil protections from the arbitrary rule of administrators. In the late 1950s, New York City teacher Albert Shanker was motivated to organize that city's United Federation of Teachers in part by his humiliating experience of working under principals who were authoritarian, played favorites among teachers, and were dismissive, unprofessional, and unhelpful for teachers who struggled with the demands of urban school teaching.[77] Particularly as more men from working-class and immigrant backgrounds became teachers in the years after the Second World War, their conflicts over authority and status with the growing cohort of male administrators increased.[78]

Unions promised a structure that would restrict the most egregious excesses of both teachers and administrators. In 1977, the union contract in one urban school district laid out a multiple-step evaluation process that clarified who would observe the teacher, what would be documented, who would accompany the teacher to the review of the observation, and, if the evaluation was unsatisfactory, when to have subsequent observations with written documentation, and procedural steps and recommendations for improvement.[79] The specificity of teacher union contracts prohibited many activities that were once in the principal's domain, including teacher transfers, evaluations, and assignments to afterschool duties. In so doing, collective bargaining contracts minimized the most irrational and autocratic of principal behavior and laid out standardized guidelines for both principals and teachers. In the best of cases, such contracts developed regular communication links between the principal and teachers who negotiated together over the work practices of the school day. Indeed, many studies of teacher unions found that, contrary to the popular image of recalcitrant union demands, teacher union contracts provided a useful road map for teachers' and principals' consultation, guiding both toward "mutual accommodation."[80] Such teacher and principal unity could also support a district's efforts for local autonomy among opponents of new federal policies such as court-ordered desegregation plans. In Atlanta, Georgia in 1970 the all-white Georgia Education Association promoted the unity of principals and teachers and their joint resistance to federal compliance plans for school desegregation. Positioning all local educators against federal bureaucrats was, the association claimed, one of the necessary "rights of educators."[81]

Nonetheless, principals, superintendents, and the public press increasingly critiqued teacher unions for encroaching upon what some saw as administrative prerogatives in schools. In 1944, only half of American teachers had even seen the blank forms on which their principals evaluated them, not to mention the actual evaluations. In contrast, in 1969, one high school principal bemoaned, perhaps hyperbolically, that he was not permitted to tell his women teachers not to wear kneesocks to school.[82] Like-minded principals referred longingly to a past when the high school principal was "a dignified, erudite, and slightly distant figure, autonomous in authority, and respected from both inside and outside the school."[83] With unions, these principals complained, that authority had been minimized and their actions confined by legalistic bureaucracy. What the principals had seen as professional autonomy was now reduced to an employer-employee relationship that radically changed the principal's professional role from an organizational leader to a bureaucratic manager following prescriptive and proscriptive guidelines.

Teacher unionization did not just change the working relationship between teachers and principals; the unionization of teachers also intensified principals' ambiguous position in the school organization. Teachers' collective bargaining occurred between the central administration and the union, leaving the principal excluded from the district-level decision making process of negotiating teachers' contracts. Many principals were uneasy about the fact that they were now required to enforce policies that had been formulated without their input and they expressed uncertainty about whether they should align with the board or the teachers, or what the consequences would be with either decision. Unions thus exacerbated what was already the untenable position of the modern school principal who stood in the middle of two negotiating parties.[84]

Statutory law did not help. Compared to court precedents that affirmed teachers' protected employment rights, the law was virtually silent on the employment rights of administrators. In most states, principals were not covered by teacher tenure laws, and they were generally considered district employees that served at the pleasure of the Board of Education, with no protective due process guidelines for demotion, transfer, or nonrenewal. Indeed, the courts tended to argue that educational administrators had an obligation of loyalty to their governing bodies that limited other rights. Even as the changing social and political conditions of schools led to increasing lawsuits against school principals, they had little representation or legal codes on which to rely.[85]

The confusion of principals' middle position between unionized teachers and the district leadership was intensified during union strikes. Principals were advised by their superiors to remember that their legal obligation was to carry out the mandate of the Board of Education, and that the principal's own professional authority was dependent on upholding district policy.[86] Still, many principals supported teachers who were their former colleagues. In the St. Paul, Minnesota teachers' strike of 1946, one of the first teacher strikes in the nation, Principal Helen Conway walked the picket line with the striking teachers, speaking publicly against the city schools' poor working conditions. Quoted in the local paper, Principal Conway asked: "How can one teacher with a class of 49 teach first-graders to learn to read and give each one individual attention?"[87] In the teachers' strike in Gary, Indiana schools in the winter of 1970, the superintendent first reprimanded the principal for offering coffee and doughnuts for teachers on the cold picket line. Later, the superintendent reflected on the ambiguous position of the principal: he had been a teacher at the school for many years before becoming assistant principal; he became principal just two years before the strike; he knew his staff well, was respected by most, a personal friend of many, and a former active teacher union member. Certainly the principal worked with his staff more closely and knew them better than he knew the superintendent, who was newly appointed to the job from another city, or school board members, who appeared at his school only on ceremonial occasions. The principal's salary was tied to the teachers' pay schedule; thus he would benefit economically if the union prevailed in its wage demands. He was wise enough, also, to know that strikes eventually ended and that he would be responsible for reopening the doors, bringing staff together, and working to heal inevitable wounds.[88] For good reason, then, did this principal literally walk the line between striking teachers and the school building.

While certainly there were principals who undercut and retaliated against striking teachers, the record is not always clear about which part of the school administration opposed teacher unions. Teachers and principals were employees of the board, and employee contracts were in the hands of the board and superintendent, and not principals. Principals could state their claim on either side and face the consequences. In 1968, Braulio Alonso was in his sixteenth year as a high school principal in Tampa, Florida, a former president of the state teachers' union in which he led the drive to racially integrate the organization, and the newly elected and first Hispanic president of the NEA. Yet when Alonso resigned as principal in solidarity with a state teachers' strike in protest over budget cuts in 1968, the county refused to rehire him.[89]

PRINCIPAL UNIONS

Principals' sense of alienation from the decision-making process of districts was one motivation for them to organize their own unions. Some principals had formed unions within the AFT and in solidarity with teachers before the Second World War. But the situation had changed with new labor laws: under the Taft-Hartley Labor Management Relations Act of 1947, which framed the federal guidelines for organized labor, supervisors were prohibited from unionization. By the late 1960s, the National Education Association had changed from a professional organization for educators, traditionally led by school administrators, to a classroom teachers' union; in 1973, the NEA disaffiliated from the national associations for elementary and secondary principals and superintendents.[90] This move led some educational administrators to blame the NEA for dividing teachers and administrators in order to strengthen their own organization.[91] But, in fact, principals were already turning to their own protective organizations. By 1975, there were over one thousand school administrator unions in twenty-four states, varying in size and structure. Over the next two years, collective bargaining units for school administrators grew by 67 percent.[92]

The movement of school principals to unionize both epitomized and challenged their traditional middle management status. A 1976 review of principals' unions described their motivation to organize:

Many school administrators feel beleaguered. The clarity and authority of command (downward from board to students) which once provided some security have been eroded. Events appear to have created a school political system so diffuse and fractured that no one is in control. For example, school boards, granted overall authority by the state, are often unable to bypass the minutiae and act effectively on issues. As part-time lay folk, they are often blissfully ignorant. Superintendents generally have the inside scoop on school problems, but they live too close to the revolving door of executive succession to take unpopular action. Parents and community people, once a supportive force (or at least a quiescent one) in educational reform, are now badly divided and often negative in dealing with schools. Even the once-close relationship between central management and supervisors, administrators, and teachers has been weakened. School systems are so large and bureaucratic that shared decision making among managers and administrators is increasingly difficult. Teacher unions and system work rules influence the interaction between administrators and teachers. It is no wonder that administrators are seeing protection in unionism.[93]

In 1965, the president of the new Federation of Principals and Supervisors in Cleveland, Ohio applauded the creation of more principals' locals, arguing that principals "have no more rapport or access to top brass than does the classroom teacher."[94] The principalship was an "institution in distress," wrote the editor of the National Association of Secondary School Principals to the membership in 1966. There was an "erosion of the principal's place in things," from the increasingly specialized district organizations on top and from organized teachers on the bottom. The district often deals directly with teachers on curriculum matters and the principal "winds up on the sidelines." Meanwhile, the bureaucratic burdens of the job kept increasing so that principals were "endlessly frustrated, forced to fritter away time on a thousand and one chores—trivial, maybe but they have to be done, and in all too many cases the principal has to do them."[95]

In smaller communities, some principals clung to a belief that teachers and principals could work together. In Council Bluffs, Iowa a strong AFT local was founded in the 1930s with over 90 percent of teachers belonging to the union. As some of those union teachers rose through the ranks to principal, they founded a principals' local and, according to one of the founding members of that union, "the two groups worked hand in hand and we made a tremendous impact on the educational system." But by the 1960s, the principals' union felt abandoned by the AFT national office that considered the principals to be "on the side of management." Such an antagonistic model did not fit with the Council Bluffs educational community, this principal asserted in a letter to AFT national in 1971: The principals had come up through the teacher union "and want no part of management. We know the problems of the teachers and want to work *with* them." But now the principals were beginning to feel threatened, both by the central district administration and by the local and national AFT. The principal pleaded to the AFT national office for "ammunition to *hold it together*. . . . will we be backed by the National Organization if the need arises?"[96]

For all the goodwill between locals described by this principal in Iowa, relations between principals' and teachers' unions became increasingly strained, due to the structural dynamic that forced them to fight against each other for recognition. In 1964, a member of the East St. Louis Principal's Union crossed his striking teachers' picket line in spite of an agreement made between the two unions. The president of national AFT was incensed and wrote the principal's union president: "This is the type of situation which makes it difficult for us to justify the existence of principal's locals."[97]

New York City's administrative union, the Council of Supervisory Associations, formally recognized as a bargaining unit in 1965, faced its first major challenge during the 1968 strike of the United Federation of Teachers over the school board's approval of three experimental community school boards to hire and fire teachers and administrators, bypassing the teacher unions' contract. In the face of a rising tide of demands for community control and associated racial tensions, the administrative council was caught in the middle of the citywide conflict between racial minority communities demanding changes in local schools and the teachers' union demanding that its bargained authority be upheld. Because the new community school boards demanded the replacement of white with black principals, overstepping regular appointment policies, the council opposed the city's authorization of community school boards; but even as many principals supported the teachers' strike, the council was unable to forge a stable alliance with the teachers' union.[98]

CONCLUSION

By the 1970s, schools were commonly portrayed in popular culture as tragic comedies where educators braced themselves against the double onslaught of rebellious youth culture and dysfunctional bureaucracy. The principal was implicated in this chaos, an iconic representative of the school out of control. Two films from the period encapsulate this popular tone.

Up the Down Staircase, a film released in 1967 two years after the publication of the novel, follows a young idealistic English teacher in her first year teaching in an inner-city high school. She is quickly disillusioned by the combination of school bureaucracy, her students' apathy, and her colleagues' incompetence. The novel is written entirely in the form of memos, student essays, and notes between the teacher and her friends. Central to the dark comedy of the story is the predominance of inane bureaucracy—the title refers to a memo from the never-seen principal whose presence exists only in the sending of memos about ridiculous rules.

In the 1979 film *Rock and Roll High School*, the core story is the battle between the principal and modern student youth culture, as encapsulated in a particularly vivacious student's passion for the punk rock band, the Ramones. Vince Lombardi High School already has a bad record when the new principal, Miss Togar, takes over, ending her first visit to the Board of Education with a military salute to the former principal, who sits in a comatose state in a straightjacket at the end of the table, presumably driven insane by the students. Ultimately, Principal Togar is herself driven crazy by her obsessive hatred for rock and roll and ends the movie in her own straightjacket. The double themes of strangling school bureaucracy and incompetent school principals was perhaps an understandable response to the massive changes that impacted schools and principals in the thirty years after the Second World War.

Since the common school reforms of the mid-nineteenth century, educators had promoted the school as a rational organization that functioned best under a bureaucracy with increasing emphasis on school leaders' technical skills and rational planning. Although sharing little else, John Dewey and Ellwood Cubberley agreed that principals could, with proper training and reflection, work effectively in a smoothly functioning and self-generating organizational system. The professionalization movement in educational administration sought to perfect this system so that schools would become finely tuned organizations where all players knew and skillfully played out their parts.

By the 1950s, there were cracks in that system, and those cracks let in a tidal wave of other influences to schools. Critics charged that school bureaucracy was a thin shell that hid a chaotic and inequitable interior, a mechanism by which teachers, students, and minority communities had been abused, student learning opportunities lost, communities ignored, and fiscal resources wasted. Through the 1970s, there were public demands for more access to and responses from schools and their leaders, much like the direct line between community and schools in the past. But enough had changed to prevent the return to such community control of schools, as the increased policy demands that began in the 1980s would make clear.

For principals, these disruptions introduced a contradictory combination of control and chaos, both of which limited principals' individual initiatives. Principals stood at the bull's eye of attention from district, state, and federal initiatives designed to standardize the work of local schools, and from local community and parent initiatives that promoted their own interests. By the 1970s, the increased state and federal proceduralism of the school system was so thick that school principals' work was oriented almost entirely toward understanding and applying the guidelines of the established system. "At one time we considered ourselves educators," reported one principal in 1971. But now "the problem is much too complicated, the organization is much too vast, the ramifications are too great, the partners in the enterprise are too many for us any longer to serve as educators."[99] In the swirl of modern popular culture, principals were seen as rigid disciplinarians and bureaucrats, "like a giant policeman who sits behind a desk far away and makes all the rules."[100] Successful principals were able to transcend their tortured position between district and community only by focusing aggressively on educational issues, often battling both state and community forces.

As we will see in the next chapter, the challenges facing school principals under civil rights legislation and community movements of the 1960s and '70s presented an even more complicated dynamic for school principals.

CHAPTER FIVE

BEARING THE BURDEN

The School Principal and Civil Rights

In the winter of 1971, when Alton Rison began his job as the first African American principal of Francis Scott Key Junior High School 117 in the Bedford Stuyvesant District of Brooklyn, New York, he faced an angry group of parents, a divided teaching force, and a school that had by all accounts become an "educational disaster area." The school was located in a notorious urban ghetto fraught with crime, persistent underemployment, and fractured families; the students in the local school district were 90 percent black and Latino, and over 75 percent of their families lived below the poverty line. As principal, Rison was caught in the middle of a newly reorganized, community-controlled school district that was still recovering from a massive teacher strike. Community control was a victory accomplished by black and Latino activists who had argued that the long-standing New York City centralized school district was a racist, top-down bureaucracy that abandoned minority children. Parents of Junior High School 117 knew this only too well from Rison's predecessor, a white male principal who had allowed the school to deteriorate to a chaotic condition with students trafficking drugs in the hallways and teachers' high absentee rates and abuse of students.

Under community control, new principals were expected to change everything. Hired as the first African American principal of the school, by the first African American superintendent of the district, Rison was seen as both an answer to community problems and a representative of the community that he served. Yet unlike earlier generations of community-minded principals, Rison came to school with virtually no resources, a divided and rebellious teacher staff, and a suspicious community, in a climate that was electric with racial and class conflict. And the school was literally crumbling. Rison described what he saw:

> There were piles of papers everywhere, strewn and tattered textbooks, pieces of desks, broken bottles, papers and shards of metals, and utter slop up and down the sidewalks and walls. There were shattered windows and boards. . . . and the building looked smoky, and it was sooted and singed, as were the boards, some blackened, cracking and peeling. . . . The guys of the school were hanging and falling all over the place. And there were shrieks and screams of children gone wild, shivering in the already frigid air and flattening the tunes of the constant false alarms clanging through windowless frames.[1]

Principal Rison set to work, surprising many by, instead of instituting radical race-based initiatives, enforcing traditional bureaucratic systems: for teachers, he monitored attendance, set a dress code and a regular contact schedule with parents, and required lesson plans, monthly tests of student content knowledge, and a biweekly report on students called "teacher predictions and projections." He conducted and documented supervision of teachers three times a year from which he developed a "Statistical Array Rank Order of Teacher Productivity Levels." In a public space in his office, he posted a nine-foot wall chart that ranked teachers, indicated in code, alongside student scores. He instituted an annual "Accountability Day" each spring when parents and community leaders were invited to "inspect" and "examine" classroom work.

Rison's traditional accountability practices were balanced with the adoption of progressive curriculum revisions. He supported teachers' development of new coursework, encouraged teachers to make classrooms more attractive, and offered demonstration teaching lessons and links to community agencies for enrichment programs. Rison also applauded students' creative work and encouraged the incorporation of black and Puerto Rican culture into the school.

Rison's strategy of documenting and making public student and teacher performance data echoed some of the traditional practices of earlier educators like Ellwood P. Cubberley, a comparison that was not lost on Rison's detractors who accused him of being a "paper pusher" just like the white bureaucrats that community activists had fought to replace. Albert Shanker, president of the United Teachers Federation, described Rison's actions as a "return to the worst practices of the nineteenth century."[2]

But it was not the nineteenth century. Alton Rison's challenges as a school principal encapsulate many of the conditions facing late twentieth-century school leaders. And of all the educational changes in the decades after the Second World War, none was more explosive in public education than the racial desegregation of schools and the political organization for civil rights in education. While the movement for desegregation had to do primarily with the integration of white and black children in schools, the employment status of black teachers and principals was also seriously impacted. Indeed, the status of black educators had been an opening wedge for the NAACP, which had earlier in the century filed salary inequity suits against Southern school districts in which the average black teacher earned barely 60 percent of the average white teacher's wages. The NAACP strategy for dismantling racially segregated systems was to increase the district costs of maintaining two systems. Through the 1930s, the NAACP won a series of salary equity cases in state courts that raised black teacher and principals' salaries, although racist school boards inevitably found other ways to maintain segregated schools.[3]

With the Supreme Court decision of *Brown v. Board of Education* in 1954, the federal mandate for school desegregation had been set and later reinforced by subsequent court decisions. But at the state and local level, school desegregation remained a highly contentious and far more difficult goal to maneuver, leading to years of overlapping federal, state, and local mandates and community mobilization for and against school integration. Simultaneously, minority community groups fought for racial equity within school culture, arguing for changes in curriculum, staffing, school regulations, school governance, and student life. Principals stood at the center of all of these changes and conflicts, albeit in a host of contradictory ways.

DESEGREGATION AND SCHOOL PRINCIPALS

When Southern school districts were legally mandated to desegregate after the Supreme Court's 1954 *Brown v. Board of Education* decision, white leaders complied by closing segregated black schools. The result all across the South was the destruction of thousands of community-based black schools and the loss of positions for black educators. While black teachers became scarce under this process, black principals faced literal extinction. In the decade after *Brown*, the number of black principals in the South was reduced by 90 percent. In the late 1960s, when the enforcement of desegregation was at its peak in the American South, black principals were eliminated through what one investigating body called an "avalanche-like force and tempo."[4] Numbers show the stark reality: Between 1964 and 1971 in Alabama, the number of black secondary school principals fell from 134 to 14 and in Virginia, from 107 to 16. Six hundred black principals lost their jobs in Texas. In Mississippi in the two years between 1969 and 1971, the number of black principals plummeted from 168 to 19. In one county a

white athletic coach with no administrative experience replaced the black
principal; in another county, a white counselor replaced a black principal
with a master's degree and fifteen years of administrative experience. Most
black principals were reassigned to minor administrative jobs working under
white principals, or returned to the classroom, or left education altogether.[5]
In Tennessee, for example, the two-year period between 1968 and 1970 saw
the decline in the number of black principals from seventy-three to seventeen; by 1975, the number of black principals had decreased even more,
but the number of black assistant principals had increased from seven to
sixteen, primarily at previously all-white schools.[6] In Maryland, while the
number of high schools had increased between 1954 and 1968, the number
of black principals decreased from 21 percent to 10 percent. Reflecting the
changing demography of American cities, black principals disappeared from
twenty-two of Maryland's rural and suburban counties in this period, but
increased in the city of Baltimore.[7]

Black principals' careers followed various downward trajectories,
demoted to lesser positions in integrated schools or appointed principal
of schools that remained predominantly African American. Lillian Taylor Orme, for example, was appointed one of the first black principals in
Kansas City in 1952 and assigned to a predominantly black school. When
the school closed in 1955 and the students were sent to newly integrated
schools, Orme, who held a bachelor's and a master's degree, was reassigned
as a "Teaching Assistant to the Principal" at an integrated school where
she was one of only two black faculty. The following year, she became
principal of the predominantly black Dunbar School and spent the next
fifteen years in two- to three-year stints as principal of different primarily
black elementary schools in Kansas City.[8] C. Horace Gibson, principal of
the small black school in rural Woodstown, New Jersey mentioned in the
previous chapter, experienced a similar path. His school closed in June 1950,
and students merged into the Woodstown Elementary School. Mr. Gibson
became an eighth-grade science and health teacher. The following year,
the white principal recommended Gibson to be the baseball team coach.[9]

The demotion and firing of black principals did more than undermine
the careers of aspiring black educators. The maintenance of a segregated
system of schooling had ensured black principals a culturally significant role,
and the dismantling of this system destroyed.[10] It interrupted the recruitment and promotion paths for young black teachers and excluded their
voices from advocating for black children at the administrative level. It
meant not only the loss of one of the few professional positions reserved
for highly educated African Americans, but also the loss of a black professional advocate and role model for black children.[11] For districts with high
African American populations, the impact was catastrophic: by the end of

the 1970s, 54 percent of Mississippi's school population was black, but only 20 percent of principals and assistant principals were black.[12]

These changes happened even as the major burden of desegregation fell on African American communities who lobbied to force local districts to implement the federal law and battled white resistance at every level. While the most public battles over desegregation took place in the courts, school board meetings, and the streets, the principal's office played a defining role in the racial integration of schools. Positioned at the nexus of policy and the classroom, principals handled the literal translation of civil rights policy into civil rights practice, and their success or failure at doing so directly shaped the progress of racial integration in their school.

In many notable cases, white principals resisted desegregation efforts at the most immediate and human level. Once the initial battles in the courtrooms and school board offices were over, brave black students who attended previously white schools faced viciously antagonistic school cultures presided over by white principals. Black students endured harassment from their classmates and racist school policies endorsed by their white principal including racially segregated and tracked classrooms, restrooms, cafeterias, social activities and athletic teams, and harsh discipline. Some white principals were more public than others in their bigotry, but in such a charged climate, even a principal's passivity furthered active racism. In Mansfield, Texas in August 1956, for example, the federal district court's order to desegregate the school district led to immediate belligerent resistance by white community members, including the hanging from the high school flagpole of an effigy of a lynched figured marked with a sign that read "this negro tried to enter a white school." The principal refused to remove the figure on the flagpole, telling a reporter, "I didn't put it up there, and I'm not going to take it down."[13]

Two case studies from the state of Arkansas show two radically different approaches taken by white and black principals in the desegregation of schools. The most notorious and widely publicized conflict over school integration was at Central High School in Little Rock Arkansas in 1957–1958 when the school became a literal battleground between the white segregationist school board and community and the National Guard, called out by President Eisenhower to enforce the legally mandated integration of nine black students. The students faced relentless cruelty as segregationist students and community members battled with advocates of integration in public displays of hostility. The white high school principal, Jess Mathews, responded to the chaos by trying to maintain a stature of neutrality and emphasis on academic order, thereby earning the disapproval of both sides.

Matthews had been a popular principal at the all-white Central High School for many years and was proud of his school's academic and athletic record. Described by the local white community as a "gentle giant," Matthews advocated for educational excellence, earning the school a record number of National Merit finalists and scholarships. In his quest for social unity and equal opportunity, he had dismantled a socially exclusive fraternity and sorority system in the school some years earlier.[14] But Matthews' rigid approach to academic and social order imploded in the chaos of the 1957–1958 school year. Matthews' attitude was that fighting over racial integration was a distraction from the regular operations of the school, and that if students would simply focus on their studies and ignore the swirl of activities around them, all would be well. "Be responsible," he directed students in one of his many written daily bulletins with which he intended to instill discipline. "Any disorder, confusion, disagreement, or quarrelling at or around school will interfere with classroom work."[15] By avoiding the conflict, Matthews exacerbated it. His bulletins advising good behavior sailed literally over the heads of white students who assaulted black students in the halls of Central High. In his belief that "the less we discuss these matters, the better," he prevented two teacher committees from developing plans to further the integration process, and he refused to respond to black parents' pleas for more authoritative discipline and leadership on enforcing the court ruling.[16]

Principal Matthews' strategy was born in part from his attempt to walk the line between the incensed white community and the entrenched school board. Yet for all his attempts at appeasement, local segregationists sought the principal's dismissal because of what they saw as his cooperation with the integration forces, even as black parents charged him with outright negligence.[17] His work for the year consisted primarily of monitoring disciplinary disputes in his office and writing and delivering memos advising students to study.

Racial integration of the schools of Fayetteville, Arkansas, twenty miles to the northwest, took a completely different turn, in large part due to the work of two women principals. Other variables eased the transition as well: Fayetteville was a small community with a stable black and white population, including faculty and staff from the local university, which had, in the late 1940s, admitted a number of black students to selected graduate programs. In the mid-1950s the school district was run by an enlightened school board that had already authorized some interactions between the white and black elementary schools. Even with these liberal aspects, the town remained deeply segregated: black students attended a segregated elementary school located in the middle of the black residential district and traveled to a neighboring town to attend their black high school.

In May 1954, four days after the Supreme Court's decision on *Brown*, the Fayetteville School Board voted unanimously to integrate its high school at the beginning of the fall term, thereby becoming the first school district in the South to integrate. Although not uniformly approved by the community, the enrollment of seven black students into the Fayetteville High School with five hundred white students progressed without incident. Two women principals, one white, one black, played a major role: Louise Bell, principal of the all-white Fayetteville High School since 1945, and Minnie B. Dawkins, principal of the all-black Lincoln School since 1946, were well acquainted with each other. Principal Dawkins, the only black school leader in the district, was a familiar member of the district principals' organization and had coordinated with other principals in programming between schools. Bell and Dawkins spent the summer before the integration of the high school together, identifying the academic areas where the black students might need more support, indicating the courses for them to take, and introducing the black parents to the school and the teachers. In the high school, Principal Bell set up student organizations to welcome and support the black students. When the state athletic association prohibited all-white school teams from playing against teams with black players, Principal Bell took the matter to the student leadership and teams to deliberate their response. The students decided unanimously to forgo playing any team that objected to their black players.[18] Outside of the schools, church groups and the League of Women Voters sponsored race relations discussions and activities for children and adults. The result was "progressive, systematic desegregation," according to the *Northwest Arkansas Times*.[19]

The Fayetteville junior high school was integrated two years later, but the process then stalled, due in large part to the increasing tension over desegregation emerging from Little Rock and segregationist state policies enacted as a result. The integration of the elementary school proved even more challenging, particularly because its principal, Pearlie Williams, led a black community opposition to the district's desegregation plan of closing the all-black school. According to some, Principal Williams was supported by an awkward alliance between the new school superintendent, who was opposed to integration, and a group of black families who fought for the maintenance of the traditional black school.[20]

For some black principals in the South, the political dynamics of the community, state, and nation collided on them in painfully ironic ways. Like Pearlie Williams, some black principals resisted desegregation, believing that the cultural strength of the all-black school would serve black students better than forced integration with a resistant white community. Their observations of the community violence occasioned by integration and the loss of the black educational staff upon the closing of black schools contributed to their concern about racial integration, as did the intense pressure from their white superiors in district offices.

White school officials who recognized the principal's cultural authority in the black community intentionally took advantage of this tension: as the superintendent of a county school district in Mississippi wrote to the state governor in 1964, "We have got to work through the negro principals and teachers to try to help us keep our schools segregated."[21]

Those southern black principals who defended their all-black schools found themselves in the middle of an explosive political dynamic. In 1965 in Benton County in northeastern Mississippi, racial tensions were intensifying with the presence of civil rights activists from the Student Non-Violent Coordinating Committee (SNCC). W. B. "Woody" Foster, the principal of the black school, earned the ire of the local black community's Citizen's Club by recommending the nonrenewal of a black teacher who had been involved in the recent SNCC voter registration drive and by initiating the arrest of a SNCC activist who attended a school basketball game. Black parents petitioned the county school board for a number of school improvements, including the construction of a school library, and to remove Principal Foster. The white school board offered a bargain: They would follow the requests *if* the parents would desist from further efforts to desegregate the schools. The black parents refused and initiated a school boycott; the district leadership responded by firing both the activist teachers and Foster and other teachers who had supported him.[22]

On the other side of the state, O. E. Jordan, a respected principal and a former president of the black educators' Mississippi Teachers Association that supported desegregation, faced similar conflict. Three years earlier, Jordan had publicly opposed the local black community's desegregation lawsuit, which when filed had led to a white reign of terror in the community. In February 1965, he took a stand against students wearing SNCC pins in school, arguing that the students' action had "created a state of confusion and had disrupted the orderly procedure at the school." In a meeting with the students, Jordan found them disrespectful and hostile, calling him "Uncle Tom." He told them that if they returned to school wearing the buttons, he would suspend them, which he did. Teachers, students, and parents debated Jordan's actions, some defending him, with the majority choosing to boycott the school.[23]

Under legal mandates for school desegregation, the tensions of the middle managerial role of the principal were exacerbated with the increased number of political players. In New Orleans in November 1960, the principals of the two white schools designated to enroll black children received two telegrams: the first, from the federal government, informing them that their schools would be integrated the following day, and the second from the state of Louisiana, informing them that if they admitted any black students they would be arrested for violating the recently passed state law that prohibited integrated schools.[24] Principals became essentially agents of the federal court and received a level of protected status under the court's ruling even as this protection alienated them from their local community.

For example, at New Orleans' McDonogh 19, which enrolled three black girls only to have all of the white students pull out of the school for the entire school year, Principal Jack Stewart spent the year supervising nineteen faculty and three students, accompanied by a handful of federal marshals who protected the school, staff, and students.[25]

In the North, the cultural authority of the principal as a key player in desegregation was recognized by both advocates and opponents of racial integration in schools. In Boston in 1974, federal judge Arthur Garrity ruled that, although the city's schools were not legally segregated, the Boston School Committee had "knowingly carried out a systematic program of segregation."[26] Facing a violently resistant white school community in South Boston, Garrity put South Boston High School under receivership, removed the school principal, and appointed Jerome Winegar, a white former assistant principal at a junior high school in St. Paul, Minnesota who came to his new job with a number of other educators from St. Paul. As outsiders to the community, appointed by a judge, the new administrative team faced overt hostility from the community and teachers. On the first day of school, spray paint on the street and signs in the windows of neighborhood houses read, "Go home, Jerome." Protected by the court order, Winegar publicly challenged the school board, teachers, and the community, and focused on improving the curriculum, educational achievement, and student discipline.[27]

Like Jesse Mathews, Principal Winegar believed that interracial relations would improve with improved education, but unlike the Little Rock principal, Winegar and his staff focused on the high poverty and low achievement rates of the school's students and implemented procedures for improved discipline, close teacher supervision, parental and community engagement, and the development of innovative programs with local professional and community organizations. Like Alton Rison in New York City, Winegar's administration emphasized the school's responsibility and accountability to provide effective education to urban children in need. Both took the approach that inner-city communities required proactive and responsive leadership that moved beyond the politics of race and that focused on reorganizing the school to more effectively address the pressing needs of urban children. "When a child does not profit from—or even respond to—an institution, we must challenge the institution, not the child," argued Winegar, who with his staff studied educational theory and developed a ten-point guiding philosophy that included the importance of small schools and personal relations, a commitment to racial equity, a priority of teaching basic literacy, the significance of applying academic study to work in the real world, and the belief that all children can learn. The tenth point reflected Winegar's insistence on organizational change as the heart of educational change: "we believe that no change will occur in urban schools without change at the administrative level." Winegar stayed as principal at South Boston High School for thirteen years.[28]

Ironically, although racial equity advocates often considered the principal the leading edge of desegregation, in many cities, principals were excluded from federally mandated faculty and staff desegregation plans that were designed under the argument that fully integrated schools had racially integrated staff as well as students.[29] In Atlanta, for example, the city's 1970 staff desegregation plan included random assignment of teachers to schools to reach the court-designated ratio of 57 percent black and 43 percent white staff, except in the case of principals, administrative assistants, and special teachers; instead, special effort was made to keep principals at their current school.[30] Even in Chicago, the only major American city where principals were also included in faculty desegregation plans, principals were included in the planning for transferring teachers, thereby implicating principals in the court ruling even as they were subject to it.[31] A principal's protection by the court could lead to antagonism by the community, particularly as the principal was looked to as a symbol of the school's level of acceptance of court orders and community values.

In their identification as the point person of racial change in a community, principals could also be the first victim of racist backlashes to desegregation. On April 3, 1971, R. Wiley Brownlee, the white principal of Willow Run High School in Ypsilanti Michigan, was kidnapped at gunpoint, tarred, and feathered by members of the Ku Klux Klan. In his six months as principal, Brownlee had publicly supported the school busing plan for desegregation. The story was reported widely around the country publicizing for both defenders and critics the potential risks of leading racial desegregation in schools.[32]

CIVIL RIGHTS, SELF-DETERMINATION, AND SCHOOL LEADERSHIP

In addition to the legal fight to desegregate schools, civil rights initiatives in education through the 1970s focused on opening enrollment and changing curriculum, teacher practices, and school policies. Central to all of these political movements was the identity and role of the school principal. Civil rights activists believed that the principal held the technical power to make or break initiatives in schools, and they also recognized the symbolic power of the principal's identity. In multiple civil rights cases across the country in the 1960s and '70s, the racial identity of the principal became a powerful symbol of political movements to change the education of minority youth.

In the late 1960s, Chicano high school students across the nation organized to change the culture and practices at local schools. The movement

Figure 13. L.A. principal blowout. Man in the middle: Principal Reginald Murphy addressing students during student "blowout," Garfield High School, Los Angeles, California, March 7, 1968. Courtesy of the Los Angeles Public Library Collection.

was sparked in March 1968 in student "blowouts" in five predominantly Mexican American high schools in East Los Angeles, where thousands of students led a week-and-a-half-long strike, demanding more Mexican American teachers and principals and the introduction of classes on Mexican American history and literature. The school administration received particular criticism from the student strikers, who claimed that high school principals, well over 95 percent of whom were white, were authoritarian and ignorant of Chicano students' needs and culture.[33] Later student and community strikes in Colorado and Texas were the result of a culmination of grievances about the abuse of Chicano students and the marginalization of Chicano culture in the school curriculum, academic practices, and extracurricular activities. Central to students' demands was the appointment of Chicano administrators who, students argued, would better represent and understand the concerns of Chicano students.[34]

In Chicago in the late 1960s, civil rights activism centered on the ouster of white principals from several predominantly black schools. Black activists in Chicago continually argued that it was white leadership that kept their children from quality education, as parents and students reported racist attitudes and behaviors emanating from both the principal's office and the teachers' classrooms under the principal's purview. In 1965, Chicago parents organized to remove the white principal, Mildred Chuchut, from her position at the predominantly black Jenner Elementary School. Through the fall of 1965 and the winter of 1966, parent and student boycotts and protest rallies sought to oust the principal, leading the Chicago Board of Education to hold a closed-door session on the issue in late January. In February, Dr. Martin Luther King Jr. spoke at a Chicago rally in support of the campaign, declaring that while the struggle over the principal at Jenner School "is but a single and bitter example of the system's insensitivity and failure to educate, it is but one thread in a vast fabric of educational and administrative inadequacy, that is woven about this entire city."[35] Similar parent and student public demonstrations and boycotts led to the replacement of dozens of white principals at other predominantly black schools over the next few years in Chicago.[36] A decade later, the Chicago *Tribune* ran a six-article series on the continuing debate over community control and the ouster or transfer of principals due to community protest. Proposed in the article was that it was now principals' civil rights that were being violated when the Board of Education made personnel decisions based on "the loudness and the tenacity of small segments of the community."[37] That the author of the series, Mark Krug, was a white education professor at the elite University of Chicago who was active in the Zionist Organization of Chicago certainly did not temper the ongoing debate over race and civil rights.

The most intransigent schools misread or flatly denied the seriousness of civil rights claims. Many school boards refused to hire black principals out of concern that they would be seen as having abdicated to political pressure. Others dismissed the minority community's calls for the hiring of minority principals and teachers of color as simply a "symbol for the discontent parents feel about the entire system."[38] School administrators blamed students of color for disrupting what they saw as beneficial order, and they blamed social unrest on outside agitators. From an older generation, trained in traditional models of professional leadership, many white principals were oblivious to the urgency and breadth of student and community claims and responded with either inappropriate informality, bad timing, or severity. Administrators often reduced civil rights demands for participation in school governance as disrespectful and ignorant challenges to their own professional authority.

All of these inept responses were played out in school administrators' responses to African American student protests at East High School in Waterloo, Iowa in 1968. In spite of the fact that for over a year, the city's black community had publicly complained about the absence of racial balance in schools, housing, and employment, and that black students at

East High School had taken a lead in creating peaceful memorial events in response to the assassination of Dr. Martin Luther King Jr. the previous spring, white school administrators remained dismissive of black students' concerns at the school. In August 1968, when two black students presented a list of grievances to Principal Lawrence Garlock, they were all but dismissed and told that a faculty group would review the grievances later in the school year. Garlock and his superiors continued their flat-footed responses through the increasingly tense fall: they cancelled classes when they feared student protests, alerted the local police about potential trouble, and set a harsh disciplinary policy directed at student activists that essentially criminalized organized student protest. Simultaneously, school administrators assured students that their concerns would be met by following "established procedures such as the student organizations and the administration."[39] Principal Garlock made a habit of addressing the black students' behavior as deviant: he denied one of the core student demands for the creation of a black student union because he could not permit "a racially segregated club," and at an all-school assembly, he characterized students' protest activities as a "lack of normal behavior." He cancelled an interracial curriculum committee meeting of community and school members out of concern that it would provide black students the opportunity to protest. Most tellingly, Garlock and his district administrators adapted the suspension of one of the protesting students to an assignment of eighteen hours of observing the school administration at work, in order that "she may better understand the duties and responsibilities of the administration and faculty."[40]

For black students and community members who demanded not only changes in curriculum and personnel, but also in the overall culture and decision-making processes in schools, this principal represented the worst of outdated professional values that ignored the contemporary context of culturally conscious activism. As Waterloo's black parents wrote to the school administration in support of their children the following spring, students should be allowed to participate in decision making in the school, instead of being told "to go through the legal channels" only to have those legal channels ignored.[41]

The most notoriously divisive case of racial conflict in the principal's office occurred in the New York City district of Ocean Hill–Brownsville in 1968. Like many cities, New York City had centralized its school managerial control earlier in the century, but by the 1960s, the increasing size and diversity of city communities had led to conflict over racial, ethnic, and cultural values in school management. In 1967, black and Latino community groups fought to decentralize New York City school management so that they might have more control over staffing and curriculum in their local schools. The school board relented with the establishment of three experimental districts to be led by a locally elected community school board, which was given authority over the hiring, placement, and retention of teachers and administrators. In the experimental district in the Brooklyn neighborhood of Ocean Hill–Brownsville, the community board representing the predominantly black working-class neighborhood immediately came into conflict with the predominantly white, Jewish middle-class teachers and administrators, represented by the newly formed United Teachers Federation (UFT). When the new community school board tried to transfer out some white teachers and administrators whom the community saw as racially intolerant, the UFT objected, citing its contract with the central board that prohibited such transfers without just cause and due process.[42] In protest, the UFT led a strike in the fall of 1968 that shut down the entire city school system for months.

Central to the Ocean Hill–Brownsville conflict was the role of the principal. Of the six hundred licensed elementary principals in New York City at the time, only five were black and none were Puerto Rican, a rate even worse than the teaching staff where 13 percent were black or Latino. And while two-thirds of the city's white teachers were Jewish, a full 90 percent of administrators were Jewish.[43] Black community leaders objected to the city's arduous examination and appointment process for principals, arguing that such tests were prejudiced against black educators, and they argued that school leadership should be chosen by the community, not professionals in faraway offices. That one-third of the city's temporarily appointed "acting principals" were black and Latino educators without administrative licenses proved the point that it was the examination process—not the quality of the applicant—that kept minority educators from administrative roles.[44]

The conflict over the racial identity of the school leader was not unique to the Ocean Hill–Brownsville district. Two years earlier, when black and Puerto Rican enrollments in New York City schools had passed 50 percent, some city communities had organized civil rights campaigns to end overcrowded and understaffed schools in the poorest city neighborhoods and de facto segregated schools.[45] Such locally oriented groups played a role in the creation of a new junior high school, IS 201, scheduled to open in East Harlem in the fall of 1966. For years, black community leaders and parents, organized in an ad hoc parents' council, had lobbied for the school, arguing with the school board over a plan for racially balanced enrollment, the name of the school, the level of community participation in school management, and finally, and most explosively, the principal. Following its usual procedure, the board reviewed their administrative eligibility lists and chose Stanley Lisser, a white Jewish principal who previously had worked in Harlem schools. Lisser handpicked the staff, which was almost equally white and black, and chose a black woman as assistant principal. But the parents' council objected to the board appointment of a white principal and organized a boycott to pressure the board to transfer Lisser out. The teachers, emboldened by the UFT, reacted with their own boycott and picketed the headquarters of the Board of Education with signs that read "All of us or none of us" and "Should principals be ousted because they are not black?" In the fray, race, gender, and professional loyalties became entangled. Black teachers in IS 201 defended Lisser, and the black female assistant principal refused to take over the principal's office, objecting to being selected on the basis of "color, not competence." In turn, the parents' council and local black groups ridiculed the black teachers as "color-blind" sellouts who were bought out by the UFT against their community interests. As Lisser maintained the principalship, the parents' council intensified its call for "a Negro or Puerto Rican male heading the school."[46]

Across the country, self-determination and independence movements in schools often started through the appointment of a principal from the petitioning group. Rough Rock Elementary School in Arizona opened in 1966 as the first American Indian–controlled school. After almost one hundred years of Anglo control of Native schools, Rough Rock was founded by Navajo leaders who applied for funding from the Federal Economic Opportunity Act for demonstration projects in poverty areas. Rough Rock was the first school to have an all-Navajo governing board and the first to teach Navajo native language and culture. Central to the organization of the school was the intentional creation of an administrative entity that was separate from the Federal Bureau of Indian Affairs. In 1969, the Navajo board appointed as director Navajo educator Dillon Platero, and in so doing, Navajo people claimed they had "taken the final step in achieving control and direction over their own education."[47] Teaching cultural curriculum was one thing; the appointment of Platero made public the faith that Native people could run their own schools.

Other Native American communities in the 1960s and '70s, too, saw the appointment of Native school teachers and administrators as a central component of their movement to replace the century-old white-controlled education of assimilation with education for Native cultural and political autonomy. Studies in the late 1960s connected the high dropout rates and low achievement levels of Native children in federally controlled schools to the absence of Native educators: One 1969 report found that only 1 percent of Native children in elementary schools had Native teachers or principals. The activism of the American Indian Movement in the early 1970s inspired a number of Native student protests, including the 1972 student walkout at Window Rock High School in Ft. Defiance, Arizona, where Navajo students protested the lack of Native American recognition and coursework. The walkout led to the election of Native Americans to the school board and the hiring of the first Native American superintendent and principal.[48] Recognizing the need for Native leadership, in the early 1970s some universities began educational leadership programs for Native American administrators and guidance counselors.[49] Such leadership was particularly essential after the passage of the federal Indian Self-Determination and Education Assistance Act in 1975, which enabled tribes and other Native communities to operate their own schools and other social services.[50]

So, too, in San Luis, Colorado in the 1950s was the leadership of a principal from the local Hispanic culture interpreted as the cornerstone of community autonomy. San Luis was a community that was historically controlled by Hispanics, although because it had no high school, its students had to travel to neighboring white communities for their secondary education. In 1953, Hispanic residents created their own high school, which by 1960 had 242 students, mostly Hispanic; 10 teachers, half of whom were Hispanic; and a Hispanic principal and assistant principal. Principal Abie Duarte agreed with many in the community that Hispanic youth performed well at the school because so many of the educators at the school—teachers, administrators, and school board members—were Hispanic. Speaking about both students and educators, Duarte asserted that at his school "there was no one here to put us down." Hispanic school leadership both set the tone and policies and acted as a symbolic figurehead for the community, allowing students and parents to feel comfortable, respected, and full of pride.[51]

The leadership of Marcus Foster, African American principal in Philadelphia in the 1960s, is a good example of how the self-determination of minority communities intersected with the movement for school leaders to take an assertive role in student achievement. Born and raised in Philadelphia and educated in predominately black schools and colleges, Foster infused the message of "racial uplift" that dominated black educational thought at the time. Foster incorporated this commitment to high achievement and character development into his educational philosophy that black youth needed to "intellectualize their everyday lives. . . . and in so doing build up their self-esteem and curiosity."[52]

As school principal in Philadelphia in the 1950s and '60s, Foster worked in the context of the Great Society federal reforms and civil rights agenda, carefully walking the line between contemporary debates on the role of the school in achieving racial equity, the structure of the black family, and the responsibility of society to address racism. Foster insisted on the school's responsibility to overcome class and racial inequities, but he also demanded that government and society make a greater commitment to improving urban education. Foster's emphasis was always on the intellectual and personal growth of his students; he emphasized personal academic achievement above all else, folding social and cultural reform initiatives and community engagement into his educational programming. Epitomizing this work was Foster's creation of "storefront schools," created as a response to the alienation of the modern school and principal's office. To gain access to his office, he once wryly commented, "you had to come up the marble staircase, past the Winged Victory standing there ominously, through twelve secretaries out in the outer pool, and there I was back in the inner sanctum, cogitating." In contrast, the storefront school was a place where community members, pregnant teenagers who were excluded from school, parents, guardians, and dropouts had full access by simply walking in off the street.[53]

Recognizing the enormous pressures against his students, Foster's leadership strategy was that "a school is like a piece of delicate machinery: when it doesn't work, the last thing you want to do is force it. What's needed is some careful investigation followed by some gently, if profound, retooling."[54] With this philosophy, Foster negotiated through often conflicting demands and constituencies, including an emerging black power movement. The results were dramatic: A colleague of Foster's described how he had made "a garden in the middle of bleakness . . . there was color, there was light" in the form of student work, community volunteers, engaged staff, and collaboration.[55]

Foster's strength, and ultimately his lesson for contemporary educators, was in the melding of diverging civil rights agendas in response to the urban crisis of schooling: he used motivational and compensatory education programs long advocated by white liberals while simultaneously emphasizing academic excellence that black parents had long demanded of public schools. According to Foster, urban schools needed to be accountable to the public: "Inner-city folks . . . want people in there who can get the job done, who get youngsters learning *no matter what it takes*. They won't be interested in beautiful theories that explain why the task is impossible. The people believe that the job can be done. And they want it done now."[56]

Later, as superintendent of schools in Oakland, California, Foster enacted his belief in parental and student engagement in schools by establishing committees of parents, teachers, and students to recommend the appointment of new principals to the superintendent, who would make the final hiring decision. To Foster, the strategy for resolving conflicts—including racial conflict—was to incorporate all participants into the local decision making of significant issues in order to address the concerns of the community and to build a culture of trust. Such community engagement and advocacy through networking, partnering, and negotiating became a central part of successful principals' work, particularly for principals of color in urban school districts. For example, Gertrude Williams, principal of the racially integrated Barclay School in inner-city Baltimore from 1973 to 1998, believed that the job of the principal was to make the school central to the community, or as she put it, to make Barclay "everybody's business."[57]

Central to these principals' strategies was to draw on federal educational enrichment programs of the late 1960s and early 1970s that were designed to ease racial segregation in schools by providing educational enrichment and community engagement. In Dayton, Ohio, for example, elementary principal Gregory Caras enhanced his overcrowded inner-city school with the support of federal funding to hire extra teaching aids and develop special services and curricular programming. Caras publically promoted his school's new programs, welcoming parents into the school and expanding the school curriculum. As the school's record became public, white teachers were more willing to accept transfers to Longfellow Elementary under the city's faculty desegregation order.[58] By the end of the 1970s, the negotiation of federal engagement in, regulation of, and funding for public education had become a critical piece of principals' work.

Figure 14. Principal Marcus Foster and students cleaning a storefront school, circa 1966. Courtesy of Special Collections Research Center, Temple University Libraries, Philadelphia, Pennsylvania.

CONCLUSION

Civil rights initiatives, including school desegregation, impacted principals in a variety of ways. For black principals in the South, school desegregation led to the wholesale closure of black schools and the loss of their leadership positions. Black principals bore the burden of such change, sacrificing their own professional roles for the greater good of school integration. Yet the social and political change occasioned by the civil rights movement brought other educators of color the opportunity to lead and represent their community, although they also faced the challenges of leading in the context of conflicted communities, established bureaucratic systems, and the highly charged racial climate of the late 1960s and early 1970s.

The racial integration of schools was only one reform objective of civil rights advocates. As important as the end of segregated school buildings was to people of color, the recognition and support of minority cultures in schools and a change in the dominant structure and attitude of schools was equally important. After the initial struggle for racial integration was over, white and black principals alike wrestled with the dynamics of changing culture in their schools, as articulated by activist students, parents, and community groups.

The most effective of these school leaders did not see desegregation as the main problem of the principal's office. Indeed, as principals, they were excluded from most of the policy making, legal maneuvering, and bureaucratic management of desegregation orders—work that fell mostly to superintendents, school boards, and governmental officials who received and managed, or tried to avoid, court orders and decrees. These principals took as their charge the improvement of learning for the children in their schools, focusing on instituting rigorous and innovative curricula and developing positive educational links with the local community and parents. In this work, they echoed the "culturally responsive" educators described in chapter 3, as well as generations of principals who negotiated their leadership between the intersecting and often conflicting demands of bureaucratic requirements and educational objectives. Supported by federal funding that was designed to ease the political strains of desegregation, the best principals developed small pockets of light in otherwise economically devastated inner-city school districts, yet often at great personal cost. With the loss of much of those federal compensatory funding programs and racial integration initiatives in the increasingly conservative late 1970s and 1980s, and the further economic decline of inner cities, these pockets of light became increasingly rare. Furthermore, by the mid-1980s, principals' attention had been turned from the challenge of achieving equity in schools to alignment with new state and federal demands for accounting for students' academic achievement.

CHAPTER SIX

INSTRUCTIONAL LEADERS IN
HIGH-STAKES SCHOOLS

In a high-poverty elementary school in Annapolis, Maryland in the 2005–2006 academic year, principal Tina McKnight oriented the bulk of her attention to supervising teachers in a highly scripted math and reading curriculum required by the district. When McKnight started her position at the school five years earlier, less than 20 percent of students performed satisfactorily on the state exam, the lowest performance in the county. McKnight developed a strategy of what she called "laser-sharp focus" toward improving student test scores. With the support of a new superintendent, she introduced extra reading and math instruction, special attention to failing students, and programs to teach testing strategies to students, including a set formula for crafting written responses. By cutting back on all activities that did not directly relate to the tests—field trips, talent shows, career days—McKnight directed her teachers and students to focus entirely on the state tests in the spring. In the process, the school became more orderly, with a collective culture and a common vocabulary aimed toward the test. After one year of this intensive and rigid structure, the school achieved what one local newspaper called a "minor miracle" with over 70 percent passing scores in reading and math across the school. Principal McKnight became a finalist for county principal of the year, and the school's success was broadcast widely.[1]

Principal McKnight recognized both the limitations and the possibilities of improving test scores. The state tests were, she said, "just the bottom of what kids should know," and her hope was that preparation for the tests would provide students with the skills and motivation to learn more, as well as initiate a revived public faith in the school. She empathized with her teachers that the increase in reading and math scores happened at the expense of science experiments, group social studies activities, learning

131

games, and topics that were not on the test. She admitted that she did not always like the curriculum plans that she rallied her teachers to follow, and that even though students learned to pass a written test, they had not really learned to write.

But the principal's job was to raise test scores, and that she did, even at her own expense. At fifty-six years old, Tina McKnight lived alone, worked constantly, and ignored her own health. She gave up her season tickets to the theater, took no vacation days, and struggled to find time to care for her aging mother and to emotionally support her adult son in medical school. Working without an assistant principal, she usually stayed at school past ten o'clock on weeknights and weekends. As an African American woman, Principal McKnight felt a special passion for her students at Tyler Heights Elementary School, most of whom were black, Hispanic, or non-English-speaking youth who lived below the poverty level. "I'm a realist," McKnight told her teachers, as she urged them in their work of preparing students for the required test, even as she publicly expressed her concern about the unintended consequences and constrained expectations of students that the test preparation involved.[2]

In an inner-city Philadelphia high school the following year, another principal faced similar challenges but came to the job with less leadership skills and a more antagonistic work environment. In a school racked by poverty and violence, the principal was hired only weeks before school started and faced rebellious students, untrained teachers, and a district leadership that threatened her with dismissal if she did not improve test scores. A white woman in a predominantly Hispanic school, she was the only white principal among the neighborhood schools, which kept her personally and professionally isolated in her district. Within her school, she was disliked by teachers who resented her pressure to pass all students in order to raise the school's ranking. As principal, she was responsible for the testing outcomes of her school, but had no input in the design or implementation of the tests, could not hire or fire her own staff, and had no financial rewards at her disposal.[3]

School principals after the early 1980s faced many of the similar types of challenges as earlier school heads, in addition to unique working conditions brought on by waves of educational reforms that placed principals in the middle of a number of paradoxical positions. The reforms were driven by an intensifying national concern about what was billed as a "crisis" in schools, represented by American school children's poor performance on standardized tests and ongoing social anxiety about youth both inside and outside schools. Political and educational leaders channeled this public concern into schoolwide assessments that included the identification of targeted outcomes, data reports, and gradated steps of rewards and punishments for individual schools.[4] These assessments were intended to hold schools accountable to the public who supported them, with specific repercussions for those schools and personnel that did not achieve the stated goals. The delineation of consequences for failure led the later reforms to be identified as "high-stakes testing."

Public schools after the 1980s were also subject to new state and federal programs that introduced elements of free-market competition into public education. These policy initiatives, collectively known as "school choice," included school vouchers, tuition tax credits, charter schools, and public school open enrollment policies. Public financing of private education through tuition tax credits was first developed by Southern whites in the 1950s and '60s who sought methods of avoiding court-ordered desegregation by providing public funding for private, racially segregated education. Across the country in subsequent years, school choice policies developed as part of an effort to free schools from bureaucratic regulations, particularly the liberal federal provisions enacted in the 1960s and '70s. Driving this wide range of reforms, which included tuition vouchers, charter schools, district and mayoral takeover of schools, school-based management, and the creation of alternative and small schools, was the theory that the large bureaucracy of public school systems strangled individual educational initiatives in a maze of regulations that restricted parental and student options. According to its advocates, such market-based incentives would infuse a competitive spirit into public schooling and encourage better performance by all educators, thus changing public education "from a provider-driven system to a consumer-driven one."[5]

School choice policies in the 1970s and '80s attracted a broad collection of supporters, including black parents who objected to the economic and academic decline of urban public schooling, religious educators, advocates for school decentralization, and alternative community school advocates. Supported by political figures who saw school choice as a method of reversing federal social welfare involvement in schools, the school choice movement reach one milestone in 1990 with the legislative approval of the Milwaukee Parental Choice program, sponsored by that city's black community that sought relief from the poor academic performance of their city schools. A second milestone was reached in 2002 with the U.S. Supreme Court approval of the application of public voucher funds to religious schools in Cleveland, Ohio.[6] Charter school legislation allowed for the creation of publicly funded schools that were free from some of the rules, regulations, and statutes that applied to other public schools; in 1991, Minnesota became the first state to pass a law to authorize the creation of charter schools. By fall 2001, there were 2,300 charter schools in the United States; that number more than doubled within five years.[7]

This collective array of reforms presented school principals with contradictory directives. Under standardized assessment programs, principals were required to follow rigid guidelines in student testing and school management. At the same time, school choice initiatives required principals to act as innovative and entrepreneurial agents in an increasingly competitive environment. These contradictory, often mutually opposing expectations were added to principal's ongoing work of mediating educational, legal, fiscal, and cultural dynamics. Located in the middle of a swirling high-stakes work environment, modern principals learned how to be even better jugglers than their predecessors.[8]

EFFECTIVE SCHOOLS, INSTRUCTIONAL LEADERSHIP, AND TRANSFORMATIONAL LEADERSHIP

The educational reform movements that began in the 1980s drew on newly articulated understandings that schools were complex organizations in need of complex leadership strategies. Effective schools, the new research showed, were learning organizations led by principals who were effective in leading instruction. The notion of principals as instructional leaders was not completely new: In 1953, the curriculum scholar Ralph Tyler called for the principal to take on the responsibility of establishing educational objectives and continually evaluating student performance.[9] Going against the grain of the popular emphasis on principals as managerial leaders, Tyler argued that school leaders needed to focus less on administration and more on improving curriculum and instruction.

The changing demography, politics, and economics of schooling in the 1970s furthered the momentum for principals to focus on instruction, particularly in underperforming urban schools. In the 1970s, a body of empirical studies referred to as Effective Schools research concluded that strong administrative leadership was among a number of factors that had an impact on student learning. Researchers paid particular attention to the leadership of the school principal who, it was argued, played a critical role in the organizational culture of the school. Exploring the links between principals' behavior and students' academic performance, the Effective Schools research introduced a notion of the principal who was not a bureaucratic administrator who managed technical tasks but an educational leader who served as a resource for teachers and developed an organizational culture of high expectations.[10] The principal in such schools, argued one of the movement's leading researchers, Ron Edmonds, was "an instructional leader, more assertive in his or her institutional leadership role who assumed responsibilities for the evaluation of achievements of basic objectives."[11] Effective principals were responsible for communicating vision and goals, building school climate and culture, and organizing the school around instruction.

Many of these studies of the 1970s and '80s were later critiqued for their weak data analysis methods and the simplicity of the popular "principal principle"—that a strong principal could make all the difference.[12] Nonetheless, the Effective Schools research was a turning point in focusing school reformers' attention to the impact of principals' leadership on student learning. For the first time, empirical evidence identified the principal as a central player in student achievement, and the momentum of this research continued for subsequent decades.

Educators' attention to the organizational complexities of schools furthered their understanding of the pivotal role of the principal in school improvement. By the 1970s, educational researchers no longer conceived of schools as bureaucratic factory-like organizations where every piece had a function, but rather as "loosely coupled" organizations that were highly influenced by and context dependent on multiple players.[13] This understanding of school culture furthered the call for the principal to be a generative force who was adaptive in the complex work of instructional leadership. School principals should be "transformative" in that they should be able to mobilize schools and their communities toward creating a learning culture of shared values around high expectations for student learning.[14] Rather than focusing specifically on direct coordination, control, and supervision, transformational leaders were expected to motivate the school's innovative capacity.

ACCOUNTABILITY, STANDARDS, AND THE SCHOOL LEADER

The emphasis of school leaders' impact on schools came at a time of increasing scrutiny on the value and quality of public schooling, both in urban districts that became increasing crippled by the postwar phenomenon of "white flight" and economic decline and in expanding middle-class suburban school districts. The link between school expenditures and student performance translated into a new word—accountability. President Nixon first introduced the term to educational policy makers in 1970, arguing that educators should not only be *responsible* for performing their work well, but also *accountable* to their students and taxpaying communities. To hold educators accountable, districts began to design performance objectives and assessments of students, educators, and the school organization.[15]

The new economic and political context of public education in the late 1970s and early 1980s accelerated the public's interest in accountability

measures. By the mid-1970s, the postwar baby boom was over, leading to
a significant drop in public school enrollments. In Fairfax County, Virginia, outside of Washington, D.C., for example, school district enrollment
dropped 16 percent between the 1974–1975 and the 1982–1983 academic
years. Simultaneously, school districts experienced tightening budgets due to
a number of factors including the national economic recession of the mid-
1970s, higher energy and fuel prices, economic inflation, and heightened
demands of unionized school workers. Also impacting school budgets was
the gradual decrease of federal funding—from a high of almost 10 percent of
public school revenue in 1980 to 6.1 percent ten years later—and the gradual enactment of largely unfunded federal policies for the support of bilingual
education, special education, and antipoverty programs, first initiated in the
1960s and early '70s.[16] As school districts struggled to cover costs by raising
local school funds, taxpayers paid increasing attention to school quality in
their residential choices, spurring the real estate industry to promote newly
available school performance indicators as part of their advertising drives.
Whereas in the early 1970s, school test scores were largely inaccessible
to the public, by the late 1980s, school performance data were publicized
widely by education officials as a requirement of educational accountability
policies, and by real estate agents who identified the quality of schools as
a variable for potential homeowners.[17]

The explosive release of the federal report *A Nation at Risk* in 1983
occurred in this context. Written by the National Commission on Excellence in Education under President Reagan's secretary of education, *A Nation
at Risk* was a response to a perceived decline in American students' academic
performance. The report described the problem with more heat than light,
asserting in alarmist rhetoric that "the educational foundations of our society are presently being eroded by a rising tide of mediocrity that threatens
our very future as a nation and a people." The report linked the nation's
educational record with national security, claiming that the United States
had been "committing an act of unthinking, unilateral educational disarma-
ment" with its mediocre academic performance. To address these problems,
the report recommended "high expectations and disciplined effort needed
to attain them" through a renewed emphasis on curricular and teaching
standards. The report effectively shifted the impetus of federal legislation
in schools from civil rights to the monitoring of K-12 school performance.[18]

A Nation at Risk set a reform fire under educational policy makers.
Between 1983 and 1990, every American president and almost every state
established a task force to raise educational standards in schools and to
devise methods of assessment and enforcement. The question of how to
evaluate student performance on these standards was quickly reduced to
clearly measurable assessments on standardized tests that could provide pub-

lic access to school performance. This initiative was ultimately formalized at a national level in the 2001 reauthorization of the federal Elementary and Secondary Education Act, entitled "No Child Left Behind," which required a raft of measurement templates for different levels of performance of local schools. What came to be called "high-stakes accountability" reform elements referred to delineated consequences for schools in which students persistently failed or underperformed on standardized tests. Schools were required to issue annual "report cards" on students' test performance and graduation rates, teachers' qualifications, and other school managerial practices; schools that consistently performed poorly could suffer decreased funding, the loss of students, and ultimately school closure. The laws' advocates argued that such competitive measures would force schools to improve their performance. Critics argued that the punitive measures further undercut troubled schools and strangled educators in more bureaucracy, and that standardized testing was not an effective measure of teacher or student performance. Critics also argued that such "high-stakes testing" was based on the assumption that failing schools were the result of ineffective educators, not children's broader social and economic handicaps or schools' economic and structural deficits.[19]

Nonetheless, under the No Child Left Behind Act of 2001, testing became "the crucial hinge" on which turned "the fate of students and the reputations and futures of their teachers, principals, and schools."[20] While the emphasis on educational accountability by standardized testing was most notably directed at teachers whose responsibility it was to prepare their students for tests, principals were responsible for the performance of the entire school, and many responded to the new requirements by totally reorienting the school toward test preparation. As Principal Tina McKnight fully recognized, the worst case scenario of high-stakes testing—that educators could lose jobs and communities could lose schools—raised the stakes on principals' ability to prepare teachers to prepare students for standardized tests.

Accordingly, school district plans included the realignment of principals' work to respond to district, state, and federal directives. In New York City in 1987, for example, District Superintendent Anthony Alvarado introduced a districtwide literacy program that required all teachers and principals to focus on a specific instructional plan. District-appointed school coaches were required to make classroom "walk throughs" to make sure every teacher was using the district-approved methods. Such practices were reminiscent of the old supervisors, who extended the authoritative arm of the superintendent around the principal and into the school and prioritized district policy over local initiatives. Yet principals were also expected to be instructional leaders who reinvigorated schools' academic culture. As Superintendent Alvarado argued, principals "have to know what good teaching is, and they have to know what to do to improve instruction. If they can't do that, then they can't ultimately get better student achievement results."[21]

The work of the principal of a high-poverty elementary school in Alvarado's New York City district is a good example of how one school leader acted out this vision of weaving district requirements into a positive culture of the school. In the mid-1990s, Principal Marguerite Straus of PS 1, an elementary school of seven hundred largely Chinese immigrant students in the middle of New York's Chinatown, promoted the school as a learning community. Principal Straus' emphasis developed from her understanding of the school as an organization in which everything from the most routine administrative work to classroom décor was developed with the consideration of how it would impact the learning environment of the school. Straus instituted teacher teams that studied student work and developed literacy practices for students with limited English proficiency. Over time, with ongoing professional development and the hiring of new teachers, Straus reshaped the collective culture of the school organization around the district standards of literacy, creating consensus and common goals among staff. Adults served as models for student learning, emphasizing reading, engagement in cultural activities around the city, and collective problem solving. Teachers met regularly to plan curriculum and review student progress, and they engaged in continual reflection and collaboration on their work. The principal served as the generative engine of cultural change in the school, using her own individual leadership skills to achieve district goals.[22]

In the case of PS 1, district mandates were the carrot that led the internal reforms in the schools. Yet in other districts, such mandates served more as a stick, pushing principals, teachers, and communities to follow new requirements at the expense of students. Most notable among these cases took place in Houston, Texas in the late 1990s and early 2000s. Under the 1994 Texas Assessment of Academic Skills program, student test scores had risen and dropout rates had declined, earning national recognition for Texas and its governor, George W. Bush, who used the results as part of his successful presidential bid in 2000. In 2003, the Houston school district reported a dropout rate for Hispanic students of only 1.2 percent, when the national dropout rate for Hispanic students typically ranged from 10 percent to as high as 60 percent. At Houston's Sharpstown High School, which served many low-income students of color, the reported dropout rate was zero. Sharpstown's assistant principal, Robert Kimball, a former dropout himself, suspected that school administrators were pushing lower-performing students out of school before they dropped out, thus artificially keeping dropout rates low. When senior administrators ignored his complaint, Kimball contacted the media, and the district eventually confirmed that the miraculous dropout rates were faked. Kimball risked his career by blowing the whistle on the

"Texas Miracle"; he was removed from his duties as a high school assistant principal and placed in a windowless room for four months with no duties, then reassigned to small primary schools where his salary was reduced.[23]

The unmasking of the "Texas Miracle" revealed that under the culture of accountability, school principals, like the students taking the tests and the teachers administering the tests, were experiencing their own version of high-stakes testing. School leaders who had previously been evaluated along a range of indicators that represented the complexity of their job were now being measured solely on their school's performance along a narrow spectrum of activities.[24] The Texas debacle foreshadowed subsequent episodes of school administrators manipulating school data, fixing student test results, and punishing whistle-blowers in order to reach their accountability goals and thereby avoid repercussions.

Whatever the impact, the significance of standards-based reforms for principals was that it was a district initiative, assigned to principals to implement. The role of the school principal was to apply and connect the district initiative to the classroom. It was the principal who connected the district plan with students; it was also the principal who felt the consequences of failure.

SCHOOL RESTRUCTURING AND THE PRINCIPAL

Accompanying school reform initiatives for the standardized assessments of student performance was the introduction of structural changes in school funding, organization, and governance as part of the broad school choice movement. Most notable of these reforms were charter schools and voucher programs that diverted public funding to private schooling for the purpose of allowing more options in public education. Central to the promotion of school choice was a revised role of the principal as entrepreneurial leader. In their 1990 book that helped invigorate the modern school choice movement, John E. Chubb and Terry M. Moe argued that America's lowest-performing schools were for the large part headed by principals who acted like middle managers, focusing on the bureaucratic relations between the district and the school, and not on student performance.[25] Because under school choice policies students took their allocated school funding with them, principals needed to be proactive leaders, advocating for their schools in order to compete in the new educational marketplace.

Under market-based school reforms, the principal was both an educational leader and a business leader, promoting both the high achievement of students in order to reach district and state test goals and developing fiscal initiatives from local businesses and the community. All principals worked in a competitive environment where they fought for academically high-performing students at the same time that they tried to engage their entire community in the advancement of all students. For example, when appointed principal of a middle school in New York City in 2003, Ramón Gonzalez saw himself more as a community activist than a CEO, continually urging parents, community members, and local institutions to support his school and students. But Gonzalez also experienced the contradictions of the city's school reform initiatives. While he supported the increased independence he was given to shape his own school, he knew that the ultimate goal of his academic year was high results on the city and state tests. Furthermore, the city's promotion of competitive, market-based initiatives such as charter schools were pulling the strongest students in his community away from his school, leaving him with the academically weakest students.[26]

Other school restructuring efforts included state policies to reconstitute schools and districts that consistently failed standardized assessments in what came to be called "educational bankruptcy." The reconstitution process could and often did include the creation of a new curriculum and the firing of staff. The first state takeover of a school occurred in 1989 when New Jersey took over the Jersey City schools; by the year 2000, twenty-two states had laws authorizing state takeovers.[27] A related effort in urban districts was the small schools movement in which reformers argued that smaller organizational units would allow for more engaged teaching, enriched curriculum, family involvement, and improved working conditions for teachers and leaders. Beginning in the 1980s some school districts began to create smaller public schools, often by dividing larger schools into smaller groups within the same building.[28]

Across the nation, school choice and other restructuring reforms put principals under the same scrutiny as teachers in the review of students' test scores. Unlike most teachers with union contracts, however, principals could be fired or transferred if their school did not perform up to expectations, and districts under reform initiatives experienced significant principal turnover. Over the course of the eleven-year tenure of New York City's reformist district superintendent Alvarado, for example, two-thirds of the district principals and about half the teaching force were replaced.[29] In Atlanta and San Diego in the late 1990s, 90 percent of the city's principals were replaced.[30] In Dallas, annual principal turnover increased from 5 percent before a district reform initiative to 25 percent afterward.[31] Less clear was the extent to which principals were demoted, reassigned, or fired because they were deemed ineffective by the community or because they did not lead their school to increased test scores. Certainly one impact was that principals became less secure about their jobs and were more inclined to reorient their work toward assessment results and not the overall school quality that they themselves envisioned.[32]

The increased attention on the principal in school improvement was also operationalized in legislative policy. Between 1975 and 1990, state-mandated principal evaluations increased from nine to forty states.[33] Illinois State Bill 730, approved by that state's legislative body in 1985, is a good example. The bill required that the local Board of Education specify in their formal job descriptions for principals "that their primary responsibility is the improvement of instruction and that a majority of their time shall be spent on curriculum and staff development." Given the majority phrase, the law was commonly known as the 51 percent law.[34] The Massachusetts Education Reform Act of 1993 strengthened the superintendent's control over the appointment of educational personnel, especially principals who were prohibited from collective bargaining.[35] In Detroit, the 1999 Michigan Public Law 10 gave the superintendent the power to fire and hire teachers and principals and to waive union contracts in order to reconstitute failing schools.[36]

For principals, this collection of reform initiatives presented a series of contradictory messages. On one hand, accountability measures tied local school performance to the strict expectations of central agencies; on the other hand, reforms that promoted alternative governance were often predicated on a more autonomous and entrepreneurial school principal. This tension over principals' role in modern school reform remained unresolved in a parallel reform movement for local control of schools.

SHARED DECISION MAKING AND PRINCIPALS' AUTHORITY

In a number of large cities, the new consumer-driven model of public schooling emphasized local control as a response to the common critique that urban schools had become too bureaucratic to be responsive to communities. In these governance reorganization schemes, responsibility and decision making over school operations was transferred from district offices to principals, teachers, parents, and other school community members. Although billed as collaborative community ventures, many local control initiatives were designed along business models that emphasized independent entrepreneurial development.[37] Under such a model, explained one district leader, the school principal would be transformed "from an agent of the bureaucracy to a CEO of his or her school."[38] But free market capitalism only went so far in public school policy: Even though local control gave principals more autonomy, their schools were still monitored by district and state standardized assessments.

One of the most radical local control initiatives was Chicago's School Reform Act of 1988 in which democratically elected Local School Councils (LSC), comprised of a majority of parents and community members, had the authority to establish a school improvement plan and budget. One goal of the act was to break the often repressive and independent control of principals over their schools, and the LSC was authorized to hire and fire the principal, even while the principal sat on the LSC.[39] In 1995, teacher and principal unions successfully lobbied the mayor to take control over some aspects of local school councils' power over personnel, although LSCs retained the authority to hire and fire school principals.[40]

The positioning of the principal as a lightning rod in the struggle over control of schools came to a head in Chicago in spring 2007 when the LSC of Curie High School fired its longtime principal. Jerryelyn Jones had spent twenty-five years at Curie, one of the largest high schools in the city—twelve years as a teacher, five as an assistant principal, and eight as a principal. An African American woman, Jones led a school that was 65 percent Hispanic. The majority of the LSC was Hispanic, including the chair whom Jones had earlier accused of bribing a school vendor. At her contract renewal hearing before the LSC, all the Hispanic members of the LSC voted against rehiring Jones. The local press publicized the case as one of ethnic conflict, and the mayor called the firing "a national disgrace" and used it as part of his and the school board's effort to restrict LSC authority in the appointment of principals. Other community groups, including one progressive wing of the teacher union, accused the central board of manipulating the case in order to gain more authority over local schools.[41] Echoing earlier community conflicts over who controlled the appointment of the principal, the employment of this principal became a battleground for interest groups.

Principals' position in the local control movement had played out in a different scenario a decade earlier in Seattle. Retired military general John Stanford, who had been appointed superintendent in July 1995, led a school reform movement in which principals were given more discretion over their budgets, the selection of new teachers, and school-site professional development programs. Having assigned authority to principals, Stanford was then critiqued by the community for not reviewing them. In 1998, his third year as superintendent, Stanford had not fired one principal, and most principals had been evaluated only irregularly; one-third of all principals had not been evaluated at all. As city officials, parents, and teachers lobbied the superintendent to review and fire some principals, the superintendent's appointments and renewals of principals became powerful public symbols of his ability to exercise authority over the school bureaucracy.[42] Indeed, much of Stanford's initial popularity emanated from his identity as a former general and an outsider, who many hoped would come into the district and "clean house." Stanford himself recognized this attitude, noting that "Because I am a general, people wanted me to come in here and fire people"—which he resisted with his own leadership line of "love 'em and lead 'em."[43] After

Stanford's death in 1998, subsequent superintendents removed principals whose schools performed poorly on the state standardized tests.[44]

In Seattle as in other communities, popular initiatives to localize school control were tempered by public concerns about local principals' authority. Such tensions begged the larger question: Were school principals part of the local community or part of district administration?

Another form of local control was the development of teacher participation in school decision making. What was called the "new unionism" of the 1980s was a move away from the traditional adversarial industrial union focus on jobs and benefits and toward collaborative relationships between teachers and administrators.[45] Teachers' increased opportunity to participate in school decision making challenged the traditional authority structure in schools and often implied a critique of principals' capabilities.[46] Some of those critiques were explicit. For example, in Cincinnati's reforms of 1980s, a peer evaluation program gave teachers a supervisory role over their peers, because, as the Cincinnati teacher union president stated: "A principal of a modern school faces too many administrative tasks. . . . [and] schools are too large and teaching fields too specialized for a principal to provide the instructional leadership that is needed."[47]

In 1987, the Rochester Teachers' Association in upstate New York achieved a radical new contract: In exchange for higher salaries, teachers would address schools' declining academic performance by obtaining more control over their work through peer evaluation and school-based planning teams. Rochester's principals' legally challenged the teachers' union over what they saw as an infringement of their contractual rights and an attack on "the very heart of administrative functions." As the president of the Rochester school administration association stated it, many principals longed for the good old days before 1987 when "everyone knew his role."[48]

Common to all of these reform initiatives—from standardized accountability measures to the restructuring of school control—was the incentive-laden performance evaluation. The impact was that principals became more externally focused, paying attention to the rewards system and evaluations originating outside of the school more so than to professional and moral accountability.[49]

THE CRISIS IN THE PRINCIPAL'S OFFICE

As defined by A Nation at Risk in 1983 and No Child Left Behind eighteen years later, the popular narrative of the chronic failure of American schooling led to a crisis mentality in professional and popular representations of the school principal. In higher education and professional organizations, reformers renewed their critique of principal preparation programs as either too technical or too theoretical and as altogether ineffective and irrelevant to contemporary needs.[50] Many critiques of principal preparation programs adopted a language of sustained invective, using pejorative terms, contemptuous and derisive of educational leadership. All portrayed a sense of urgency and immediate crisis, that the problem was unprecedented and so deserved crisis management. For example, one 2005 study charged that American principal preparation programs ranged from "inadequate to appalling," citing low standards, weak faculty, poor research, and irrelevant and incoherent curriculum that collectively engaged in a "race to the bottom."[51] Another educator began his 2006 article in the popular *Phi Delta Kappan*: "it is no longer necessary to belabor the catastrophe that is the education, certification, and licensure of school leaders in the US."[52] All the reports relied on the undocumented and ahistorical assumption that there had been glory decades of effective leadership preparation sometime in the past, although significantly, none of the studies offered any empirical correlation between principal preparation programs and improved student achievement.[53]

In the 1990s, some school districts established their own principal preparation programs in which district leaders identified promising teachers and paid full or partial tuition for a program that was designed jointly by the district and a university. This model of "homegrown leadership" developed widely thereafter, the argument being that such embedded leadership training better prepared principals for the specific roles of the district. Later iterations of these alternative programs were nonprofit "leadership academies" established by a combination of educators and business leaders.[54]

More critical than the cry to change the quality of principal preparation programs was the need to attract more applicants to the principalship. Through the 1990s, school districts reported a shortage in the labor pool for open elementary and secondary principal positions due to declining interest in the profession that was known for its high stress, low compensation, and extended work hours.[55] In the early 2000s, 20 percent of all principals left their jobs each year, and more than half of all principals had less than four years' experience on the job.[56]

The numerical shortage was worsened by a scarcity of women and people of color in the principal's office in a time period when the number of students of color was increasing. The need was especially great in cities: In the early 1960s, over 50 percent of Philadelphia's students were African American, but only 18 out of 145 principals, or 7.5 percent, were black. In Detroit, 57 percent of student enrollment was black, and only 6 percent of school principals were black. In New York City in 1965, only three of the full-time principals were black, and in Newark, New Jersey, there were no black principals in 1967.[57] Organized recruitment led to some increases in black principals in northern cities, although even in 1994, less than 10 percent of all principals were African American, and only 4 percent were Hispanic at a time when students of color constituted a majority of enrollment in urban public school systems. In 1990, only 14 percent of all public schools with high Native American enrollment had a Native American principal.[58]

Women also remained a minority in school administration, even in the elementary principalship, which women had dominated well through World War II. In the early 1970s only 20 percent of elementary principals and 3 percent of high school principals were women. By the 1990s, women's presence had increased to 30 percent of elementary principalships and 10 percent of high school principalships, even though women remained over three-fourths of all teaching staff.[59] Furthermore, upon their first appointment, all women principals were older and had more experience than their male peers, indicating a tendency for districts to "fast track" male applicants into school administration.[60]

There were good reasons why educators were turning away from the principalship. Principals complained about insufficient compensation and too much stress and time demands, including an average sixty hours a week spent on administrative duties, followed by attendance at student programs and special events. Principals also noted how the intensifying demands for high-stakes accountability policies further complicated their jobs.[61]

IMAGES OF THE PRINCIPAL AT RISK

Nor did popular culture portray an attractive image of the school principal. In television and Hollywood movies after 1983, the prevailing image of education was of schools out of control with a principal who literally personified the dysfunctional school system.[62] A series of psychologically unstable school principals appeared in popular television, including the high-strung Principal McViker in *Beavis and Butt-head*, the popular animated television series that aired between 1993 and 1997, in which the principal regularly downed handfuls of pills and bottles of whisky in his ongoing battle with two obnoxious students. Many Hollywood principals were also military veterans, such as Mr. Weatherbee in *Archie* comics and Principal Skinner in *The Simpsons*, both of whose attempts to instill rigid school discipline were constantly foiled by student pranks, thus furthering the popular imagery of schools as poorly run military regimes deserving of rebellion.

Principals' incompetence was often portrayed as the result of their slavish obsession with bureaucracy and legalistic rules that suffocated the inspirational work of gifted teachers. In the 1995 film *Dangerous Minds*, an inspired ex-Marine female teacher struggled to make a difference in her urban school *in spite* of her principal who was fixated on protocol and lawsuits at the expense of student learning.[63] African American principals were particularly characterized as authoritarian, as they trudged through impersonal and chaotic urban schools filled with underachieving and misbehaving poor African American students whom they often literally whipped into shape.[64] In virtually none of the popular media through the 1990s were principals seen as charismatic leaders, community engagers, or intellectual role models.

The most famous American principal of the 1980s silver screen was a rebellious iconoclast who bucked the bureaucratic system, representing the entrepreneurial ideology that animated market based school reforms. *Lean on Me* was the popular 1989 biographical-drama Hollywood film that was loosely based on the story of Joe Clark, an inner-city high school principal in Patterson, New Jersey whose school was at risk of being taken over by the state government unless students improved their test scores. The Hollywood story line centers on the now familiar chaotic urban school, with a special plague of drug dealers. A new principal is hired to bring strict order to the school, and he does so notoriously by breaking the fire safety code and locking all the building doors shut to keep drug dealers out. The new principal fires teachers and expels students and is ultimately under threat of being fired himself until enough students pass the basic skills exam. Although testing was the disagreeable goal for the principal to achieve, *Lean on Me* was less a critique of rigid standardized testing and more a critique of bureaucracy that had reduced schools to chaos. The film applauded independent, entrepreneurial, and male school leaders, who efficiently solve social problems by bucking central bureaucracy. Indeed, after Principal Clark learns that the school will not fall into receivership, he yells, "You can tell the state to go to Hell!"[65]

Principal Clark reflected the popular political argument advocated by President Ronald Reagan that public education was in a crisis that could only be solved by good old-fashioned masculine heroes. Reagan's secretary of education William Bennett, who assertively promoted this agenda, compared the two extremes of educational leadership, stating that "sometimes you need Mr. Chips and sometimes you need Dirty Harry," referring to the intellectually inspiring and effete Mr. Chips from the British novel and film and the tough policeman, Dirty Harry, played by Clint Eastwood in the 1971 Hollywood movie.[66] In *Lean on Me*, the problem is weak people, including single mothers, a football coach with a losing team, compromising politicians, and a female music teacher who insists on teaching classical music. "Forget about the way it used to be," the Hollywood Clark insists, "This is not a damn democracy. We are in a state of emergency."[67] The militaristic, "can do" Joe Clark appealed to a public that was already imbued with images of schools as war zones and suspicious of government institutions that were too domesticated, too feminine, and too weak. Rather than work to change the school system, drawing on the civic goodwill and resources of the community as advocated in the earlier Effective School literature, the Joe Clark model principal was an aggressive zealot who led autocratically, as if fighting fire with fire in the battle for learning.[68]

But this image of a tough and efficient principal who cleaned house was largely a fictional invention of Hollywood. In reality, many dynamic principals who sought to make radical change were constricted by the demands of their community. Such was the experience of Dennis Littky, who in 1981 became principal of Thayer Junior/Senior High School in rural Winchester, New Hampshire. Upon his arrival, Littky found a school that was physically dilapidated and culturally conflicted: 20 percent of students dropped out before graduation and only 11 percent of graduating seniors enrolled in college. Littky began his work by addressing personal relations and school climate. He drew on research in human behavior and learning theory to reshape the school culture toward one of learning, responsiveness to student and teacher interests, and community engagement. As a symbol of his leadership style, one of Principal Littky's first actions was to hire one student to paint a mural—of anything he wished—on the cafeteria wall. By listening to teacher and student concerns, Littky rescheduled the curriculum to fewer and longer curriculum blocks, and he developed internships in local community centers and businesses. As he attracted like-minded teachers, Littky expanded the interdisciplinary curriculum and set up small advisory groups where students and teachers had time for regular conversation. Seeing school as "a living organism that has got to be changing all the time," Littky raised the school's graduation rate to 95 percent, with over 60 percent of graduating seniors going on to college. But the local school board objected to Littky's changes, arguing that the principal had experimented too radically with the curriculum and student activities and criticizing his relaxed style. In March 1986, the board voted against renewing Littky for another five-year contract, even as a majority of the school's students and a large number of parents signed petitions in his support. A judge overturned the nonrenewal decision, because the board violated state law by not holding a public hearing, and Littky retained his position, albeit with continued conflict between the central board and the school.[69]

In cities, high-stakes legislation could be as restrictive as a local school board. In San Francisco in the early 1990s, Ken Romines struggled to improve student performance at a school that was called the worst school in California. Test scores were so low that the school faced the threat of reconstitution, a legally imposed mandate to address poorly performing schools by removing all teachers, administrators, and staff and starting over. Principal Romines made valiant efforts to motivate students with a culture of learning that crossed race, class, and language identities, involve parents and community agencies, and reenergize teachers' morale and performance. Within two years, student test scores improved for the first time in more than a decade and in an improved school environment. Although change was evident, the school board still recommended reconstitution. Principal Romines moved on to help another struggling elementary school in the city improve, an itinerate, problem-solving career path that many other talented principals would follow.[70]

CONCLUSION

Hundreds of school principals in the 1980s made changes in their schools by successfully negotiating with their communities, including Tony Cook, the Indiana high school principal who in 1986 led his school community to welcome student Ryan White with open arms after he had been chased out of his past school for having AIDS, and Deborah Meier who worked with teachers and community members to develop a progressive public elementary school in Harlem in the 1980s.[71] For these principals, school leadership began with organizational change in and with the school community, echoing the work of generations of earlier progressive principals.

Yet such innovations were increasingly difficult to achieve in the years after 1983, as schools became targets of high-stakes standardized assessments. Principal Anabel Garza's 2009–2010 academic year at the John H. Reagan High School in Austin, Texas epitomizes some of the cruel ironies of principals' work in early twenty-first-century America. The school was in its fourth year as "academically unacceptable" by the state and so would be shut down and the staff and students dispersed if its test scores, attendance, and graduation rates did not improve by spring 2010.

At the risk of heightening her blood pressure, Principal Garza, herself a former teen mother from a working-class family on the Texas-Mexico border, poured herself into her school that year, translating the schools' objectives to Spanish-speaking parents, encouraging her teachers, and nurturing school pride in classrooms, sports teams, and the community. She also drove around the district looking for students because, in addition to improved text scores, Reagan High School needed to improve students' attendance and completion rates. Working with her dropout intervention specialist, Principal Garza was often on the telephone calling parents, making home visits, and finding students on the city streets. On the major testing day in the spring, the search mission intensified, particularly for those academically capable students who might lift the school's test scores. As soon as teachers reported who was missing from the testing hall, the principal drove off to knock on students' doors to urge them to come to school. On one of those days, Principal Garza, an educator with advanced degrees and twenty years of experience in the district, including fifteen years as a school administrator, stood at the side of an apartment building, rapping at a student's bedroom window, urging her to wake up and come to school to take the test.[72]

Modern public school principals shared with their predecessors the responsibility for the success and survival of the school. Yet for modern school leaders, that responsibility was complicated by the stringent requirements of local, district, state and federal requirements, and community expectations. As one veteran of school reforms in the 1980s and '90s observed, school principals who tried to make changes at modern schools often found themselves in a "battleground" and a "no-win situation, caught between the needs and interests of their schools' stakeholders, forced to decide what will help children most and infuriate the fewest parents, teachers, district personnel, [and] school board members." The work lives of such principals make clear that the "childhood image of the principal as a figure of awesome, ubiquitous power is, in fact, a myth."[73]

CONCLUSION

IN THE PRINCIPAL'S OFFICE

As I was completing this history of American school principals, I read an article in my local newspaper on the changing roles of principals that began in this way:

> There was a time when principals were mostly known as building managers, the guys in charge of making sure of two things: maintaining discipline when a student became too disruptive for the teacher and making sure there were enough office supplies.

Today, however, the article continued, the image of the principal has changed to a "hard-charging leader capable of single-handedly turning around a low-performing school."[1] In a similar vein, former students often recall times in the past when the principal's role centered on paddling, caning, and other punishments in the dark privacy of the principal's office.

While many principals have certainly emphasized building management and student discipline, one of my goals in writing this book is to revise this simplistic understanding of one of the most prominent roles in American education. Although certainly there have been many principals who served merely as building managers and ruled their teachers and students with domineering behaviors, American school principals have long played active and productive roles in the development of public education. Their ranks have include "hard-charging" men and women, all former teachers, who struggled to make progressive educational change, address community needs, and improve academic instruction. They have held multiple roles as they managed a large institution of adults and children while responding to the demands of multiple constituencies outside their building. Their work is notoriously busy, messy, multifaceted, and intense. And it has always been so. One purpose of this book is to simply chronicle the rich, complicated, and dynamic history of school leaders.

History also helps us to understand the present, and a second purpose of this book is to provide insight into the significance and challenges of contemporary principals' work. In *The Principal's Office*, I have argued that the principalship has played a central role in the development of American schooling because of its unique position in the middle of the public education system. Like other middle managers, principals are positioned between administrator and administered, responsible for policy directives from a distant central office and for overseeing daily dynamics in the workplace. From this central position, principals have stood literally at the front door of educational change. Principals' ability to exact such change has depended on the context of the many different elements that surround them—school, community, students, district, state—as well as their own professional and personal capabilities. Contemporary school reformers who are considering the best combination of regulations and supports for school leaders would do well to reflect on the complicated dynamics that have historically impacted principals' work.

Finally, this historical study has revealed ways in which the principal's office carries within itself many of our deepest questions about public education. Indeed, the history of school principals epitomizes the many conflicts and contradictions, highs and lows, of American public schooling. How are community and national values about education translated into day-to-day activities in schools? How important are the daily operations of schools— the proverbial delivery of beans, bells, and buses—in the implementation and maintenance of those values? What is the role of leadership in helping a school community collectively deliberate its educational goals? What is the most effective, equitable, and ethical balance between local control and central control, and how much freedom should local school leaders have in interpreting that measure? To what extent is the social and political context of schooling significant in educational planning, and how can the energies of communities be effectively marshaled to serve democratic civic ends? Such questions intersect educational philosophy, administrative management, and community relations. And all of these questions rest at the heart of the principal's office.

NOTES

INTRODUCTION

1. Nelson Lichtenstein, "'The Man in the Middle': A Social History of Automobile Industry Foreman," in *On the Line: Essays in the History of Auto Work*, ed. Nelson Lichtenstein and Stephen Meyer (Urbana: University of Illinois Press, 1989), 161–62; C. Wright Mills, *White Collar: The American Middle Classes* (New York: Oxford University Press, 1951), 74; Alfred Chandler, *The Visible Hand: The Managerial Revolution in American Business* (Cambridge, MA: Belknap Press, 1977).

2. Larry Cuban, *The Managerial Imperative and the Practice of Leadership in Schools* (Albany: State University of New York Press, 1988), 61.

CHAPTER ONE. PRECEPTORS, HEAD TEACHERS, AND
PRINCIPAL TEACHERS: SCHOOL LEADERSHIP
THROUGH THE LATE NINETEENTH CENTURY

1. Rosetta M. Cohen and S. Scheer, eds., *The Work of Teachers in America: A Social History Through Stories* (Mahwah, NJ: Lawrence Erlbaum, 1997), 24.

2. Cohen and Scheer, *The Work of Teachers in America*, 21.

3. R. Carlyle Buley, *The Old Northwest Pioneer Period, 1815–1840* (Indianapolis: Indiana University Press, 1950), Vol. II, 370–71; see also Richard Hofstadter, *Anti-Intellectualism in American Life* (New York: Random House, 1963), 299–316.

4. Franklin Parker, "Ezekiel Cheever: New England Colonial Teacher," *Peabody Journal of Education* 37 (May 1960): 355–60.

5. Kim Tolley, "Mapping the Leadership of Higher Schooling, 1727–1850," in *Chartered Schools: Two Hundred Years of Independent Academies in the United States, 1727–1925*, ed. Nancy Beadie and Kim Tolley (New York: Routledge, 2002), 19.

6. *100th Anniversary of the Caledonia County Grammar School* (Peacham, VT: Alumni Association, 1900), 25.

7. Melissa Ladd Teed, "Crafting Community: Hartford Public High School in the Nineteenth Century," in *Schools as Imagined Communities: The Creation of Identity, Meaning, and Conflict in U.S. History*, ed. Dierdre Cobb-Roberts, Sherman Dorn, and Barbara Shircliffe (New York: Palgrave, 2006), 51–77.

8. Lynne Templeton Brickley, "The Litchfield Female Academy," in *"To Ornament Their Minds": Sarah Pierce's Litchfield Female Academy, 1792–1833*, ed. The Litchfield Historical Society (Litchfield, CT: Litchfield Historical Society, 1993), 20–81.

9. James McLachlan, *American Boarding Schools: A Historical Study* (New York: Charles Scribner, 1970), 93.

10. McLachlan, *American Boarding Schools*, 99.

11. Kim Tolley and Margaret A. Nash, "Leaving Home to Teach: The Diary of Susan Nye Hutchison, 1815–1841," in Beadie and Tolley, *Chartered Schools*.

12. Tolley and Nash, "Leaving Home,"163, 165.

13. Teri L. Castelow, "'Creating an Educational Interest': Sophia Sawyer, Teacher of the Cherokee," in Beadie and Tolley, *Chartered Schools*.

14. Castelow, "'Creating an Educational Interest,'" 203.

15. Christopher Span, "Alternative Pedagogy: The Rise of the Private Black Academy in Early Postbellum Mississippi, 1862–1870," in Beadie and Tolley, *Chartered Schools*, 215.

16. Ronald E. Butchart, *Schooling the Freed People: Teaching, Learning, and the Struggle for Black Freedom, 1861–1876* (Chapel Hill: University of North Carolina Press, 2010), 17–51; Ronald E. Butchart, "Edmonia G. and Caroline V. Highgate: Black Teachers, Freed Slaves, and the Betrayal of Black Hearts," in *Portraits of African American Life Since 1865*, ed. Nina Mjagkij (Wilmington, DE: Scholarly Resources, Inc., 2003), 1–13.

17. I am grateful to Laura K. Muñoz for introducing me to Solomon Coles. Moses N. Moore Jr. and Yolanda Y. Smith, "Solomon M. Coles: Preacher, Teacher, and Former Slave—The First Black Student Officially Enrolled in Yale Divinity School," Unpublished manuscript, Yale University, http://www.yale.edu/divinity/storm/Coles_5_1_07.pdf; Edna Jordan, *Black Tracks to Texas: Solomon Melvin Coles* (Corpus Christi: Golden Banner Press, 1977).

18. Solomon Coles, "Doubt in the Negro's Capabilities a Hindrance to His Higher Development," *Lincoln University Alumni Magazine* 1 (November 1884): 14–18; Solomon Coles, "Colored Teachers," *Lincoln University Alumni Magazine* 1 (February 1885): 49–51; Solomon Coles, "Caste in Colored Institutions," *Lincoln University Alumni Magazine* 1 (November 1885): 124–29.

19. Adah Ward Randolph, "Building Upon Cultural Capital: Thomas Jefferson Ferguson and the Albany Enterprise Academy in Southeast Ohio, 1863–1886," *Journal of African American History* 87 (Spring 2002): 182–95.

20. Tolley and Nash, "Leaving Home to Teach," in Beadie and Tolley, *Chartered* Schools, 175.

21. Quoted in Tolley and Nash, "Leaving Home to Teach," in Beadie and Tolley, *Chartered Schools*, 175.

22. Silas Hertzler, *The Rise of the Public High School in Connecticut* (Baltimore: Warwick and York, 1930), 27–28.

23. Melissa Ladd Teed, "'If Only I Wore a Coat and Pants': Gender and Power in the Making of an American Public High School, 1847–1851," *Gender and History* 16 (April 2004): 135.

24. Teed, "'If Only I Wore a Coat and Pants,'" 137.

25. McLachlan, *American Boarding Schools*, 99.

26. Lawrence Grossman, "In His Veins Coursed No Bootlicking Blood: The Career of Peter H. Clark," *Ohio History* 86 (Spring 1977): 79–95.

27. Ann Hassenpflug, "Murder in the Classroom: Privilege, Honor, and Cultural Violence in Antebellum Louisville," *Ohio Valley History* 4 (Summer 2004): 5–26.

28. Carl F. Kaestle, *Pillars of the Republic: Common Schools and American Society, 1780–1860* (New York: Hill and Wang, 1987), 132–34.

29. As quoted in Selwyn K. Troen, *The Public and the Schools: Shaping the St. Louis System, 1838–1920* (Columbia: University of Missouri Press, 1975), 146.

30. Troen, *The Public and the Schools*, 150–51.

31. "Henry Barnard on the Significance of School Grading," in *Education in the United States: A Documentary History*, Vol. 3, ed. Sol Cohen (New York: Random House: 1974), 1322.

32. David B. Tyack, *The One Best System: A History of American Urban Education* (Cambridge: Harvard University Press, 1974), 44–45; David L. Angus, Jeffrey E. Mirel, and Maris A. Vinovskis, "Historical Development of Age Stratification in Schooling," *Teachers College Record* 90 (Winter 1988): 211–36; Frederick Dean McClusky, "Introduction of Grading into the Public Schools of New England," *The Elementary School Journal* 21 (October 1920): 132–45.

33. Michael B. Katz, "The Emergence of Bureaucracy in Urban Education: The Boston Case, 1850–1884, Part 1," *History of Education Quarterly* 8 (Summer 1968): 157–60.

34. Katz, "The Emergence of Bureaucracy, Part 1," 166–68.

35. Louise Durham, *The Old Market Street School, 1872–1920* (Memphis: Memphis State University, 1953).

36. Horace Mann, *Sixth Annual Report: Massachusetts Board of Education* (Boston: Dutton and Wentworth, 1843), 28.

37. Richard J. Altenbaugh, *The American People and Their Education: A Social History* (Columbus, OH: Merrill Prentice Hall, 2003), 114.

38. Quoted in Willard Elsbree, *American Teacher: Evolution of a Profession in a Democracy* (New York: Greenwood Press, 1970), 201.

39. Katz, "The Emergence of Bureaucracy, Part 1," 166.

40. Michael B. Katz, "The Emergence of Bureaucracy in Urban Education: The Boston Case, 1850–1884, Part 2," *History of Education Quarterly* 8 (Autumn 1968), 327.

41. Paul Revere Pierce, *The Origin and Development of the Public School Principalship* (Chicago: University of Chicago, 1935), 62.

42. *Seventeenth Annual Report of the Board of Education of St. Louis, Missouri, 1871*, 188. Quoted in Cuban, *The Managerial Imperative*, 58.

43. Tyack, *One Best System*, 45–46.

44. David Tyack, "Bureaucracy and the Common School: The Example of Portland, Oregon, 1851–1913," *American Quarterly* 19 (Autumn 1967): 48.

45. McClusky, "Introduction of Grading into the Public Schools of New England," 141.

46. Pierce, *Origin and Development of the Public School Principalship*, 11–12, 26–27.

47. Pierce, *Origin and Development of the Public School Principalship*, 27.

48. A. T. Andreas, *History of Chicago*, Vol. 2 (Chicago: A. T. Andreas Publishers, 1885), 214.

49. Pierce, *Origin and Development of the Public School Principalship*, 18–19.

50. John Rury, *Education and Social Change: Themes in the History of American Schooling* (Mahwah, NJ: Lawrence Erlbaum, 2002), 80–82.

51. Clarence Ray Aurner, *History of Education in Iowa*, Vol. II (Iowa City: State Historical Society, 1914), 94–102.

52. Pierce, *Origin and Development of the Public School Principalship*, 28; Thomas Fleming, "British Columbia Principals: Scholar-Teachers and Administrative Amateurs in Victorian and Edwardian Eras, 1872–1918," in *School Leadership: Essays on the British Columbia Experience, 1872–1995*, ed. Thomas Fleming (Mill Bay, British Columbia: Bendall Books, 2001), 251–52.

53. Pierce, *Origin and Development of the Public School Principalship*, 154–155.

54. Chester C. Dodge, *Reminiscences of a School Master* (Chicago: Ralph Fletcher Seymour, 1941), 21–47.

55. John Swett, *Public Education in California: Its Origin and Development, with Personal Reminiscences of Half a Century* (New York: American Book Co., 1911, reprinted by New York: Arno Press, 1969), 105, 121, 132, 234.

56. Kate Rousmaniere, "School Segregation in Oxford, Ohio: The Perry Gibson Case of 1887," *The Oxford Press* (March 7, 2003), A5.

57. Spencer Maxcy, "Progressivism and Rural Education in the Deep South, 1900–1950," in *Education and the Rise of the New South*, ed. Ronald K. Goodenow and Arthur O. White (Boston: G. K. Hall, 1981), 47–71; William A. Link, *A Hard Country and a Lonely Place: Schooling, Society, and Reform in Rural Virginia, 1870–1920* (Chapel Hill: University of North Carolina Press, 1986); James L. LeLoudis, *Schooling in the New South: Pedagogy, Self, and Society in North Carolina, 1880–1920* (Chapel Hill: University of North Carolina Press, 1996).

58. Joseph Mayer Rice, *The Public-School System of the United States* (New York: Arno Press, 1969), 113, 149.

CHAPTER TWO. THE MAKING OF THE PRINCIPAL'S OFFICE, 1890–1940

1. Roald F. Campbell, *The Making of a Professor: A Memoir* (Salt Lake City: Westwater Press, 1981), 49–77.

2. Roy A. Crouch, "Status of the Elementary School Principal," *Fifth Yearbook, Department of Elementary School Principals* (July 1926), 208.

3. Paul H. Hanus, "High-School Pioneering: Denver High School, District 2, 1886–90," *The School Review* 45 (June 1937): 417–28.

4. James F. Hosic, "College Course for Elementary School Principals," *Teachers College Record* 27 (1926): 792.

5. John Rufi, *The Small High School* (New York: Teachers College, Contribution to Education, 1926), 58–59.

6. Eugene M. Hinton, "An Investigation of the High School Principalship as a Profession," *Phi Delta Kappan* 5 (November 1922): 19.

7. Miss C. I. Mathis to Mr. Stecker, 17 June 1921. Box 19 AFT Series VI, Local #156 Principal's Union of Washington, D.C. American Federation of Teachers Archives, Walter Reuther Library, Wayne State University, Detroit.

8. Susie P. Watkins to Atlanta Public School Teachers Association, 1935, Box 2009, Folder 9, Atlanta Education Association papers, Southern Labor Archives, Georgia State University.

9. *Report on the Committee of Salaries, Tenure, and Pensions of Public School Teachers in the United States to the National Council of Education* (Washington, DC: National Education Association, 1905), 52.

10. Thomas Goebel, "The Uneven Rewards of Professional Labor: Wealth and Income in the Chicago Professions, 1870–1920," *Journal of Social History* 29 (Summer 1996): 749–77.

11. David B. Tyack, *The One Best System: A History of American Urban Education* (Cambridge: Harvard University Press, 1974), 126–29.

12. Keith Goldhammer, "Evolution in the Profession," *Educational Administration Quarterly* 19 (Summer 1983): 249–72; B. H. Peterson, "Certification of School Administrators in the United States," *School and Society* 45 (1937): 784–86.

13. Tyack, *The One Best System*, 185.

14. Tyack, *The One Best System*, 183.

15. Jesse B. Sears and Adin D. Henderson, *Cubberley of Stanford and His Contribution to American Education* (Stanford, CA: Stanford University Press, 1957), 130–31.

16. Ellwood P. Cubberley, "The Principal and the Principalship," *The Elementary School Journal* 23 (January 1923): 342.

17. William A. Link, "The School That Built a Town: Public Education and the Southern Social Landscape, 1880–1930," in *Essays in Twentieth-Century Southern Education*, ed. Wayne J. Urban (New York: Garland, 1999), 19–42.

18. Paul Revere Pierce, *The Origin and Development of the Public School Principalship* (Chicago: University of Chicago, 1935), 47–48. See also Antonio Viñao, "The School Head's Office as Territory and Place: Location and Physical Layout in the First Spanish Graded School," in *Materialities of Schooling: Design, Technology, Objects, Routines*, ed. Martin Lawn and Ian Grosvenor (Oxford: Symposium Books, 2005), 47–70.

19. "The Principal and the Community," *Bulletin of the Department of Elementary School Principals* (National Education Association) 7 (April 1928): 249–53.

20. Charles Lyle Spain and Arthur B. Moehlman, *The Public Elementary School Plant* (New York: Rand McNally, 1930), 255–57.

21. W. C. Reavis and Robert Woellner, "Labor-Saving Devices Used in Office Administration in Secondary Schools," *The School Review* 36 (November 1928): 736–37.

22. As quoted in Pierce, *Origin and Development of the Public School Principalship*, 82.

23. William McAndrew, *The Public and Its School* (Yonkers-on-Hudson, NY: World Book Co., 1917), 50–51.

24. As quoted in Larry Cuban, *The Managerial Imperative and the Practice of Leadership in Schools* (Albany: State University of New York Press, 1988), 58–59.

25. "Functions of the High School Principal in Curriculum-Making," *National Association of Secondary School Principals Eighth Yearbook* (Chicago: National Association of Secondary School Principals, 1924), 13–14.

26. W. S. Deffenbaugh, "Administration of Schools in the Smaller Cities," *Bureau of Education Bulletin* 2 (1922): 59; William C. Reavis, "According the Principal a Larger Autonomy in His Own School," *Fundamentals in a Democratic School*, University of Pennsylvania Bulletin, March 30–April 2, 1938.

27. Ella Flagg Young, as quoted in Pierce, *The Origin and Development of the Public School Principalship*, 49.

28. John Guy Fowlkes, *The Report of a Study of the New Castle Schools* (New Castle, PA: Board of School Directors, 1944), 133.

29. Report of Principals' Meeting, 8 March 1930, Box 58, Folder January-March 1930, Chicago Teachers' Federation Papers, Chicago Historical Society.

30. "A Study of Clerical Help for Elementary School Principals," *Sixth Yearbook of the Department of Elementary School Principals* 6 (April 1927): 230.

31. Pierce, *Origin and Development of the Public School Principalship*, 52–53.

32. Jeffrey Glanz, *Bureaucracy and Professionalism: The Evolution of Public School Supervision* (Madison, NJ: Farleigh Dickinson University Press, 1991), 43; Joseph Mayer Rice, *The Public-School System of the United States* (New York: Arno Press, 1969), 14–17, 96–98.

33. Lotus D. Coffmann, "The Control of Educational Progress Thru School Supervision," in *Proceedings and Addresses of the Annual Meeting of the National Education Association of the United States* (Washington, DC: National Education Association, 1917), 194.

34. Ross L. Finney, *A Sociological Philosophy of Education* (New York: Macmillan, 1928), 539.

35. Worth McClure, "The Organizing and Administrative Work of the School Principal," in *Modern School Administration: Its Problems and Progress*, ed. John C. Almack (Boston: Houghton Mifflin, 1933), 119.

36. Willard S. Elsbree and E. Edmund Reutter Jr., *Principles of Staff Personnel Administration in Public Schools* (New York: Teachers College, 1954), 231.

37. George S. Counts, *School and Society in Chicago* (New York: Harcourt Brace and Co., 1928), 127.

38. Victoria-María MacDonald, "The Paradox of Bureaucratization: New Views on Progressive Era Teachers and the Development of a Woman's Profession," *History of Education Quarterly* 39 (Winter 1999): 427–53.

39. Julius Arp, *Rural Education and the Consolidated School* (Yonkers on Hudson, NY, 1918), 146–50.

40. Ellwood P. Cubberley, *Rural Life and Education: A Study of the Rural-School Problem as a Phase of the Rural-Life Problem* (Boston, 1914), 283, 320; Kathleen Weiler, "Women and Rural School Reform: California, 1900–1940," *History of Education Quarterly* 34 (Spring 1994): 25–47.

41. Jeffrey Glanz, "Beyond Bureaucracy: Notes on the Professionalization of Public School Supervision in the Early 20th Century," *Journal of Curriculum & Supervision* 5 (Winter 1990): 150–70; Tracy L. Steffes, "Solving the 'Rural School Problem': New State Aid, Standards, and Supervision of Local Schools, 1900–1933," *History of Education Quarterly* 48 (May 2008): 181–220.

42. W. E. Chancellor, *Our Schools: Their Administration and Supervision* (Boston: D.C. Heath, 1908).

43. Jeffrey Glanz, "Histories, Antecedents, and Legacies of School Supervision," in *Handbook of Research on School Supervision*, ed. Gerald R. Firth and Edward F. Pajak (New York: Macmillan, 1998), 64.

44. Fred C. Ayer, "The Rise of Supervision," in *Educational Supervision: A Report of Current Views, Investigations, and Practices*, ed. James Fleming Hosic (New York: Teachers College, 1928), 13–17; Glanz, *Bureaucracy and Professionalism*, 85–86.

45. Kent Peterson, "An Examination of the Introduction of Music Instruction into the Core Curriculum of the Hamilton Schools, 1878–1933," paper for EDL 629, History of American Education, Miami University, Oxford, Ohio, Spring 2008.

46. Ron Cohen, *Children of the Mill: Schooling and Society in Gary, Indiana, 1906–1960* (Bloomington: Indiana University Press, 1990), 41.

47. C. W. Crandell, "The Relationship between Principals and Supervisors," *Bulletin of the Department of Elementary School Principals* 8 (April 1929): 169–78; Rudolph D. Lindquist, *Effective Instructional Leadership: A Study of the Problem of Integration* (New York: Teachers College Press, 1933), 72; Glanz, *Bureaucracy and Professionalism*, 111.

48. Fred Engelhardt and Ernest Melby, "The Supervisory Organization and Instructional Program, Albert Lea, Minnesota," *Bulletin of University of Minnesota* 17 (August 1928): 8–9, 17.

49. Minutes of Meeting of the Teachers' Elementary General Council with the Superintendent of Schools of Chicago, 18 November 1922, Box 50, Folder November-December 1922, CTF General Files, Chicago Historical Society.

50. Engelhardt and Melby, "The Supervisory Organization and Instructional Program, Albert Lea, Minnesota," 17.

51. A. K. Savoy, President, Elementary School Principal's Union, Local #147 Washington, DC to F. G. Stecker, Secretary AFT, 26 February 1920, Box 19, AFT Series VI, Local American Federation of Teachers Archives, Walter Reuther Library, Wayne State University, Detroit.

52. Francis T. Spaulding and L. Leland Dudley, *A Survey of the School System of Concord Massachusetts* (Cambridge, MA: Harvard University, 1927), 45.

53. Spaulding and Dudley, *A Survey of the School System of Concord*, 45–46.

54. M. R. Trabue, "The Activities in Which Principals Are Actually Engaged," in *Educational Supervision*, ed. Hosic, 130.

55. Ellwood P. Cubberley, *The Portland Survey* (Yonkers-on-Hudson, NY: World Book, 1916), as quoted in Tyack, *The One Best System*, 192.

56. Marian Dogherty, "The First Class: A Reminiscence," in Nancy Hoffman, *Women's "True" Profession: Voices from the History of Teaching* (New York: Feminist Press, 2003), 278.

57. Norwood M. Cole, "The Licensing of Schoolmasters in Colonial New England," *History of Education Journal* 8 (Winter 1957): 70.

58. Frank W. Hart, "Special Certification as a Means of Professionalizing Educational Leadership," *Teachers College Record* 27 (1925): 121.

59. *Public Education in Indiana: Report of the Indiana Education Survey Commission* (New York: General Education Board, 1923), 283; F. Herrick Connors and J. Cayce Morrison, "A Contrast of the Preparation and Work of Men and Women Elementary School Principals," *Educational Research Bulletin* 4 (November 18, 1925): 355–360; John S. Thomas, "The Status of the Michigan Principalship," *The National Elementary Principal* 12 (October 1932): 16–19.

60. B. H. Peterson, "Certification of School Administrators in the United States," *School and Society* 45 (1937): 784–86.

61. Leonard V. Koos, *The High School Principal: His Training, Experience, and Responsibilities* (Boston: Houghton Mifflin, 1924), 40.

62. Hart, "Special Certification as a Means of Professionalizing Educational Leadership," 121.

63. Thomas E. Glass, *The History of Educational Administration Viewed through Its Textbooks* (Lanham, MD: Scarecrow Education, 2004), 62.

64. James F. Hosic, "Appropriate Graduate Work for Elementary School Principals," *Teachers College Record* 33 (1931): 45–51.

65. Frank Kale Foster, "Status of the Junior High School Principal," Bulletin No. 18 (Washington: U.S. Department of the Interior, 1930), 22.

66. Arthur G. Powell, *The Uncertain Profession: Harvard and the Search for Educational Authority* (Cambridge: Harvard University Press, 1980), 64–70.

67. Dan Harrison Eikenberry, *Status of the High School Principal* (Washington: Department of the Interior, Bureau of Education, 1925, No. 24), 62.

68. Peterson, "Certification of School Administrators."

69. Hosic, "College Course for Elementary School Principals."

70. "The Content of Professional Courses," *Elementary School Principals 7th Yearbook* (Washington: NEA Department of Elementary School Principals, 1928), 466–67; Hart, "Special Certification as a Means of Professionalizing Educational Leadership," 121; Hosic, "College Course for Elementary School Principals," 792.

71. Hart, "Special Certification as a Means of Professionalizing Educational Leadership," 121.

72. Peterson, "Certification of School Administrators in the United States," 784–86.

73. Pierce, *Origin and Development of the Public School Principalship*, 175–76.

74. Eikenberry, "Status of the High School Principal," 62; Glass, *History of Educational Administration Viewed through Its Textbooks*, 62; Peterson, "Certification of School Administrators in the United States," 784–86.

75. David Tyack and Elisabeth Hansot, *Managers of Virtue: Public School Leadership in America, 1820–1980* (New York: Basic Books, 1982), 183; Bess Goodykoontz and Jessie A. Lane, *The Elementary School Principalship*, Bulletin No. 8 (Washington: U.S. Department of the Interior, 1938), 12; Pierce, *Origin and Development of the Public School Principalship*, 172.

76. Kathleen C. Berkeley, " 'The Ladies Want to Bring about Reform in the Public Schools': Public Education and Women's Rights in the Post–Civil War South," *History of Education Quarterly* 24 (Spring 1984): 45–58.

77. Louise Durham, *The Old Market Street School, 1872–1920* (Memphis, TN: Memphis State University, 1953).

78. Doris Hinson Pieroth, *Seattle's Women Teachers of the Interwar Years: Shaper of a Liveable City* (Seattle: University of Washington Press, 2004), 103.

79. William J. Kritek and Delbert K. Clear, "Teachers and Principals in the Milwaukee Public Schools," in *Seeds of Crisis: Public Schooling in Milwaukee since 1920*, ed. John L. Rury and Frank A. Cassell (Madison: University of Wisconsin Press, 1993), 166.

80. Tyack and Hansot, *Managers of Virtue*, 183; Eikenberry, "Status of the High School Principal," 43; Andrew Fishel and Janice Pottker, "Women in Educational Governance: A Statistical Portrait," *Educational Researcher* 3 (July–August 1974): 4–7; David Dana White, *The Status of the High School Principal in Alabama*, University of Alabama, MA thesis, 1931, 8.

81. Pierce, *Origin and Development of the Public School Principalship*, 188.

82. Salary Survey of Southern Districts, Box 2008, Folder 6, Atlanta Public School Teachers Association Papers, Southern Labor Archives, Georgia State University.

83. Rosalind Rosenberg, *Changing the Subject: How the Women of Columbia Shaped the Way We Think about Sex and Politics* (New York: Columbia University Press, 2004), 114–17.

84. Fred C. Ayer, "The Duties of the Public School Administrator, III," *American School Board Journal* 78 (April 1929): 40.

85. Peterson, "Certification of School Administrators in the United States," 785.

86. Connors and Morrison, "A Contrast of the Preparation and Work of Men and Women Elementary School Principals," 355–60.

87. Pierce, *Origin and Development of the Public School Principalship*, 163.

88. State of Vermont, Fifth Biennial Report of the State Board of Education, 1922–1924 (Rutland, Vermont, 1924), 17; John W. Withers, *A Report of the Survey of Public Schools in Cleveland Heights, Ohio* (Cleveland Heights, OH: Board of Education, May 1922), 38.

89. Pierce, *Origin and Development of the Public School Principalship*, 175–76.

90. For one unique exception to the exclusion of women through certification, see Anne Drummond, "Gender, Profession, and Principals: The Teachers of Quebec Protestant Academies, 1875–1900," *Historical Studies in Education* 2 (Spring 1990): 59–71.

91. "Male Teachers Needed," *American School Board Journal* 37 (December 1908): 8.

92. William E. Chancellor, *Our Schools: Their Administration and Supervision* (Boston: D.C. Heath and CO, 1915), 183.

93. Jackie M. Blount, "Manliness and the Gendered Construction of School Administration in the USA," *International Journal of Leadership in Education* 2 (April–June 1999): 64.

94. Margaret Smith Crocco, "The Price of an Activist Life: Elizabeth Almira Allen and Marion Thompson Wright," in *Pedagogies of Resistance: Women Educator Activists, 1880–1960*, ed. Margaret Smith Crocco, Petra Munro, and Kathleen Weiler (New York: Teachers College Press, 1999), 56.

95. Wayne Urban, *Why Teachers Organized* (Detroit: Wayne State University Press, 1982), 32.

96. Jonathan Sher and Rachel Tompkins, "Economy, Efficiency, and Equality: The Myth of Rural School and District Consolidation," in *Education in Rural America*, ed. Jonathan Sher (Boulder, CO: Westview Press, 1977), 164.

97. Kathleen Weiler, *Country Schoolwomen: Teaching in Rural California, 1850–1950* (Stanford, CA: Stanford University Press, 1998), 240.

98. Tyack and Hansot, *Managers of Virtue*, 183.

99. *The W.H.S. Alumni Centennial Booklet, 1854–1954* (Woodstock, VT: Alumni Association of Woodstock High School, 1954), 16; *Vermont Standard*, 4 February 1965, 12; Dorothy Cook, "My First Four Years at Woodstock High School," *The Vermont Standard: Special Edition: Woodstock Union High School*, 10 October 1957, 53.

100. Bessie Kidder Thomas alumni file, Wellesley College Archives, Wellesley, Massachusetts.

101. Hosic, "College Course for Elementary School Principals," 792.

102. Goodykoontz and Lane, *The Elementary School Principalship*, 4.

103. William Oscar Hampton, "How Public School Principals Use Their Time," PhD diss. University of North Carolina, 1926, as reviewed in "Studies on

the Principalship," Chapter 25, 7th *Bulletin of the Department of Elementary School Principals* (April 1928): 506.

CHAPTER THREE. OUTSIDE THE PRINCIPAL'S OFFICE: PRINCIPALS, DEMOCRATIC LEADERSHIP, AND COMMUNITY CHANGE

1. Adah Ward Randolph and Stephanie Sanders, "In Search of Excellence in Education: The Political, Academic, and Curricular Leadership of Ethel T. Overby," *Journal of School Leadership* 21 (July 2011): 521–47. See also Adah L. Ward Randolph, " 'It's Better to Light a Candle Than to Curse the Darkness': Ethel Thompson Overby and Democratic Schooling in Richmond, Virginia, 1910–1958," *Educational Studies* 48 (November 2012): 220–43.

2. John Dewey, "Democracy in Education," in *Teachers, Leaders, and Schools: Essays by John Dewey*, ed. Douglas J. Simpson and Sam F. Stack Jr. (Carbondale: Southern Illinois University Press, 2010), 146.

3. Dewey quoted in Simpson and Stack, *Teachers, Leaders, and Schools*, 118.

4. John Dewey, "Toward Educational Statesmanship," in Simpson and Stack, *Teachers, Leaders, and Schools*, 132; William G. Wraga, "Making Educational Leadership 'Educational,' " *Journal of School Leadership* 14 (January 2004): 105–21; William G. Wraga, "Democratic Leadership in the Classroom: Lessons from Progressives," *Democracy and Education* 14 (2001): 29–32.

5. John Dewey, "Democracy in Education," in Simpson and Stack, *Teachers, Leaders, and Schools*, 124.

6. Samuel Everett, ed., *The Community School* (New York: D. Appleton-Century Co., 1938), 58–61.

7. Everett, ed., *The Community School*, 124; Michael C. Johanek and John L. Puckett, *Leonard Covello and the Making of Benjamin Franklin High School: Education as if Citizenship Mattered* (Philadelphia: Temple University Press, 2007), 33–35.

8. George Strayer, *The Report of a Survey of the Public Schools of Pittsburgh, Pennsylvania*, (New York: Teachers College Press, 1940), 301.

9. George D. Strayer and N. L. Engelhardt, *The Report of a Survey of the Public Schools of Newark, New Jersey* (New York: Teachers College, 1942), 49.

10. Clyde M. Hill and S. M. Brownell, *Report of the Co-Operative Study of the Lincoln Schools, 1945–46* (Lincoln, NE: Board of Education, 1946), 69.

11. William C. Reavis, "Democratic Ideals in Teaching and Administration," in *Education in a Democracy*, ed. Newton Edwards (Chicago: University of Chicago Press, 1941), 107.

12. *Report of the Committee of Fifteen of the California High School Teachers' Association on Secondary Education in California* (San Francisco: California High School Teachers Association, 1924), 68.

13. "The Principal and the Community," *Yearbook of the Bulletin of the Department of Elementary School Principals* 7 (April 1928): 249–53.

14. Wayne J. Urban and Jennings L. Wagoner Jr., *American Education: A History* (New York: McGraw Hill, 2004), 235.

15. Alan Semel and Susan Sadovnik, *Schools of Tomorrow, Schools of Today: What Happened to Progressive Education* (New York: Peter Lang, 1999).

16. Craig Kridel and Robert V. Bullough Jr., *Stories of the Eight-Year Study: Reexamining Secondary Education in America* (Albany: State University of New York Press, 2007).

17. Covello quoted in Johanek and Puckett, *Leonard Covello and the Making of Benjamin Franklin High School,* 143; Nicolas V. Longo, *Why Community Matters: Connecting Education with Civic Life* (Albany: State University of New York Press, 2007), 31–33.

18. Johanek and Puckett, *Leonard Covello and the Making of Benjamin Franklin High School,* 220.

19. James Chreitzberg, "A Rural High School and Its Community," *The Southern Association Quarterly* 3 (1939): 469–71; Ralph W. Tyler, "The Responsibility of the School for the Improvement of American Life," *The School Review* 52 (September 1944): 400–05; William Burt Lauderdale, *Progressive Education: Lessons from Three Schools* (Bloomington, IN: Phi Delta Kappa Educational Foundations, 1981).

20. Lewis E. and Rae Harris, *Bootstraps: A Chronicle of a Real Community School* (Cable, WI: Harris Publications, 1980); Thomas P. Thomas, "The Difficulties and Successes of Reconstructionist Practice: Theodore Brameld and the Floodwood Project," *Journal of Curriculum and Supervision* 14 (Spring 1999): 260–82; Craig Kridel, "Theodore Brameld's Floodwood Project: A Design for America," in *Educational Reconstruction,* ed. Frank Andrews Stone (Storrs, CT: Varousia Press, 1977), 81–91.

21. Arthur Zilversmit, *Changing Schools: Progressive Education Theory and Practice, 1930–1960* (Chicago: University of Chicago Press, 1993), 46; Lawrence A. Cremin, *The Transformation of the School: Progressivism in American Education, 1876–1957* (New York: Vintage, 1964), 295–99.

22. Quoted in Sheila MacDonald Stearns, "S.R. Logan: Educator for Democracy, 1885–1970," PhD diss., University of Montana, 1983, 127.

23. Quoted in Stearns, "S. R. Logan: Educator for Democracy," 146.

24. Stearns, "S. R. Logan: Educator for Democracy," 169–70.

25. Stearns, "S. R. Logan: Educator for Democracy," 133.

26. Stearns, "S. R. Logan: Educator for Democracy," 226.

27. Miles E. Cary, "Intergroup and Inter-racial Education," *Proceedings of the Thirty-Second Annual Convention,* National Association of Secondary School Principals (March 1948), 43; Alan R. Shoho, "Ethical Leadership: The Principalship of Miles Cary at McKinley ('Tokyo') High School." Paper presented at the meeting of the American Educational Research Association, Chicago, IL, March 1997.

28. Miles E. Cary, "Learning Comes through Living," *Educational Leadership* 4 (May 1947): 491.

29. Eileen Tamura, "The Struggle for Core Studies: Miles Cary at McKinley High School in the Territory of Hawai'i," *Pacific Educational Research Journal* 8 (1996): 22–23.

30. Miles Cary, "'Final Authority' and the Schools," *Educational Administration and Supervision* 33 (1946): 480.

31. Cary quoted in Tamura, "The Struggle for Core Studies," 24.

32. Cary, "Learning Comes through Living," 493–94.

33. Cary, "Learning Comes through Living," 492; Tamura, "The Struggle for Core Studies," 24, 26.

34. Tamura, "The Struggle for Core Studies," 30.

35. Miles E. Cary, "Initiating Creative Curriculum Development," *The North Central Association Quarterly* 23 (April 1949): 345–46.

36. Lauri Johnson, "Making Her Community a Better Place to Live: Lessons from History for Culturally Responsive Urban School Leadership," in *Keeping the Promise: Essays on Leadership, Democracy, and Education*, ed. Dennis Carlson and C. P. Gause (New York: Peter Lang, 2007).

37. Judy A. Alston, "Tempered Radicals and Servant Leaders: Black Females Persevering in the Superintendency," *Educational Administration Quarterly* 41 (October 2005): 675–88; Linda C. Tillman, "African American Principals and the Legacy of Brown," *Review of Research in Education* 28 (2004): 101–46; Dionne Danns, "Thriving in the Midst of Adversity: Educator Maudelle Brown Bousfield's Struggles in Chicago, 1920–1950," *The Journal of Negro Education* 78 (Winter 2009): 3–19.

38. *The Complete Report of Mayor LaGuardia's Commission on the Harlem Riot of March 19, 1935*, reprinted as *Mass Violence in America* (New York: Arno Press, 1969), 79.

39. Lauri Johnson, "A Generation of Women Activists: African American Female Educators in Harlem, 1930–1950," *The Journal of African American History* 89 (Summer 2004): 229.

40. Vanessa Siddle Walker, *Their Highest Potential: An African American School Community in the Segregated South* (Chapel Hill: University of North Carolina Press, 1996); Carter Julian Savage, "Cultural Capital and African American Agency: The Economic Struggle for Effective Education for African Americans in Franklin, Tennessee, 1890–1967," *The Journal of African American History* 87 (Spring 2002), 206–35; Frederick A. Rodgers, *The Black High School and Its Community* (Lexington, MA: Lexington Books, 1975); Vivian Gunn Morris, *The Price They Paid: Desegregation in an African American Community* (New York: Teachers College Press, 2002).

41. Vanessa Siddle Walker with Ulysses Byas, *Hello Professor: A Black Principal and Professional Leadership in the Segregated South* (Chapel Hill: University of North Carolina Press, 2009), xiii.

42. "Inequalities of Educational Opportunity," *NEA Research Bulletin* 14–15 (1936): 160–69.

43. APSTA Salary Survey of Southern Districts, 1929, Box 2008, Folder 6, Atlanta Education Association Papers, Southern Labor Archives, Georgia State University.

44. Siddle Walker with Byas, *Hello Professor*, 46.

45. Siddle Walker, *Their Highest Potential*, 107.

46. Siddle Walker, *Their Highest Potential*, 16–70.

47. Johnson, "Making Her Community a Better Place," 276–78.

48. Gertrude Ayer quoted in Johnson, "Making Her Community a Better Place to Live," 276.

49. Marian J. Morton, *Women in Cleveland: An Illustrated History* (Bloomington: Indiana University Press, 1995), 204–06.

50. Hazel Mountain Walker quoted in Summary Report of the Joint Project of R. B. Hayes School and Karamu House, June 1941, Folders 673 and 678, Karamu House Collection, Western Reserve Historical Society, Cleveland, Ohio.

51. Summary Report of the Joint Project of R. B. Hayes School and Karamu House, June 1941. Folders 673 and 678, Karamu House Collection, Western Reserve Historical Society, Cleveland, Ohio.

52. David Sandor, " 'Black Is as Good a Color as White': The Harriet Beecher Stowe School and the Debate Over Separate Schools in Cincinnati," *Ohio Valley History* 9 (Summer 2009): 27–53.

53. Mark Naison, *Communists in Harlem during the Depression* (Urbana: University of Illinois Press, 1983), 214; Lauri Johnson, " 'Making Democracy Real': Teacher Union and Community Activism to Promote Diversity in the New York City Public Schools, 1935–1950," *Urban Education* 37 (November 2002): 566–87.

54. Naison, *Communists in Harlem*, 215; Jonna Perrillo, *Uncivil Rights: Teachers, Unions, and Race in the Battle for School Equity* (Chicago: University of Chicago Press, 2012), 15–20.

55. Johnson, " 'Making Democracy Real,' " 569.

56. Gustav Schoenchen to "My Dear Colleagues," January 27, 1937, cited in Robert Iverson, *The Communists and the Schools* (New York: Harcourt, Brace and Co., 1959), 106–07.

57. Michael E. James, *The Conspiracy of the Good: Civil Rights and the Struggle for Community in Two American Cities, 1875–2000* (New York: Peter Lang, 2005), 311–23.

58. Group Council 29, Bryn Mawr School, Chicago, 21 October 1921, Box 48, Folder August–October 1921, Chicago Teachers Federation General Files, Chicago Historical Society.

59. "Master and Servant," *The American Teacher* 2 (January 1913): 11.

60. W. C. Bagley, "The Status of the Classroom Teacher," *NEA Proceedings* (1918): 384.

61. Margaret K. Nelson, "From the One-Room School House to the Graded School: Teaching in Vermont, 1910–1950," *Frontiers: A Journal of Women's Studies* 7 (1983): 14–20; Richard Quantz, "The Complex Visions of Female Teachers and the Failure of Unionization in the 1930s: An Oral History," *History of Education Quarterly* 25 (Winter 1985): 439–58.

62. Wayne Urban, *Why Teachers Organized* (Detroit: Wayne University Press, 1982), 30.

63. Principal Nellie Fields, Anniversary Luncheon of Chicago Teachers Federation, January 21, 1928, Box 55, Folder January–March 1928, Chicago Teachers Federation General Files, Chicago Historical Society.

64. Angelo Patri, *A Schoolmaster of a Great City* (New York: Macmillan, 1921), 29–30.

65. Minnie J. Reynolds, *The Crayon Clue* (New York: Mitchell Kennerley, 1915), 7.

66. Letter from United Brotherhood of Carpenters and Joiners of America, Waycross, Georgia to Allie Mann, 1931, Box 2009, Folder 1, Atlanta Education Association Papers, Southern Labor Archives, Georgia State University.

67. Charles Stillman to Margaret Haley, 3 August 1916, Box 45, Folder 3, Chicago Teachers Federation Papers, Chicago Historical Society; Lulu M. McDonald,

Grade Teachers Union of Washington D.C. to Charles Stillman, AFT, 11 February 1920, Box 19, Series VI, Local #156 Principals Union of Washington, D.C., American Federation of Teachers Archives, Walter Reuther Library, Wayne State University, Detroit.

68. James Barron, President APSTA to Mr. J. W. Harrah, President, Akron Teachers' Association, Akron, Ohio, 5 May 1927, Box 2008, Folder 4, Atlanta Education Association Papers, Southern Labor Archives, Georgia State University.

69. "To the members of the Joint Conference," 17 March 1931, The Joint Conference of Principals and Teachers of the Chicago Public Schools, Box 60, Folder February–April 1931, Chicago Teachers Federation General Files, Chicago Historical Society.

70. Margaret Smith Crocco, "The Price of an Activist Life: Elizabeth Almira Allen and Marion Thompson Wright," in *Pedagogies of Resistance: Women Educator Activists, 1880–1960*, ed. Margaret Smith Crocco, Petra Munro, and Kathleen Weiler (New York: Teachers College Press, 1999), 52–53.

71. Elizabeth Almira Allen quoted in Crocco, "The Price of an Activist Life," 54.

72. Crocco, "The Price of an Activist Life," 55.

73. Crocco, "The Price of an Activist Life," 54.

74. Joseph W. Newman, "Religious Discrimination, Political Revenge, and Teacher Tenure," in *The Teacher's Voice: A Social History of Teaching in Twentieth Century America*, ed. Richard J. Altenbaugh (Washington, DC: Falmer Press, 1992), 90–106.

75. Newman, "Religious Discrimination," 105.

76. Joseph W. Newman, "Mary C. Barker and the Atlanta Teachers' Union," in *Southern Workers and Their Unions, 1880–1975*, ed. Merl E. Reed, Leslie S. Hough, and Gary M. Fink (Westport, CT: Greenwood Press, 1981), 61–77.

77. William B. Thomas and Kevin J. Moran, "Reconsidering the Power of the Superintendent in the Progressive Period," *American Educational Research Journal* 29 (Spring 1992): 22–50.

78. Olive M. Jones, "The Principal's Multiple Functioning," *Bulletin of the Department of Elementary School Principals* (NEA: Department of Elementary School Principals), 2 (April 1923); Olive M. Jones obituary, *New York Times*, 12 August 1953.

79. Nelson Lincoln Burbank, "The Cincinnati Elementary School Principals' Club History: 1923–1957 (Cincinnati, OH: Cincinnati Elementary School Principals' Club, 1957).

80. Olive Wilson, Principal of Roosevelt School, Vallejo California to F. G. Stecker, 12 April 1920. Box 19, AFT Series VI, Local #168, American Federation of Teachers Archives, Walter Reuther Library, Wayne State University, Detroit.

81. Local #147, Elementary School Principals' Union, D.C. (colored), and Local #156, Principal's Union of Washington, D.C., Box 19, AFT Series VI, Walter Reuther Library, Wayne State University, Detroit.

82. Margaret Gribskov, "Adelaide Pollock and the Founding of the NCAWE," in *Women Educators: Employees of Schools in Western Countries*, ed. Patricia Schmuck (Albany: State University of New York Press, 1987); Patricia Schmuck, "Advocacy Organizations for Women School Administrators, 1977–1993," in *Women Leading in Education*, ed. Diane M. Dunlap and Patricia A. Schmuck (Albany: State University of New York Press, 1995).

83. Judith Rosenberg Raftery, *Land of Fair Promise: Politics and Reform in Los Angeles Schools, 1885–1941* (Stanford, CA: Stanford University Press, 1992), 103–05; Kathleen Weiler, "Women and Rural School Reform: California, 1900–1940," *History of Education Quarterly* 34 (Spring 1994): 28–29.

84. Edgar B. Wesley, *NEA: The First Hundred Years* (New York: Harper and Brothers, 1957), 393–96.

85. Carol Karpinski, *"A Visible Company of Professionals": African Americans and the National Education Association during the Civil Rights Movement* (New York: Peter Lang, 2008).

86. Siddle Walker with Byas, *Hello Professor*, 124–58.

CHAPTER FOUR. CRACKS IN THE SYSTEM: SCHOOL LEADERSHIP, 1945–1980

1. Principal's monthly reports, 1947, 1949–50, Woodstown Elementary School, Woodstown, NJ, Pluma Batten Papers, MS 1156, New Jersey Historical Society, Newark, NJ.

2. Lynn G. Beck and Joseph Murphy, *Understanding the Principalship: Metaphorical Themes, 1920–1990s* (New York: Teachers College Press, 1993), 115.

3. Gerald Grant, *The World We Created at Hamilton High* (Cambridge, MA: Harvard University Press, 1988), 17–19; Gordon L. McAndrew, "The High-School Principal: Man in the Middle," *Daedalus* 110 (Summer 1981): 106–07.

4. Robert Hampel, *The Last Little Citadel: American High Schools Since 1940* (New York: Houghton Mifflin, 1986), 14–15, 46.

5. David L. Angus and Jeffrey E. Mirel, *The Failed Promise of the American High School, 1890–1995* (New York: Teachers College Press, 1999), 114–15, 132–35; Arthur G. Powell, Eleanor Farrar, and David K. Cohen, *The Shopping Mall High School: Winners and Losers in the Educational Marketplace* (Boston: Houghton Mifflin, 1985).

6. Wayne J. Urban, *More Science than Sputnik: The National Defense Education Act of 1958* (Tuscaloosa, AL: University of Alabama Press, 2010).

7. Quoted in Judith Kafka, *The History of "Zero Tolerance" in American Public Schooling* (New York: Palgrave, 2011), 57.

8. Judith Kafka, "Shifting Authority: Teachers' Role in the Bureaucratization of School Discipline in Postwar Los Angeles," *History of Education Quarterly* 49, 3 (August 2009): 345; Donald W. Robinson, "Police in the Schools," *Phi Delta Kappan* 48 (February 1967): 278–80.

9. Stanley M. Elam, Lowell C. Rose, and Alec M. Gallup, "The 25th Annual Phi Delta Kappa/Gallup Poll of the Public's Attitudes Toward Public Schools," *Phi Delta Kappan* 75 (1993): 137–54.

10. James S. Coleman, et al., *Equality of Educational Opportunity* (Washington, DC: Government Printing Office, 1966), 3–20.

11. Wayne J. Urban, *Gender, Race, and the National Education Association* (New York: Routledge Falmer, 2000).

12. Coleman et al., *Equality of Educational Opportunity*.

13. Jon C. Teaford, *The Metropolitan Revolution: The Rise of Post-Urban America* (New York: Columbia University Press, 2006), 78–79; Jack Dougherty, "Shopping for

Schools: How Public Education and Private Housing Shaped Suburban Connecticut," *Journal of Urban History* 38 (2012): 205–24.

14. Carol Mason, *Reading Appalachia from Left to Right: Conservatives and the 1974 Kanawah County Textbook Controversy* (Ithaca, NY: Cornell University Press, 2009).

15. Connaught Coyne Marshner, *Blackboard Tyranny* (New Rochelle: Arlington House Publishers, 1978).

16. Mary Anne Raywid, *The Ax-Grinders* (New York: Macmillan, 1963); Albert Lynd, *Quackery in the Public Schools* (Boston: Little Brown, 1953), 46.

17. Arthur Bestor, *The Restoration of Learning: A Program for Redeeming the Unfulfilled Promise of American Education* (New York: Knopf, 1955), 53, quoting A. E. Lauchner, "How Can the Junior High School Curriculum Be Improved?" *Bulletin of the National Association of Secondary School Principals* 37 (March 1951): 299–300.

18. Raywid, *The Ax-Grinders*; Arthur Bestor, *Educational Wastelands* (Urbana: University of Illinois Press, 1953); Mortimer Smith, *And Madly Teach: A Layman Looks at Public School Education* (Chicago: H. Regnery Co., 1949).

19. Sloan Wilson, "It's Time to Close Our Carnivals," *Life Magazine*, 24 March 1958, 36.

20. Arthur S. Trace, *What Ivan Knows that Johnny Doesn't* (New York: Random House, 1961).

21. Robert W. Iverson, *The Communists and the Schools* (New York: Harcourt, Brace and Co., 1959), 264–65.

22. Iverson, *The Communists and the Schools*, 344; Stuart J. Foster, *Red Alert! Educators Confront the Red Scare in American Public Schools, 1947–1954* (New York: Peter Lang, 2000).

23. Ronald E. Butchart, "Punishment, Penalties, Prizes and Procedures: A History of Discipline in U.S. Schools," in *Classroom Discipline in American Schools: Problems and Possibilities for Democratic Education*, ed. Ronald E. Butchart and Barbara McEwan (Albany: State University of New York Press, 1998), 19–49; Richard M. Ritchie and Ritchard M. Ritchie, "Due Process and the Principal," *Phi Delta Kappan* 54 (June 1973): 697–98.

24. Hampel, *The Last Little Citadel*, 95; Ronald K. Olson, "Tinker and the Administrator," *School and Society*100 (February 1972): 86–89.

25. Virginia Lee, "A Legal Analysis of *Ingraham v. Wright*," in *Corporal Punishment in American Education*, ed. Irwin A. Hyman and James H. Wise (Temple University Press, Philadelphia, 1979), p. 188–189.

26. J. Lloyd Trump and Jane Hunt, *Report on a National Survey of Secondary School Principals on the Nature and Extent of Student Activism* (Washington, DC: National Association of Secondary School Principals, 1969).

27. Report by the Committee on Internal Security, House of Representatives, Ninety-First Congress, 1969, as quoted in *Student Dissent in the Schools*, ed. Irving G. Hendrick and Reginald L. Jones (Boston: Houghton Mifflin, 1972), 289–303; J. Edgar Hoover, "The SDS and the High Schools: A Study in Student Extremism," *The PTA Magazine* 64 (January–February, 1970): 2–5, 8–9.

28. Hendrick and Jones, eds., *Student Dissent in the Schools*, 311–43.

29. Frances Wurtz and Geraldine Fergen, "Boards Still Duck the Problem of Pregnant Schoolgirls," *American School Board Journal* 157 (April 1970): 22–24; Hendrick and Jones, eds., *Student Dissent in the Schools*, 88–130.

30. T. D. Schelhardt, "Losing the Reins: Principals' Rules Erodes as Students, Teachers, Parents, Attack Them," *Wall Street Journal*, 25 February 1970, 1, 22.

31. L. Bruder, "Students Support Defiant Principal," *New York Times*, 24 March 1976, 82.

32. Craig Peck, "'Carry Me Out Piece by Piece:' Fighting for Principal Power in New York City, 1966–1977," paper delivered at American Educational Research Association Annual meeting, April 2011, New Orleans; Howard Hurwitz, *The Last Angry Principal* (Portland, OR: Halcyon House, 1988).

33. Peck, "'Carry Me Out Piece by Piece,'" 12–13.

34. Quoted in Philip Cusick, *The Educational System: It's Nature and Logic* (New York: McGraw Hill, 1992), 114–15; Nat Hentoff, Profiles, "The Principal," *The New Yorker*, 7 May 1966, 52.

35. Fred M. Hechinger, "Call for New Breed of School Leader: Principals," *New York Times*, 21 March 1971, E7.

36. Arthur J. Vidich and Charles McReynolds, "Rhetoric versus Reality: A Study of New York City High School Principals," in *Anthropological Perspectives on Education*, ed. Murray L. Wax, Stanley Diamond, and Fred O. Gearing (New York: Basic Books, 1971), 195.

37. B. C. Watson, "The Principal in the System," in *The Principal in Metropolitan Schools*, ed. Donald A. Erickson and Theodore L. Reller (Berkeley, CA: McCutchan, 1978), 40.

38. Quoted in Michael S. Kimmel, *Manhood in America: A Cultural History* (New York: Oxford University Press, 2006), 82–83.

39. Thomas C. Cochran, *Business in American Life: A History* (New York: McGraw Hill, 1972), 252–53, 271.

40. Susan Faludi, *Stiffed: The Betrayal of the American Man* (New York: William Morrow, 1999), 74–77.

41. Norman Mailer, *The White Negro* (San Francisco: City Lights Books, 1957), quoted in Kimmel, *Manhood in America*, 242.

42. Raywid, *The Ax-Grinders*, 6–7, 72.

43. "It's Time to Fight Back, Fellow Scapegoats!" *Phi Delta Kappan* 39 (February 1958), 193–94.

44. Patricia Sexton, *The Feminized Male: Classrooms, White Collars, and the Decline of Manliness* (New York: Random House, 1969), 97.

45. Patrick Ryan, "A Historiography of Media Representations of the Teacher," History of Education Society Annual Meeting, Tampa, Florida, 2008; Jean-Paul Gabilliet, *Of Comics and Men: A Cultural History of American Comic Books* (Jackson, MS: University of Mississippi Press, 2010), 24.

46. Karen Graves, *'And They Were Wonderful Teachers': Florida's Purge of Gay and Lesbian Teachers* (Urbana: University of Illinois Press, 2009), 17.

47. Quoted in Catherine A. Lugg, "Sissies, Faggots, Lezzies, and Dykes: Gender, Sexual Orientation, and the New Politics of Education?" *Educational Administration Quarterly* 39 (February 2003): 95–134.

48. Victor E. Leonard, "No Man's Land," *American School Board Journal* 113 (September 1946): 21.

49. Quoted in Jackie Blount, *Destined to Rule the Schools: Women and the Superintendency, 1873–1995* (Albany: State University of New York Press, 1998),

108. Marriage remained a virtual prerequisite for male principals: In the late 1970s, over 90 percent of men principals surveyed were married, compared to less than half of the women principals surveyed. "Principalship Offers Upward Mobility for Many Families," *Phi Delta Kappan* 61 (May 1980): 645.

50. John W. Dalton, "Mice or Men (A Reaction to 'Teaching as a Man's Job')" *Phi Delta Kappan* 23 (January 1941): 197.

51. Catherine Lugg, "Our Strait-Laced Administrators: The Law, Lesbian, Gay, Bisexual and Transgendered Educational Administrators and the Assimilationist Imperative," *Journal of School Leadership* 13 (January 2003), 61, 67.

52. Lugg, "Our Strait-Laced Administrators," 51–85; Karen M. Harbeck, "Gay and Lesbian Educators: Past History/Future Prospects," in *Coming Out of the Classroom Closet: Gay and Lesbian Students, Teachers, and Curriculum*, ed. Karen M. Harbeck (New York: Harrington Park Press, 1992), 127–29.

53. Rose Terlin, "New Horizons for Educated Women," presentation at National Council of Administrative Women in Education annual meeting, Atlantic City, February 1965, Series 34 National Council of Administrative Women in Education, 1922–1978, Box 1790, Folder 2, National Education Association Archives, George Washington University, Washington, D.C.

54. Suzanne E. Estler, "Women as Leaders in Public Education," *Signs* 1 (Winter 1975): 371–73.

55. Estler, "Women as Leaders in Public Education," 376.

56. Thomas E. Glass, *The History of Educational Administration Viewed through Its Textbooks* (Lanham, MD: Scarecrow Education, 2004), 62; "The Woman Principal," *National Elementary Principal* 45 (April 1966): 10.

57. Keith Goldhammer, John E. Suttle, William D. Aldridge, and Gerald L. Becker, *Issues and Problems in Contemporary Educational Administration* (Eugene, OR: The Center for the Advanced Study of Educational Administration, 1967), 1–2.

58. National Conference of Professors of Educational Administration, *Providing and Improving Administrative Leadership in America's Schools*, The Fourth Report (New York: Teachers College, Columbia University, 1951).

59. Martin B. Garrison, "An Analysis of the Preparation Program in Educational Administration at George Peabody College for Teachers," George Peabody College for Teachers master's thesis 1956, 53–56; "Regional Action for Professional Progress: Activities-Outcomes-Impact of the Southern States Cooperative Program in Educational Administration," *Bulletin of the Bureau of School Service* 29 (December1956): 5–26.

60. Lawrence G. Derthick, "A Superintendent Looks at the CPEA," *The School Executive* 71 (1952): 74.

61. Estler, "Women as Leaders in Public Education," 371–74.

62. Elliott J. Gorn and Warren Goldstein, *A Brief History of American Sports* (New York: Hill and Wang, 1993), 180.

63. NEA Research Division, "Salary Schedule Supplements for Extra Duties, 1969–70: Public-School Salaries Series, Research Report 1970-R4" (Washington, DC: NEA, 1970).

64. Estler, "Women as Leaders in Public Education," 374.

65. Liliana Rodriguez-Campos, Rigoberto Rincones-Gomez, and Jianping Shen, "Principals' Educational Attainment, Experience, and Professional Development," in *School Principals*, ed. Jianping Shen (New York: Peter Lang, 2005), 36–38.

66. National Education Association Research Report, *26th Biennial Salary and Staff Survey of Public School Professional Personnel, 1972–73*; Estler, "Women as Leaders in Public Education," 364.

67. Andrew Fishel and Janice Pottker, "Women in Educational Governance: A Statistical Portrait," *Educational Researcher* 3 (July–August 1974): 6.

68. "State Report Finds Few Women Hold Top School Posts," *New York Times*, 4 October 1972, 50.

69. "Chronicle of Sex, Race and Schools," *Integrated Education* 79 (January–February 1976): 50.

70. Christina Collins, *"Ethnically Qualified": Race, Merit, and the Selection of Urban Teachers, 1920–1980* (New York: Teachers College Press, 2011), 166.

71. In these same years, elementary principals earned little more than a half of superintendents' average salaries. Educational Research Service, "Salaries Scheduled for Administrative and Supervisory Personnel in Public Schools, 1973–74," Educational Research Service: Arlington, Virginia, 1973, Box 1662, Series 19, Folder 9, National Education Association Archives, George Washington University, Washington, D.C.; Bill Pharis, "How to Know if You Need a Raise: The Latest Scoop on Salaries," *The National Elementary Principal* 59 (March 1980): 40–44.

72. Abe Feuerstein, "School Administration and the Changing Face of Masculinity," *Journal of School Leadership* 16 (January 2006): 4–33; Myra H. Strober and David Tyack, "Why Do Women Teach and Men Manage? A Report on Research on Schools," *Signs* 5 (Spring 1980): 494–503.

73. Rose Terlin, "New Horizons for Educated Women," presentation at National Council of Administrative Women in Education annual meeting, Atlantic City, February 1965, NEA, Series 34, National Council of Administrative Women in Education, 1922–1978, Box 1790, Folder 2, National Education Association Archives, George Washington University, Washington, D.C.

74. Quoted in Richard J. Altenbaugh, "Teachers and the Workplace," in *The Teacher's Voice: A Social History of Teaching in Twentieth-Century America*, ed. Richard J. Altenbaugh (Washington, DC, The Falmer Press, 1992), 162.

75. Quoted in Howard S. Becker, "Role and Career Problems of the Chicago Public School Teacher," PhD diss., University of Chicago, 1951, 126

76. Quoted in John F. Lyons, *Teachers and Reform: Chicago Public Education, 1929–1970* (Chicago: University of Illinois Press, 2008), 143.

77. Richard D. Kahlenberg, *Tough Liberal: Albert Shanker and the Battles over Schools, Unions, Race, and Democracy* (New York: Columbia University Press, 2007), 32–34.

78. Dan C. Lortie, *Schoolteacher: A Sociological Study* (Chicago: University of Chicago Press, 1975), 35; Michael Betz, "Inter-Generational Mobility Rates of Public School Teachers," *The Journal of Educational Research* 67 (September 1973): 3–8.

79. Susan Moore Johnson, *Teacher Unions in Schools* (Philadelphia: Temple University Press, 1984), 120.

80. Michael J. Murphy and Neil Ellman, "The Building Principal and the Union: A Study in Mutual Accommodation," *IAR Research Bulletin* 14 (June 1974): 3–5; Paul Berg, "The Impact of Collective Bargaining upon the Principal," *Administrator's Notebook* 21 (September, 1972–June 1973): 1–4.

81. "Georgia Education Association Memo: A Chance to Make a Difference," 19 January 1970, Box 2043, Folder 12, Atlanta Education Association Papers, Southern Labor Archives, Georgia State University.

82. Robert Hampel, *The Last Little Citadel: American High Schools Since 1940* (Boston: Houghton Mifflin, 1986), 96–97.

83. Vidich and McReynolds, "Rhetoric versus Reality: A Study of New York City High School Principals," 198.

84. Bruce S. Cooper, "Collective Bargaining Comes to School Middle Management," *Phi Delta Kappan* 58 (October 1976): 202; William P. Knoester, "Administrative Unionization: What Kind of Solution?" *Phi Delta Kappan* 59 (February 1978): 419–22; Luverne L. Cunningham, "Collective Negotiations and the Principalship," *Theory into Practice* 7 (April 1968): 62–70.

85. Gilbert R. Weldy, "Administering a Negotiated Contract," National Association of Secondary School Principals, Reston, Virginia, 1973; "Concerning Administrator's Right to Continuing Employment," *A Legal Memorandum*, National Association of Secondary School Principals, Reston, Virginia, September 1973; "A Bill of Rights for School Administrators," *Spectator*, National Association of Elementary School Principals' newsletter (December 1975).

86. Robert W. Heller, "The Principal's Role in Planning for a Teacher Strike," *NASSP Bulletin* 62 (May 1978): 98–105.

87. Kris Berggren, "Historic St. Paul Walkout," *Twin Cities Daily Planet*, 17 April 2011, http://www.tcdailyplanet.net/news/2011/04/15/historic-st-paul-walkout.

88. Gordon L. McAndrew, "The High-School Principal: Man in the Middle," *Daedalus* 110 (Summer 1981): 106–07.

89. "An Educator's Educator," *The Tampa Tribune*, 7 November 2000; "Tampan Takes NEA Reins," *St. Petersburg Times*, 8 July 1967.

90. *The Administrative Team* 1 (1971), joint newsletter of the AASA, NAESP, and NAASP, Department of Elementary School Principals, Series 14, Box 1636, Folder 8, NEA Archives, George Washington University, Washington, D.C.; *Spectator*, National Association of Elementary School Principals, Fall 1973, Department of Elementary School Principals, Series 14, Box 1637, Folder 28, NEA Archives, George Washington University, Washington, D.C.

91. Thomas A. Shannon, "Resolving Management Conflicts through Associations," Arlington VA, National Association of Elementary School Principals (1972).

92. Bruce S. Cooper, "Collective Bargaining for School Administrators Four Years Later," *Phi Delta Kappan* 61 (October 1979): 130–31; Edwin M. Bridges and Bruce S. Cooper, "Collective Bargaining for School Administrators," *Theory into Practice* 15 (October 1976): 306.

93. Cooper, "Collective Bargaining Comes to School Middle Management," 202.

94. Paul B. High, President of Local 1554, To Charles Cogan, President AFT, Local #1554 Cleveland Federation of Principals and Supervisors, AFT Office of the President, Box 20, Item 23, 30 January 1965, American Federation of Teachers Archives, Walter Reuther Library, Wayne State University, Detroit.

95. Fred T. Wilhelms, "The Principalship: An Institution in Distress?" *NASSP Spotlight* 75 (November–December 1966): 9–10.

96. Principal Ollie Clatterbuck to David Selden, president of AFT, 4 August 1971, Local #1042, Council Bluffs, Iowa, AFT Series XII, Box 18, Item 32, American Federation of Teachers Archives, Walter Reuther Library, Wayne State University, Detroit.

97. Charles Cogan, President AFT to William O. Thomas, President Local #1327, 17 December 1964, AFT Series XII, Box 86, Item Local #1327 East St. Louis Principal's Union, American Federation of Teachers Archives, Walter Reuther Library, Wayne State University, Detroit.

98. Council of School Supervisors and Administrators Records, Tamiment Library and Robert F. Wagner Labor Archives, New York University, New York; Daniel Perlstein, *Justice, Justice: School Politics and the Eclipse of Liberalism* (New York: Peter Lang, 2004), 22; Vidich and McReynolds, "Rhetoric versus Reality: A Study of New York City High School Principals," 199.

99. Vidich and McReynolds, "Rhetoric versus Reality: A Study of New York City High School Principals," 200.

100. Sidney Trubowitz, "Confessions of a Ghetto Administrator," *Phi Delta Kappan* 53 (December 1971): 210.

CHAPTER FIVE. BEARING THE BURDEN: THE SCHOOL PRINCIPAL AND CIVIL RIGHTS

1. Heather Lewis, "'There Are No More Hiding Places—Even in Bedford Stuyvesant': The School Leader at the Nexus of Bureaucracy and Accountability in the 1970s," paper presented at History of Education Society Annual Meeting, Tampa, Florida, 2008, 8; Heather Lewis, *The "Bad Old Days": The Community Control Movement and Its Legacy in New York City Schools* (New York: Teachers College Press, 2013).

2. Lewis, "'There Are No More Hiding Places,'" 17.

3. Scott Baker, "Testing Equality: The National Teacher Examination and the NAACP's Legal Campaign to Equalize Teachers' Salaries in the South, 1936–63," *History of Education Quarterly* 35 (Spring 1995): 49–64.

4. Cited in Linda C. Tillman, "African American Principals and the Legacy of *Brown*," *Review of Research in Education* 28 (2005): 112.

5. Carol F. Karpinski, "Bearing the Burden of Desegregation: Black Principals and *Brown*," *Urban Education* 41 (May 2006): 251; Charles C. Bolton, *The Hardest Deal of All: The Battle Over School Desegregation in Mississippi, 1870–1980* (Jackson: University of Mississippi Press, 2005), 214; Robert Hooker, "Displacement of Black Teachers in the Eleven Southern States," *Afro-American Studies* 2 (December 1971): 165–80; Everett E. Abney, "The Status of Florida's Black School Principals," *The Journal of Negro Education* 43 (Winter 1974): 3–8.

6. Sonya Ramsey, *Reading, Writing and Segregation: A Century of Black Women Teachers in Nashville* (Champaign: University of Illinois Press, 2008), 116.

7. Samuel B. Ethridge, "Maryland Study on Principal Displacement," National Education Association, Center for Human Relations, 9 February 1970 memo, Box 2015, Folder 6, Atlanta Education Association Papers, Southern Labor Archives, Georgia State University.

8. Lillian Taylor Orme Collection, Kansas Collection, Kenneth Spencer Research Library, University of Kansas, Lawrence, Kansas.

9. Pluma Batten Papers, MS 1156, New Jersey Historical Society, Newark, NJ.

10. Adah Ward Randolph, "The Memories of an All-Black Northern Urban School: Good Memories of Leadership, Teachers, and the Curriculum," *Urban Education* 39 (November 2004); Vanessa Siddle Walker, "Organized Resistance and Black Educators' Quest for School Equality," *Teachers College Record* 107 (March 2005): 355–88.

11. Tillman, "African American Principals," 112–13.

12. Bolton, *The Hardest Deal of All*, 215.

13. Robyn Duff Ladino, *Desegregating Texas Schools: Eisenhower, Shivers, and the Crisis at Mansfield High* (Austin: University of Texas Press, 1996), 96–100.

14. Beth Roy, *Bitters in the Honey* (Fayetteville: University of Arkansas Press, 1999), 232.

14. Roy, *Bitters in the Honey*, 373; Elizabeth Huckaby, *Crisis at Central High, Little Rock, 1957–58* (Baton Rouge: Louisiana State University Press, 1980), 64.

16. Karen Anderson, *Little Rock: Race and Resistance at Central High School* (Princeton: Princeton University Press, 2010), 100–03.

17. Elizabeth Jacoway, *Turn Away Thy Son: Little Rock, the Crisis That Shocked the Nation* (New York: Free Press, 2007), 58, 217–18, 225.

18. Julianne Lewis Adams and Thomas A. DeBlack, *Civil Obedience: An Oral History of School Desegregation in Fayetteville, Arkansas, 1954–65* (Fayetteville: University of Arkansas Press, 1994), 13, 61.

19. Willard B. Gatewood, "School Desegregation in Fayetteville: A Forty-Year Perspective," in Adams and DeBlack, *Civil Obedience*, 1–28.

20. Adams and DeBlack, *Civil Obedience*, 159.

21. Cited in Bolton, *The Hardest Deal of All*, 163.

22. Bolton, *The Hardest Deal of All*, 145–47.

23. Bolton, *The Hardest Deal of All*, 100, 143–45.

24. Alan Wieder, "The New Orleans School Crisis of 1960," in Alan Wieder, *Race and Education: Narrative Essays, Oral Histories and Documentary Photography* (New York: Peter Lang, 1997), 81.

25. Alan Wieder, "A School Principal and Desegregation," *Equity & Excellence in Education* 22 (Summer 1986): 127.

26. Carey Goldberg, "Judge W. Arthur Garrity Jr. Is Dead at 79," *New York Times*, 18 September 1999.

27. Susan Greenblatt, "The School Principal as Adversary: Innovation and Factionalism at a Desegregated High School," in *The School Principal and Desegregation*, ed. George W. Noblit and Bill Johnston (Springfield, IL: Charles C. Thomas, 1982), 43–60.

28. Geraldine Kozberg and Jerome Winegar, "The South Boston Story: Implications for Secondary Schools," *Phi Delta Kappan* 62 (April 1981): 566; Diego Ribadeneira, "Winegar Leaving S. Boston High Post," *Boston Globe*, 15 November 1989.

29. Michael Rebell and Arthur Block, "Faculty Desegregation: The Law and Its Implementation," Columbia University Teachers College, ERIC Clearinghouse on Urban Education, 1983.

30. Memo to all school personnel, 6 January 1970, from Superintendent John W. Letson, Subject: Proposed Plans—Staff Integration, Box 2019, Folder 4, Atlanta Education Association Papers, Southern Labor Archives, Georgia State University.

31. Dionne Danns, "Northern Desegregation: A Tale of Two Cities," *History of Education Quarterly* 51 (February 2011): 77–104.

32. "Michigan Principal Tarred, Feathered," *New York Times*, 3 April 1971, 23; *Tuscaloosa News*, 2 April 1971; *Pittsburg Post-Gazette*, 3 April 1971; *Atlanta Daily World*, 4 April 1971.

33. Johns H. Harrington, "L.A.'s Student Blowout," *Phi Delta Kappan* 50 (October 1968): 74–79; Judith Kafka, "'Sitting on a Tinderbox': Racial Conflict, Teacher Discretion, and the Centralization of Disciplinary Authority," *American Journal of Education* 114 (March 2008): 247–70.

34. John Staples Shockley, *Chicano Revolt in a Texas Town* (Notre Dame, IN: University of Notre Dame Press, 1974); Miguel A. Guajardo and Francisco J. Guajardo, "The Impact of *Brown* on the Brown of South Texas: A Micropolitical Perspective on the Education of Mexican Americans in a South Texas Community," *American Educational Research Journal* 41 (Autumn 2004): 501–26; Carlos Muñoz, *Youth, Identity, and Power: The Chicano Movement* (New York: Verso Press, 2007), 79–80; Johns H. Harrington, "L.A.'s Student Blowout," *Phi Delta Kappan* 50 (October 1968): 74–79.

35. Dionne Danns, "Chicago High School Students' Movement for Quality Education, 1966–71," *The Journal of African American History* 88 (Spring 2003): 140; Casey Banas, "Dr. King Backs Dissidents at Jenner School," *Chicago Tribune*, 22 February 1966, A9.

36. Danns, "Chicago High School Students' Movement for Quality Education," 140; Dionne Danns, "Black Student Empowerment and Chicago School Reform Efforts in 1968," *Urban Education* 37 (November 2002): 631–55.

37. Mark M. Krug, "Chicago: The Principals' Predicament," *Phi Delta Kappan* 56 (September 1974): 44.

38. Edith Herman, "Principals: New Victims of Protest," *Chicago Tribune*, 11 February 1973, 8.

39. DeeAnn Grove, "'That Might Not Be Soon Enough': White Administrators' Resistance to Black Student Demands for Integration, East High School, Waterloo, Iowa, 1968," paper presented at the History of Education Society Annual Meeting, Boston, November 2010, 13

40. Grove, "'That Might Not Be Soon Enough,'" 15.

41. Grove, "'That Might Not Be Soon Enough,'" 22–23.

42. Urban and Wagoner, *American Education*, 338.

43. Christina Collins, *"Ethnically Qualified": Race, Merit, and the Selection of Urban Teachers, 1920–1980* (New York: Teachers College Press, 2011), 4–5.

44. Jerry Podair, *The Strike That Changed New York* (New Haven: Yale University Press, 2002), 146; Collins, *"Ethnically Qualified,"* 146–47, 152.

45. Diane Ravitch, *The Great School Wars: A History of New York Public Schools* (New York: Basic Books, 1988), 292–305.

46. Collins, *"Ethnically Qualified,"* 173; Podair, *The Strike That Changed New York*, 159–60; Ravitch, *The Great School Wars*, 302.

47. Robert A. Roessel, "An Overview of the Rough Rock Demonstration School," *Journal of American Indian Education* 7 (May 1968): 11; Teresa McCarty, *A Place to Be Navajo: Rough Rock and the Struggle for Self-Determination in Indigenous Schooling* (Mahwah, NJ: Earlbaum, 2002).

48. Jon Allan Reyhner, *Education and Language Restoration* (Philadelphia: Chelsea House Publishers, 2006), 10, 15.

49. Utah State University and the University of Minnesota started such programs in 1970. Margaret Connell Szasz, *Education and the American Indian: The Road to Self-Determination since 1928* (Albuquerque: University of New Mexico Press, 1999), 166, 295.

50. K. Tsianina Lomawaima and Teresa L. McCarty, *To Remain an Indian: Lessons in Democracy from a Century of Native American Education* (New York: Teachers College Press, 2006), 117.

51. Rubén Donato, *Mexicans and Hispanos in Colorado Schools and Communities, 1920–1960* (Albany: State University of New York Press, 2007), 116–17.

52. John Palmer Spencer, "Caught in the Crossfire: Marcus Foster and America's Urban Education Crisis, 1941–1973," unpublished PhD diss., New York University, 2002, 67; John Spencer, "A 'New Breed' of Principal: Marcus Foster and Urban School Reform in the United States, 1966–1969," *Journal of Educational Administration and History* 41 (August 2009): 285–300.

53. Spencer, "Caught in the Crossfire," 288.

54. Spencer, "Caught in the Crossfire," 114–15

55. Spencer, "Caught in the Crossfire," 104–05

56. Foster quoted in John Spencer, "Updating 'No Child Left Behind': Change, or More of the Same?" *Origins* 3 (June 2010), http://ehistory.osu.edu/osu/origins/article.cfm?articleid=41.

57. David L. Kirp, *Just Schools: The Idea of Racial Equality in American Education* (Berkeley: University of California Press, 1982), 242; Jo Ann Robinson, with Gertrude Williams, *Education as My Agenda: Gertrude Williams, Race, and the Baltimore Public Schools* (New York: Palgrave Macmillan, 2005), 112.

58. Joseph Watras, *Politics, Race and Schools: Racial Integration, 1954–1994* (New York: Garland, 1997), 136–37.

CHAPTER SIX. INSTRUCTIONAL LEADERS IN HIGH-STAKES SCHOOLS

1. Linda Perlstein, *Tested: One American School Struggles to Make the Grade* (New York: Henry Holt, 2007), 9.

2. Linda Perlstein, "Unintended Consequences: High Stakes Can Result in Low Standards," *American Educator* 34 (Summer 2010): 6–9.

3. Christina Asquith, *The Emergency Teacher* (New York: Skyhorse, 2007).

4. Dorothy Shipps and Monica White, "A New Politics of the Principalship? Accountability-Driven Change in New York City," *Peabody Journal of Education* 84 (July 2009): 363.

5. Jonathan Mahler, "Reformed School," *New York Times Magazine*, 10 April 2011, 36.

6. Jim Carl, *Freedom of Choice: Vouchers in American Education* (Santa Barbara, CA: Praeger, 2011).

7. Diane Ravitch, *The Death and Life of the Great American School System* (New York: Basic Books, 2012), 125.

8. Judith Kafka, "The Principalship in Historical Perspective," *Peabody Journal of Education* 84 (July 2009): 318–30.

9. Ralph W. Tyler, "Leadership Role of the School Administrator in Curriculum and Instruction," *The Elementary School Journal* 54 (December, 1953): 200–01.

10. Steven T. Bossert, David C. Dwyer, Brian Rowan, and Ginny V. Lee, "The Instructional Management Role of the Principal," *Educational Administration Quarterly* 18 (Summer 1982): 36–37; Stewart C. Purkey and Marshall S. Smith, "Effective Schools: A Review," *The Elementary School Journal* 83 (1983): 429; Michael Rutter, Barbara Maughan, Peter Mortimore, and Janet Ouston, *Fifteen Thousand Hours* (Cambridge, MA: Harvard University Press, 1979).

11. Ronald Edmonds, "Effective Schools for the Urban Poor," *Educational Leadership* 37 (October 1979): 18.

12. Gerald W. Bracey, "The Principal Principle?" *Phi Delta Kappan* 69 (May 1988): 689.

13. Karl E. Weick, "Educational Organizations as Loosely Coupled Systems," *Administrative Science Quarterly* 21 (1976): 1–19.

14. Philip Hallinger, "The Evolving Role of American Principals: From Managerial to Instructional to Transformational Leaders," *Journal of Educational Administration* 30 (1992): 35–48.

15. Daniel L. Duke, *Education Empire: The Evolution of an Excellent Suburban School System* (Albany: State University of New York Press, 2005), 36–39.

16. Duke, *Education Empire*, 36–51; Joseph W. Newman, *America's Teachers: An Introduction to Education* (Boston: Allyn and Bacon, 2002), 333; Thomas B. Parrish, "Special Education Finance: Past, Present, and Future," Policy Paper Number 8 (Palo Alto, CA: American Institutes for Research in the Behavioral Sciences, Center for Special Education Finance, May 1996).

17. Jack Dougherty, "Shopping for Schools: How Public Education and Private Housing Shaped Suburban Connecticut," *Journal of Urban History* 38 (2012): 205–24.

18. Ravitch, *The Death and Life of the Great American School System*, 16–26.

19. Ravitch, *The Death and Life of the Great American School System*, 95–96.

20. Ravitch, *The Death and Life of the Great American School System*, 152.

21. Anthony Alvarado quoted in "Making Schools Work with Hedrick Smith," http://www.pbs.org/makingschoolswork/dwr/ny/alvarado.html, retrieved 21 February 2011.

22. Mary Kay Stein, "Public School 1: The Alfred E. Smith School: Community District #2: A Case Study," February 1998. University of Pittsburgh, High Performance Learning Communities Project, Learning Research and Development Center.

23. Michael Winerip, "On Education: The 'Zero Dropout' Miracle: Alas! Alack! A Texas Tall Tale," *New York Times* 13 August 2003; Gerald W. Bracey, "Kicked Down and Out by the Texas Miracle," *Phi Delta Kappan* 89 (May 2008): 699–700; Jennifer Booher-Jennings, "Below the Bubble: 'Educational Triage' and the

Texas Accountability System," *American Educational Research Journal* 42 (Summer 2005): 231–68.

24. Marla W. McGhee and Sarah W. Nelson, "Sacrificing Leaders: Villainizing Leadership: How Educational Accountability Policies Impair School Leadership," *Phi Delta Kappan* 86 (January 2005): 368.

25. John E. Chubb and Terry M. Moe, *Politics, Markets and American's Schools* (Washington DC: Brookings Institute, 1990), 85.

26. Jonathan Mahler, "Reformed School," *New York Times Magazine*, 10 April 2011, 36–37, 57.

27. James G. Cibulka, "The City-State Partnership to Reform Baltimore's Public Schools," in *Powerful Reforms with Shallow Roots*, ed. Larry Cuban and Michael Usdan (New York: Teachers College Press, 2003), 253; Simon Hakim, Daniel J. Ryan, and Judith C. Stull, eds., *Restructuring Education: Innovations and Evaluations of Alternative Systems* (Westport, CT: Praeger, 2000), 8; James G. Cibulka, "Educational Bankruptcy, Takeovers, and Reconstitution of Failing Schools," *Yearbook of the National Society for the Study of Education* 102 (April 2003): 249–70.

28. Susan F. Semel and Alan R. Sadovnik, "The Contemporary Small-School Movement: Lessons from the History of Progressive Education," *Teachers College Record* 110 (September 2008): 1744–71.

29. Ravitch, *The Death and Life of the Great American School System*, 36.

30. Ravitch, *The Death and Life of the Great American School System*, 50–53, 164; Clara Hemphill, Kim Nauer, with Helen Zelon and Thomas Jacobs, *The New Market Place: How Small-School Reforms and School Choice Have Reshaped New York City's High Schools* (New York: Center for New York City Affairs, 2009), 21.

31. Helen F. Ladd, "The Dallas School Accountability and Incentive Program: An Evaluation of Its Impact on Student Outcomes," *Economics of Education Review* 18 (1999): 1–16.

32. Deborah L. West, Craig Peck, and Ulrich C. Reitzug, "Limited Control and Relentless Accountability: Examining Historical Changes in Urban School Principal Pressure," *Journal of School Leadership* 20 (March 2012): 238–66; Helen F. Ladd and Arnaldo Zelli, "School-Based Accountability in North Carolina: The Responses of School Principals," *Educational Administration Quarterly* 38 (October 2002): 494–529.

33. Philip Hallinger and Ronald. H. Heck, "Reassessing the Principal's Role in School Effectiveness: A Review of Empirical Research, 1980–1995," *Educational Administration Quarterly* 32 (February 1996): 6.

34. Joe Murphy, "School Administration Responds to Pressures for Change," in *The Educational Reform Movement of the 1980s*, ed. Joe Murphy (Berkeley, CA: McCutchan, 1990), 318.

35. John Portz and Robert Schwartz, "Governing the Boston Public Schools: Lessons in Mayoral Control," in *When Mayors Take Charge: School Governance in the City*, ed. Joseph P. Vitteritti (Washington, DC: Brookings Institution Press, 2009), 105; Paul Reville and Celine Coggins, eds., *A Decade of Urban School Reform: Persistence and Progress in the Boston Public Schools* (Cambridge: Harvard University Press, 2007).

36. Wilbur C. Rich, "Who's Afraid of a Mayoral Takeover of Detroit Public Schools?" in *When Mayors Take Charge: School Governance in the City*, ed. Joseph P. Vitteritti (Washington, DC: Brookings Institution Press, 2009), 155.

37. Larry Cuban and Michael Usdan, eds., *Powerful Reforms with Shallow Roots: Improving America's Urban Schools* (New York: Teachers College Press, 2003), 8; G. A. Hess, *Restructuring Urban Schools: A Chicago Perspective* (New York: Teachers College Press), 49.

38. Quoted in Clara Hemphill, "Parent Power and Mayoral Control: Parent and Community Involvement in New York City Schools," in *When Mayors Take Charge: School Governance in the City*, ed. Joseph P. Vitteritti (Washington, DC: Brookings Institution Press, 2009), 203.

39. Dorothy Shipps, "Updating Tradition: The Institutional Underpinnings of Modern Mayoral Control in Chicago's Public Schools," in *When Mayors Take Charge: School Governance in the City*, ed. Joseph P. Vitteritti (Washington, DC: Brookings Institution Press, 2009), 121–22.

40. Michael W. Kirst, "Mayoral Control of Schools: Politics, Trade-Offs, and Outcomes," in *When Mayors Take Charge: School Governance in the City*, ed. Joseph P. Vitteritti (Washington, DC: Brookings Institution Press, 2009), 61.

41. Shipps, "Updating Tradition," 127–28; Mary Mitchell, "Lightning Rod: Four Takes on Jerryelyn Jones' Ouster from Curie," *Chicago Sun-Times*, 13 March 2007; Aaron Chambers, "No Traction on Plan to Strip LSC Powers," *Catalyst Chicago*, May 2007.

42. Gary Yee and Barbara McCloud, "A Vision of Hope: A Case Study of Seattle's Two Nontraditional Superintendents," in *Powerful Reforms with Shallow Roots: Improving America's Urban Schools*, ed. Larry Cuban and Michael Usdan (New York: Teachers College Press, 2003), 65–66.

43. Ruth Teichroeb, "Weak Leaders Threaten John Stanford's Goal of 'World Class" Schools in Seattle, Critics Say," *Seattle Post-Intelligencer*, 13 July 1998.

44. Debera Carlton Harrell, "Demotions of Principals Send Message to Improve," *Seattle Post-Intelligencer*, 17 May 2000.

45. Charles Taylor Kerchner and Julia E. Koppich, *A Union of Professionals: Labor Relations and Educational Reform* (New York: Teachers College Press, 1993), 15; Sharon C. Conley and Samuel B. Bacharach, "From School-Site Management to Participatory School-Site Management," *Phi Delta Kappan* 71 (March 1990): 539–44.

46. Gerald Grant and Christine E. Murray, *Teaching in America: The Slow Revolution* (Cambridge: Harvard University Press, 1999), 205; Jeanne Kohl Jenkins, "Advisory Councils and Principals in Los Angeles," *Integrated Education* 79 (January–February 1976): 27–31.

47. Tom Mooney quoted in Kerchner and Koppich, *A Union of Professionals*, 71.

48. Kerchner and Koppich, *A Union of Professionals*, 147–48; Grant and Murray, *Teaching in America*, 141–81.

49. Dorothy Shipps and Monica White, "A New Politics of the Principalship?" *Peabody Journal of Education* 84 (July 2009): 363.

50. National Commission on Excellence in Educational Administration, *Leaders for America's Schools: The Report of the National Commission on Excellence in Educational Administration* (Tempe, AZ: UCEA, 1987); Frederick M. Hess and Andrew P. Kelly, "Learning to Lead: What Gets Taught in Principal-Preparation Programs," *Teachers College Record* 109 (January 2007): 268.

51. Arthur Levine, *Educating School Leaders* (New York: The Educating School Project, 2005), 16–17.

52. Richard F. Elmore, "Breaking the Cartel," *Phi Delta Kappan* 87 (March 2006): 517.

53. Murphy, "School Administration Responds to Pressures for Change," 306–07; Stephen Davis, Linda Darling-Hammond, Michelle LaPointe, and Debra Meyerson, "School Leadership Study: Developing Successful Principals," Stanford Educational Leadership Institute, 2005: 11.

54. Richard F. Elmore and Deanna Burney, "Leadership and Learning: Principal Recruitment, Induction and Instructional Leadership in Community School District #2, New York City," University of Pittsburgh, High Performance Learning Communities Project, Learning Research and Development Center, 4.

55. Suzette Lovely, *Staffing the Principalship: Finding, Coaching, and Mentoring School Leaders* (Alexandria, VA: ASCD, 2004); Jimmy Guterman, "Where Have All the Principals Gone?: The Acute School-Leader Shortage," *Edutopia,*7 June 2007, http://www.edutopia.org/where-have-all-principals-gone; Kathryn S. Whitaker, "Exploring Causes of Principal Burnout," *Journal of Educational Administration* 34 (1996): 60–71.

56. Ashley Miller, "Principal Turnover, Student Achievement and Teacher Retention," Princeton University, 2009, http://www.ers.princeton.edu/Miller.pdf.

57. Jesse L. Colquit, "The Increase in Black Administrators in Metropolitan School Systems," *NAASP Bulletin* 59 (October 1975): 70–74; Aretha B. Pigford, "An Administrator Training Program for Minorities," *Phi Delta Kappan* 70 (April 1989): 650–51.

58. Education Writers Association, "Searching for a Superhero: Can Principals Do It All?" (New York: The Wallace Foundation, 2002), 6; D. Michael Pavel, "Comparing BIA and Tribal Schools with Public Schools: A Look at the Year 1990–91," *Journal of American Indian Education* 35 (October 1995): 10–15.

59. Carol Millsom, "Women and Education," *Educational Leadership* 31 (November 1973): 99; Thelma Sardin, "Number of Women Principals in United States Low, but Growing," *Reading Today* 12 (February–March 1995): 16.

60. *National Association of Elementary School Principals, the K–8 Principal in 2008: A 10-Year Study* (Alexandria, VA: National Association of Elementary School Principals, 2009), 69, 142.

61. G. Bottoms and K. O'Neill, *Preparing a New Breed of School Principals: It's Time for Action* (Atlanta, GA: Southern Regional Education Board, 2001).

62. Pat Thomson, Jill Blackmore, Judyth Sachs, and Karen Tregenza, "High Stakes Principalship—Sleepless Nights, Heart Attacks and Sudden Death Accountabilities: Reading Media Representations of the United States Principal Shortage," *Australian Journal of Education* 47 (2003): 128; Linda Tillman and James Trier, "Boston Public as Public Pedagogy: Implications for Teacher Preparation and School Leadership," *Peabody Journal of Education* 82 (2007): 121–49; Jeffrey Glanz, "Images of Principals on Television and in the Movies," *Clearing House* 70 (July–August 1997): 295–97.

63. Sharon H. Pristash, *What People Think Principals Do* (Lanham, MD: Scarecrow Press, 2002), 75.

64. Linda C. Tillman, "Halls of Anger: The (Mis) Representation of African American Principals in Film," in *Keeping the Promise: Essays on Leadership, Democracy, and Education,* ed. Dennis Carlson and C. P. Gause (New York: Peter Lang, 2007).

65. Kathleen Porter-Magee, "Teacher Quality, Controversy, and NCLB," *Clearing House* 78 (September–October, 2004): 26–29.

66. I. Hyman, "The 'Make Believe World' of 'Lean on Me.' *Education Week,* 26 April 1989, 27, 29.

67. Penny Smith, "Rethinking Joe: Exploring the Borders of *Lean on Me,*" in *Popular Culture and Critical Pedagogy: Reading, Constructing, Connecting,* ed. Toby Daspit and John A. Weaver (New York: Garland Press, 1999), 8.

68. Penny Smith, "Sex, Lies and Hollywood's Administrators: The (de) Construction of School Leadership in Contemporary Films," *Journal of Educational Administration* 37 (1999): 50–66.

69. Susan Kammaradd-Campbell, *Doc: The Story of Dennis Littky and His Fight for a Better School* (New York: Contemporary Books, 1989).

70. Ken Romines, *A Principal's Story: Two-Year Effort to Turn Around Edison Elementary School in San Francisco* (San Francisco: Study Center Press, 1997).

71. Ryan White and Ann Marie Cunningham, *Ryan White: My Own Story* (New York: Dial Books, 1991); George H. Wood, *Schools That Work: America's Most Innovative Public Education Programs* (New York: Plume, 1992).

72. Michael Brick, *Saving the School: The True Story of a Principal, a Teacher, a Coach, a Bunch of Kids, and a Year in the Crosshairs of Education Reform* (New York: Penguin Press, 2012), 263–65.

73. Ramon Cortines, quoted in Romines, *A Principal's Story,* 5.

CONCLUSION: IN THE PRINCIPAL'S OFFICE

1. Richard O. Jones, "Principal Roles Changing for 21st Century Schools," *Hamilton Journal News* (Ohio) 7 May 2012, C1.

SELECTED BIBLIOGRAPHY

The following selected bibliography includes major works used in this book that specifically concern the history of school principals. Researchers should also consult the journals, bulletins, yearbooks, and newsletters of the national associations of secondary school principals and elementary school principals, as well as the proceedings and professional publications of the National Education Association. Professional journals such as *Phi Delta Kappan, American School Board Journal*, and *The American Teacher* have long publication histories that document much of early school administration. All other references are cited in the notes.

Archival depositories, historical societies, and libraries consulted include: the Kenneth Spencer Research Library, University of Kansas, Lawrence, Kansas; the Western Reserve Historical Society, Cleveland, Ohio; the New Jersey Historical Society, Newark, New Jersey; the Vermont Historical Society, Barre, Vermont; the Woodstock Historical Society, Woodstock, Vermont; the Chicago Historical Society, Chicago, Illinois; the Monroe C. Gutman Library, Harvard University; and the University Library of the University of Illinois at Urbana-Champaign, Illinois. Three archival collections were especially rich for this work: the Southern Labor Archives, Georgia State University, Atlanta, Georgia; the National Education Association Archives, George Washington University, Washington, D.C.; and the American Federation of Teachers Archives at the Walter Reuther Library, Wayne State University, Detroit.

Abney, Everett E. "The Status of Florida's Black School Principals." *The Journal of Negro Education* 43 (Winter 1974).

Alston, Judy A. "Tempered Radicals and Servant Leaders: Black Females Persevering in the Superintendency." *Educational Administration Quarterly* 41 (October 2005).

Ayer, Fred C. "The Duties of the Public School Administrator." *American School Board Journal* 78 (April 1929).

Ayer, Fred C. "The Rise of Supervision." In *Educational Supervision: A Report of Current Views, Investigations, and Practices*, ed., James Fleming Hosic. New York: Teachers College Press,1928.

Beck, Lynn G., and Joseph Murphy. *Understanding the Principalship: Metaphorical Themes, 1920–1990s*. New York: Teachers College Press, 1993.

Berg, Paul. "The Impact of Collective Bargaining upon the Principal." *Administrator's Notebook* 21 (September, 1972–June 1973).

Blount, Jackie. *Destined to Rule the Schools: Women and the Superintendency, 1873–1995.* Albany: State University of New York Press, 1998.

Blount, Jackie. "Manliness and the Gendered Construction of School Administration in the USA." *International Journal of Leadership in Education* 2 (April–June 1999).

Booher-Jennings, Jennifer. "Below the Bubble: 'Educational Triage' and the Texas Accountability System." *American Educational Research Journal* 42 (Summer 2005).

Bossert, Steven T., David C. Dwyer, Brian Rowan, and Ginny V. Lee. "The Instructional Management Role of the Principal." *Educational Administration Quarterly* 18 (Summer 1982).

Bottoms, Gene, and Kathy O'Neill. *Preparing a New Breed of School Principals: It's Time for Action.* Atlanta, GA: Southern Regional Education Board, 2001.

Bracey, Gerald W. "The Principal Principle?" *Phi Delta Kappan* 69 (May 1988).

Brick, Michael. *Saving the School: The True Story of a Principal, a Teacher, a Coach, a Bunch of Kids, and a Year in the Crosshairs of Education Reform.* New York: Penguin Press, 2012.

Bridges, Edwin M., and Bruce S. Cooper. "Collective Bargaining for School Administrators." *Theory into Practice* 15 (October 1976).

Butchart, Ronald E. "Edmonia G. and Caroline V. Highgate: Black Teachers, Freed Slaves, and the Betrayal of Black Hearts." In *Portraits of African American Life since 1865,* ed. Nina Mjagkij. Wilmington, DE: Scholarly Resources, 2003.

Campbell, Roald F. *The Making of a Professor: A Memoir.* Salt Lake City, UT: Westwater Press, 1981.

Cary, Miles E. "'Final Authority' and the Schools." *Educational Administration and Supervision* 33 (1946).

Cary, Miles E. "Initiating Creative Curriculum Development." *The North Central Association Quarterly* 23 (April 1949).

Cary, Miles E. "Intergroup and Inter-racial Education." *Proceedings of the Thirty-Second Annual Convention, National Association of Secondary School Principals* (March 1948).

Cary, Miles E. "Learning Comes Through Living." *Educational Leadership* 4 (May 1947).

Castelow, Teri L. "'Creating an Educational Interest': Sophia Sawyer, Teacher of the Cherokee." In *Chartered Schools: Two Hundred Years of Independent Academies in the United States, 1727–1925,* ed. Nancy Beadie and Kim Tolley. New York: Routledge, 2002.

Chancellor, W. E. *Our Schools: Their Administration and Supervision.* Boston: D. C. Heath, 1908.

Chreitzberg, James. "A Rural High School and Its Community." *The Southern Association Quarterly* 3 (1939).

Coffmann, Lotus D. "The Control of Educational Progress thru School Supervision." In *Proceedings and Addresses of the Annual Meeting of the National Education Association of the United States* (Washington, D.C.: National Education Association, 1917).

Cole, M. Norwood. "The Licensing of Schoolmasters in Colonial New England." *History of Education Journal* 8 (Winter 1957).

Colquit, Jesse L. "The Increase in Black Administrators in Metropolitan School Systems." *NAASP Bulletin* 59 (October 1975).

Connors, F. Herrick, and J. Cayce Morrison. "A Contrast of the Preparation and Work of Men and Women Elementary School Principals." *Educational Research Bulletin* 4 (November 18, 1925).

Cooper, Bruce S. "Collective Bargaining Comes to School Middle Management." *Phi Delta Kappan* 58 (October, 1976).

Cooper, Bruce S. "Collective Bargaining for School Administrators Four Years Later." *Phi Delta Kappan* 61 (October 1979).

Crandell, C. W. "The Relationship between Principals and Supervisors." *Bulletin of the Department of Elementary School Principals* 8 (April 1929).

Crocco, Margaret Smith. "The Price of an Activist Life: Elizabeth Almira Allen and Marion Thompson Wright." In *Pedagogies of Resistance: Women Educator Activists, 1880–1960* ed. Margaret Smith Crocco, Petra Munro, and Kathleen Weiler. New York: Teachers College Press, 1999.

Crouch, Roy A. "Status of the Elementary School Principal." *Fifth Yearbook, Department of Elementary School Principals* (July 1926).

Cuban, Larry. *The Managerial Imperative and the Practice of Leadership in Schools.* Albany: State University of New York Press,1988.

Cubberley, Ellwood P. "The Principal and the Principalship." *The Elementary School Journal* 23 (January 1923).

Cunningham, Luverne L. "Collective Negotiations and the Principalship." *Theory into Practice* 7 (April 1968).

Danns, Dionne. "Thriving in the Midst of Adversity: Educator Maudelle Brown Bousfield's Struggles in Chicago, 1920–1950." *The Journal of Negro Education* 78 (Winter 2009)

Davis, Stephen, Linda Darling-Hammond, Michelle LaPointe, and Debra Meyerson. "School Leadership Study: Developing Successful Principals." Stanford Educational Leadership Institute, 2005.

Deffenbaugh, W. S. "Administration of Schools in the Smaller Cities." *Bureau of Education Bulletin* 2 (1922).

Dodge, Chester C. *Reminiscences of a School Master.* Chicago: Ralph Fletcher Seymour, 1941.

Drummond, Anne. "Gender, Profession, and Principals: The Teachers of Quebec Protestant Academies, 1875–1900." *Historical Studies in Education* 2 (Spring 1990).

Edmonds, Ronald. "Effective Schools for the Urban Poor." *Educational Leadership* 37 (October 1979).

Education Writers Association. "Searching for a Superhero: Can Principals Do It All?" New York: The Wallace Foundation, 2002.

Eikenberry, Dan Harrison. "Status of the High School Principal." No. 24, Department of the Interior, Bureau of Education, 1925.

Elmore, Richard F. "Breaking the Cartel." *Phi Delta Kappan* 87 (March 2006).

Elmore, Richard F., and Deanna Burney. "Leadership and Learning: Principal Recruitment, Induction and Instructional Leadership in Community School District #2, New York City." University of Pittsburgh, High Performance Learning Communities Project, Learning Research and Development Center.

Elsbree, Willard S., and E. Edmund Reutter Jr. *Principles of Staff Personnel Administration in Public Schools.* New York: Teachers College Press, 1954.

Engelhardt, Fred, and Ernest Melby. "The Supervisory Organization and Instructional Program, Albert Lea, Minnesota." *Bulletin of University of Minnesota* 17 (August 1928).

Estler, Suzanne E. "Women as Leaders in Public Education." *Signs* 1 (Winter 1975).

Feuerstein, Abe. "School Administration and the Changing Face of Masculinity." *Journal of School Leadership* 16 (January 2006).

Fishel, Andrew, and Janice Pottker. "Women in Educational Governance: A Statistical Portrait." *Educational Researcher* 3 (July–August 1974).

Fleming, Thomas, ed. *School Leadership: Essays on the British Columbia Experience, 1872–1995.* Mill Bay, British Columbia: Bendall Books, 2001.

Garrison, Martin B. "An Analysis of the Preparation Program in Educational Administration at George Peabody College for Teachers." George Peabody College for Teachers master's thesis, 1956.

Glanz, Jeffrey. "Beyond Bureaucracy: Notes on the Professionalization of Public School Supervision in the Early 20th Century." *Journal of Curriculum & Supervision* 5 (Winter 1990).

Glanz, Jeffrey. *Bureaucracy and Professionalism: The Evolution of Public School Supervision.* Madison, NJ: Farleigh Dickinson University Press, 1991.

Glanz, Jeffrey. "Histories, Antecedents, and Legacies of School Supervision." In *Handbook of Research on School Supervision,* ed. Gerald R. Firth and Edward F. Pajak. New York: Macmillan, 1998.

Glanz, Jeffrey. "Images of Principals on Television and in the Movies." *Clearing House* 70 (July–August 1997).

Glass, Thomas E. *The History of Educational Administration Viewed through Its Textbooks.* Lanham, MD: Scarecrow, 2004.

Goldhammer, Keith. "Evolution in the Profession." *Educational Administration Quarterly* 19 (Summer 1983).

Goldhammer, Keith, John E. Suttle, William D. Aldridge, and Gerald L. Becker. *Issues and Problems in Contemporary Educational Administration.* Eugene, OR: The Center for the Advanced Study of Educational Administration, 1967.

Goodykoontz, Bess, and Jessie A. Lane. *The Elementary School Principalship.* Bulletin No. 8. Washington, DC: U.S. Department of the Interior, 1938.

Greenblatt, Susan. "The School Principal as Adversary: Innovation and Factionalism at a Desegregated High School." In *The School Principal and Desegregation,* ed. George W. Noblit and Bill Johnston. Springfield, IL: Charles C. Thomas, 1982.

Gribskov, Margaret. "Adelaide Pollock and the Founding of the NCAWE." In *Women Educators: Employees of Schools in Western Countries,* ed. Patricia Schmuck. Albany: State University of New York Press, 1987.

Grossman, Lawrence. "In His Veins Coursed No Bootlicking Blood: The Career of Peter H. Clark." *Ohio History* 86 (Spring 1977).

Grove, DeeAnn. " 'That Might Not Be Soon Enough': White Administrators' Resistance to Black Student Demands for Integration, East High School, Waterloo, Iowa, 1968." Paper presented at the History of Education Society Annual Meeting, Boston, November 2010.

Guterman, Jimmy. "Where Have All the Principals Gone?: The Acute School-Leader Shortage." *Edutopia*, 7 June 2007, http://www.edutopia.org/where-have-all-principals-gone.

Hallinger, Philip. "The Evolving Role of American Principals: From Managerial to Instructional to Transformational Leaders." *Journal of Educational Administration* 30 (1992).

Hallinger, Philip, and Ronald. H. Heck. "Reassessing the Principal's Role in School Effectiveness: A Review of Empirical Research, 1980–1995." *Educational Administration Quarterly* 32 (February 1996).

Harris, Lewis E., and Rae Harris. *Bootstraps: A Chronicle of a Real Community School.* Cable, WI: Harris Publications, 1980.

Hart, Frank W. "Special Certification as a Means of Professionalizing Educational Leadership." *Teachers College Record* 27 (1925).

Hassenpflug, Ann. "Murder in the Classroom: Privilege, Honor, and Cultural Violence in Antebellum Louisville." *Ohio Valley History* 4 (Summer 2004).

Heller, Robert W. "The Principal's Role in Planning for a Teacher Strike." *NASSP Bulletin* 62 (May 1978).

Hentoff, Nat. "The Principal." *The New Yorker.* 7 May 1966.

Hess, Frederick M., and Andrew P. Kelly. "Learning to Lead: What Gets Taught in Principal-Preparation Programs." *Teachers College Record* 109 (January 2007).

Hinton, Eugene M. "An Investigation of the High School Principalship as a Profession." *Phi Delta Kappan* 5 (November 1922).

Hosic, James F. "Appropriate Graduate Work for Elementary School Principals." *Teachers College Record* 33 (1931).

Hosic, James F. "College Course for Elementary School Principals." *Teachers College Record* 27 (1926).

Hurwitz, Howard. *The Last Angry Principal.* Portland, OR: Halcyon House, 1988.

Hyman, I. A. "The 'Make Believe World' of 'Lean on Me.'" *Education Week*, 26 April 1989.

Jenkins, Jeanne Kohl. "Advisory Councils and Principals in Los Angeles." *Integrated Education* 79 (January–February 1976).

Johanek, Michael C., and John L. Puckett. *Leonard Covello and the Making of Benjamin Franklin High School: Education as if Citizenship Mattered.* Philadelphia: Temple University Press, 2007.

Johnson, Lauri. "A Generation of Women Activists: African American Female Educators in Harlem, 1930–1950." *The Journal of African American History* 89 (Summer 2004).

Johnson, Lauri. "Making Her Community a Better Place to Live: Lessons from History for Culturally Responsive Urban School Leadership." In *Keeping the Promise: Essays on Leadership, Democracy, and Education*, ed. Dennis Carlson and C. P. Gause. New York: Peter Lang, 2007.

Jones, Olive M. "The Principal's Multiple Functioning." *Bulletin of the Department of Elementary School Principals* 2 (April 1923).

Kafka, Judith. "The Principalship in Historical Perspective." *Peabody Journal of Education* 84 (July 2009).

Karpinski, Carol F. "Bearing the Burden of Desegregation: Black Principals and *Brown*." *Urban Education* 41 (May 2006).

Knoester, William P. "Administrative Unionization: What Kind of Solution?" *Phi Delta Kappan* 59 (February 1978).

Koos, Leonard V. *The High School Principal: His Training, Experience, and Responsibilities*. Boston: Houghton Mifflin, 1924.

Kozberg, Geraldine, and Jerome Winegar. "The South Boston Story: Implications for Secondary Schools." *Phi Delta Kappan* 62 (April 1981).

Kritek, William J., and Delbert K. Clear. "Teachers and Principals in the Milwaukee Public Schools." In *Seeds of Crisis: Public Schooling in Milwaukee since 1920*, ed. John L. Rury and Frank A. Cassell. Madison: University of Wisconsin Press, 1993.

Krug, Mark M. "Chicago: The Principals' Predicament." *Phi Delta Kappan* 56 (September 1974).

Ladd, Helen F., and Arnaldo Zelli. "School-Based Accountability in North Carolina: The Responses of School Principals." *Educational Administration Quarterly* 38 (October 2002).

Lauderdale, William Burt. *Progressive Education: Lessons from Three Schools*. Bloomington, IN: Phi Delta Kappa Educational Foundations, 1981.

Levine, Arthur. *Educating School Leaders*. New York: The Educating School Project, 2005.

Lewis, Heather. *The "Bad Old Days": The Community Control Movement and Its Legacy in New York City Schools*. New York: Teachers College Press, 2013.

Lewis, Heather. "'There Are No More Hiding Places—Even in Bedford Stuyvesant': The School Leader at the Nexus of Bureaucracy and Accountability in the 1970s." History of Education Society Annual Meeting, Tampa, Florida, 2008.

Link, William A. "The School That Built a Town: Public Education and the Southern Social Landscape, 1880–1930." In *Essays in Twentieth-Century Southern Education*, ed. Wayne J. Urban. Garland: New York, 1999.

Lovely, Suzette. *Staffing the Principalship: Finding, Coaching, and Mentoring School Leaders*. Alexandria, VA: ASCD, 2004.

Lugg, Catherine. "Our Strait-Laced Administrators: The Law, Lesbian, Gay, Bisexual and Transgendered Educational Administrators and the Assimilationist Imperative." *Journal of School Leadership* 13 (January 2003).

McAndrew, Gordon L. "The High-School Principal: Man in the Middle." *Daedalus* 110 (Summer 1981).

McAndrew, William. *The Public and Its School*. Yonkers-on-Hudson, NY: World Book Co., 1917.

McClure, Worth. "The Organizing and Administrative Work of the School Principal." In *Modern School Administration: Its Problems and Progress*, ed. John C. Almack. Boston: Houghton Mifflin, 1933.

McGhee, Marla W., and Sarah W. Nelson. "Sacrificing Leaders: Villainizing Leadership: How Educational Accountability Policies Impair School Leadership." *Phi Delta Kappan* 86 (January 2005).

Miller, Ashley. "Principal Turnover, Student Achievement and Teacher Retention." Princeton University, 2009. http://www.ers.princeton.edu/Miller.pdf.

Millsom, Carol. "Women and Education." *Educational Leadership* 31 (November 1973).

Morris, Vivian Gunn. *The Price They Paid: Desegregation in an African American Community*. New York: Teachers College Press, 2002.

Murphy, Joe. "School Administration Responds to Pressures for Change." In *The Educational Reform Movement of the 1980s*, ed. Joe Murphy. Berkeley, CA: McCutchan, 1990.

Murphy, Michael J., and Neil Ellman. "The Building Principal and the Union: A Study in Mutual Accommodation." *IAR Research Bulletin* 14 (June 1974).

National Association of Elementary School Principals. *The K-8 Principal in 2008: A 10-Year Study*. Alexandria, VA: National Association of Elementary School Principals, 2009.

National Commission on Excellence in Educational Administration. *Leaders for America's Schools: The Report of the National Commission on Excellence in Educational Administration*. Tempe, AZ: UCEA, 1987.

National Conference of Professors of Educational Administration. *Providing and Improving Administrative Leadership in America's Schools*. The Fourth Report. New York: Teachers College, Columbia University, 1951.

Newman, Joseph W. "Mary C. Barker and the Atlanta Teachers' Union." In *Southern Workers and Their Unions, 1880–1975*, ed. Merl E. Reed, Leslie S. Hough, and Gary M. Fink. Westport, CT: Greenwood Press, 1981.

Olson, Ronald K. "Tinker and the Administrator." *School and Society* 100 (February 1972).

Parker, Franklin. "Ezekiel Cheever: New England Colonial Teacher." *Peabody Journal of Education* 37 (May 1960).

Patri, Angelo. *A Schoolmaster of a Great City*. New York: Macmillan, 1921.

Peck, Craig. " 'Carry Me Out Piece by Piece': Fighting for Principal Power in New York City, 1966–1977." Paper delivered at American Educational Research Association Annual meeting, April 2011, New Orleans.

Perlstein, Linda. *Tested: One American School Struggles to Make the Grade*. New York: Henry Holt, 2007.

Peterson, B. H. "Certification of School Administrators in the United States." *School and Society* 45 (1937).

Pharis, Bill. "How to Know if You Need a Raise: The Latest Scoop on Salaries." *The National Elementary Principal* 59 (March 1980).

Pierce, Paul Revere. *The Origin and Development of the Public School Principalship*. Chicago: University of Chicago, 1935.

Pigford, Aretha B. "An Administrator Training Program for Minorities." *Phi Delta Kappan* 70 (April 1989).

Reavis, William C. "According the Principal a Larger Autonomy in His Own School." *Fundamentals in a Democratic School, University of Pennsylvania Bulletin* (March 30–April 2, 1938).

Reavis, William C. "Democratic Ideals in Teaching and Administration." In *Education in a Democracy*, ed. Newton Edwards. Chicago: University of Chicago Press, 1941.

Rebell, Michael, and Arthur Block. "Faculty Desegregation: The Law and Its Implementation." Columbia University Teachers College, ERIC Clearinghouse on Urban Education, 1983.

Ritchie, Richard M., and Ritchard M. Ritchie. "Due Process and the Principal." *Phi Delta Kappan* 54 (January 1973).

Robinson, Jo Ann, with Gertrude Williams. *Education as My Agenda: Gertrude Williams, Race, and the Baltimore Public Schools.* New York: Palgrave Macmillan, 2005.

Rodgers, Frederick A. *The Black High School and Its Community.* Lexington, MA: Lexington Books, 1975.

Rodriguez-Campos, Liliana, Rigoberto Rincones-Gomez, and Jianping Shen. "Principals' Educational Attainment, Experience, and Professional Development." In *School Principals*, ed. Jianping Shen. New York: Peter Lang, 2005.

Roessel, Robert A. "An Overview of the Rough Rock Demonstration School." *Journal of American Indian Education* 7 (May 1968).

Romines, Ken. *A Principal's Story: Two-Year Effort to Turn Around Edison Elementary School in San Francisco.* San Francisco: Study Center Press, 1997.

Sardin, Thelma. "Number of Women Principals in United States Low, but Growing." *Reading Today* 12 (February–March 1995).

Savage, Carter Julian. "Cultural Capital and African American Agency: The Economic Struggle for Effective Education for African Americans in Franklin, Tennessee, 1890–1967." *The Journal of African American History* 87 (Spring 2002).

Schelhardt, T. D. "Losing the Reins: Principals' Rules Erode as Students, Teachers, Parents, Attack Them." *Wall Street Journal*, 25 February 1970.

Schmuck, Patricia. "Advocacy Organizations for Women School Administrators, 1977–1993." In *Women Leading in Education*, ed. Diane M. Dunlap and Patricia A. Schmuck. Albany: State University of New York Press, 1995.

Shannon, Thomas A. "Resolving Management Conflicts through Associations." Arlington, VA: National Association of Elementary School Principals, 1972.

Shipps, Dorothy, and Monica White. "A New Politics of the Principalship? Accountability-Driven Change in New York City." *Peabody Journal of Education* 84 (July 2009).

Shoho, Alan R. "Ethical Leadership: The Principalship of Miles Cary at McKinley ('Tokyo') High School." Paper presented at the meeting of the American Educational Research Association, Chicago, IL, March 1997.

Siddle Walker, Vanessa. *Their Highest Potential: An African American School Community in the Segregated South.* Chapel Hill: University of North Carolina Press, 1996.

Siddle Walker, Vanessa. "Organized Resistance and Black Educators' Quest for School Equality." *Teachers College Record* 107 (March 2005).

Siddle Walker, Vanessa, with Ulysses Byas. *Hello Professor: A Black Principal and Professional Leadership in the Segregated South.* Chapel Hill: University of North Carolina Press, 2009.

Simpson, Douglas J., and Sam F. Stack Jr., eds. *Teachers, Leaders, and Schools: Essays by John Dewey.* Carbondale: Southern Illinois University Press, 2010.

Smith, Penny. "Rethinking Joe: Exploring the Borders of *Lean on Me.*" In *Popular Culture and Critical Pedagogy: Reading, Constructing, Connecting*, ed. Toby Daspit and John A. Weaver. New York: Garland Press, 1999.

Smith, Penny. "Sex, Lies and Hollywood's Administrators: The (de)Construction of School Leadership in Contemporary Films." *Journal of Educational Administration* 37 (1999).

Spencer, John P. *In the Crossfire: Marcus Foster and the Troubled History of American School Reform.* Philadelphia: University of Pennsylvania Press, 2012.

Spencer, John. "A 'New Breed' of Principal: Marcus Foster and Urban School Reform in the United States, 1966–1969." *Journal of Educational Administration and History* 41 (August 2009).

Stearns, Sheila MacDonald. "S. R. Logan: Educator for Democracy, 1885–1970," PhD dissertation, University of Montana, 1983.

Strober, Myra H., and David Tyack. "Why Do Women Teach and Men Manage? A Report on Research on Schools." *Signs* 5 (Spring 1980).

Swett, John. *Public Education in California: Its Origin and Development, with Personal Reminiscences of Half a Century.* New York: American Book Co., 1911, reprinted by Arno Press, 1969.

Tamura, Eileen. "The Struggle for Core Studies: Miles Cary at McKinley High School in the Territory of Hawai'i." *Pacific Educational Research Journal* 8 (1996).

Teed, Melissa Ladd. "Crafting Community: Hartford Public High School in the Nineteenth Century." In *Schools as Imagined Communities: The Creation of Identity, Meaning, and Conflict in U.S. History,* ed. Dierdre Cobb-Roberts, Sherman Dorn, and Barbara Shircliffe. New York: Palgrave, 2006.

Teed, Melissa Ladd. "'If Only I Wore a Coat and Pants': Gender and Power in the Making of an American Public High School, 1847–1851." *Gender and History* 16 (April 2004).

Thomas, John S. "The Status of the Michigan Principalship." *The National Elementary Principal* 12 (October 1932).

Thomas, William B., and Kevin J. Moran. "Reconsidering the Power of the Superintendent in the Progressive Period." *American Educational Research Journal* 29 (Spring 1992).

Thomson, Pat, Jill Blackmore, Judyth Sachs, and Karen Tregenza. "High Stakes Principalship—Sleepless Nights, Heart Attacks and Sudden Death Accountabilities: Reading Media Representations of the United States Principal Shortage." *Australian Journal of Education* 47 (2003).

Tillman, Linda C. "African American Principals and the Legacy of *Brown.*" *Review of Research in Education* 28 (2005).

Tillman, Linda C. "Halls of Anger: The (Mis)Representation of African American Principals in Film." In *Keeping the Promise: Essays on Leadership, Democracy, and Education,* ed. Dennis Carlson and C. P. Gause. New York: Peter Lang, 2007.

Tillman, Linda, and James Trier. "Boston Public as Public Pedagogy: Implications for Teacher Preparation and School Leadership." *Peabody Journal of Education* 82, 2007.

Tolley, Kim. "Mapping the Leadership of Higher Schooling, 1727–1850." In *Chartered Schools: Two Hundred Years of Independent Academies in the United States, 1727–1925,* ed. Nancy Beadie and Kim Tolley. New York: Routledge, 2002.

Tolley, Kim, and Margaret A. Nash. "Leaving Home to Teach: The Diary of Susan Nye Hutchison, 1815–1841." In *Chartered Schools: Two Hundred Years of Independent Academies in the United States, 1727–1925,* ed. Nancy Beadie and Kim Tolley. New York: Routledge, 2002.

Trabue, M. R. "The Activities in Which Principals Are Actually Engaged." In *Educational Supervision: A Report of Current Views, Investigations, and Practices*, ed. James Fleming Hosic. New York: Teachers College Press, 1928.

Trubowitz, Sidney. "Confessions of a Ghetto Administrator." *Phi Delta Kappan* 53 (December 1971).

Trump, J. Lloyd, and Jane Hunt. Report on a National Survey of Secondary School Principals on the Nature and Extent of Student Activism. Washington, DC: National Association of Secondary School Principals, 1969.

Tyack, David, and Elisabeth Hansot. *Managers of Virtue: Public School Leadership in America, 1820–1980*. New York: Basic Books, 1982.

Tyler, Ralph W. "Leadership Role of the School Administrator in Curriculum and Instruction." *The Elementary School Journal* 54 (December, 1953).

Urban, Wayne. *Why Teachers Organized*. Detroit: Wayne State University Press, 1982.

Vidich, Arthur J., and Charles McReynolds. "Rhetoric versus Reality: A Study of New York City High School Principals." In *Anthropological Perspectives on Education*, ed. Murray L. Wax, Stanley Diamond, and Fred O. Gearing. New York: Basic Books, 1971.

Viñao, Antonio. "The School Head's Office as Territory and Place: Location and Physical Layout in the First Spanish Graded School." In *Materialities of Schooling: Design, Technology, Objects, Routines*, ed. Martin Lawn and Ian Grosvenor. Oxford: Symposium Books, 2005.

Wallace, James M. *The Promise of Progressivism: Angelo Patri and Urban Education*. New York: Peter Lang, 2006.

Ward Randolph, Adah, and Stephanie Sanders. "In Search of Excellence in Education: The Political, Academic, and Curricular Leadership of Ethel T. Overby." *Journal of School Leadership* 21 (July 2011).

Ward Randolph, Adah. " 'It Is Better to Light a Candle Than to Curse the Darkness': Ethel Thompson Overby and Democratic Schooling in Richmond, Virginia, 1910–1958." *Educational Studies* 48 (2012).

Ward Randolph, Adah. "Building upon Cultural Capital: Thomas Jefferson Ferguson and the Albany Enterprise Academy in Southeast Ohio, 1863–1886." *Journal of African American History* 87 (Spring 2002).

Ward Randolph, Adah. "The Memories of an All-Black Northern Urban School: Good Memories of Leadership, Teachers, and the Curriculum." *Urban Education* 39 (November 2004).

Watson, B. C. "The Principal in the System." In *The Principal in Metropolitan Schools*, ed. Donald A. Erickson and Theodore L. Reller. Berkeley, CA: McCutchan, 1978.

Weick, Karl E. "Educational Organizations as Loosely Coupled Systems." *Administrative Science Quarterly* 21 (1976).

Weldy, Gilbert R. "Administering a Negotiated Contract." National Association of Secondary School Principals, Reston, Virginia, 1973.

West, Deborah L., Craig Peck, and Ulrich C. Reitzug. "Limited Control and Relentless Accountability: Examining Historical Changes in Urban School Principal Pressure." *Journal of School Leadership* 20 (March 2012).

Whitaker, Kathryn S. "Exploring Causes of Principal Burnout." *Journal of Educational Administration* 34 (1996).

Wieder, Alan. "A School Principal and Desegregation." *Equity & Excellence in Education* 22 (Summer 1986).

Wilhelms, Fred T. "The Principalship: An Institution in Distress?" *NASSP Spotlight* 75 (November–December 1966).

Wolcott, Harry F. *The Man in the Principal's Office: An Ethnography.* New York: Holt, Rinehart and Winston, 1973.

Wraga, William G. "Democratic Leadership in the Classroom: Lessons from Progressives." *Democracy and Education* 14 (2001).

Wraga, William G. "Making Educational Leadership 'Educational.'" *Journal of School Leadership* 14 (January 2004).

INDEX